The Blackest Thing in Slavery Was Not the Black Man

THE BLACKEST THING IN SLAVERY WAS NOT THE BLACK MAN

THE LAST TESTAMENT OF ERIC WILLIAMS

EDITED BY BRINSLEY SAMAROO

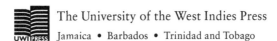

The University of the West Indies Press
Jamaica • Barbados • Trinidad and Tobago

The University of the West Indies Press
7A Gibraltar Hall Road, Mona
Kingston 7, Jamaica
www.uwipress.com

© 2022 by The Estate of Eric Williams

All rights reserved. Published 2022

A catalogue record of this book is available from the National
Library of Jamaica.

ISBN: 978-976-640-747-6 (print)
978-976-640-749-0 (ePub)

Cover design by Robert Harris

Printed in the United States of America

The University of the West Indies Press has no responsibility for
the persistence or accuracy of URLs for external or third-party
internet websites referred to in this publication and does not
guarantee that any content on such websites is, or will remain,
accurate or appropriate.

Contents

Preface / vii

Introduction / 1

1. Europe 1492: Slavery and Racism / 21

2. The European Exodus / 55

3. The Amerindians / 91

4. African Slavery in the New World / 115

5. European Christianity and African Slavery / 138

6. The Calvary of Free Blacks / 161

7. Asiatic Labour / 181

8. Black Power / 204

Notes / 219

Bibliography / 225

Index / 227

Preface

A few years ago, responding to a request for some words about Eric Williams for a forthcoming book of essays by him, I wrote about myself as a fourteen-year-old boy, living in relative poverty in Greenhill Village in Diego Martin and attending St Mary's College in Port of Spain, and the extent to which I was overwhelmed in 1956 by Williams's dynamism as he rose that year to political power. "Single-handedly and single-mindedly, Eric Williams transformed our lives," I wrote. "He swept away the old and inaugurated the new. He made us proud to be who we were, and optimistic as never before about what we were going to be, or could be. 'Bliss was it in that dawn to be alive', and nothing that has transpired since in Trinidad can negate Williams' gift to his people, or his triumph of intellect and spirit."

Since I wrote those words, nothing has made me want to repudiate them. The more I became a scholar interested in race and culture, the more I admired Williams's own efforts over a lifetime to devote his energy and skills as a historian to the task of critically recording the impact of Africa around the world. These elements include the African past before the start of the Atlantic slave trade; the iniquitous, world-blighting trade itself; its sustenance and its decline and fall in various parts of the world, especially in Britain and its colonies, white and "coloured", and also throughout the entire Americas; the moral claims for abolitionism that Williams challenged in his masterwork, *Capitalism and Slavery*; and the major effects of all of this history on the world in general, but on the Caribbean especially.

From 1956 until his death in 1981, Williams was the leading political figure in Trinidad and Tobago, notably as chief minister, premier and finally prime minister upon the achievement of independence in 1962. In his busy political career he never ceased to function also in some capacity as a historian, but inevitably paid the price exacted by the demands of his leadership of a fractious nation in a fractious world. In his last years, however, after distinct political setbacks despite maintaining his high office, he turned for refuge to what he cherished most – the life of the historian challenging dogmas about the past, especially the past involving Africa and the African diaspora. Now, in a blessed surprise, he has left us a

viii | Preface

gift that attests to his uniquely vigorous prophetic power anchored both in scholarship and in polemics.

The Blackest Thing in Slavery documents Williams's dedication to political resistance in fighting the monstrous notion of white racial supremacy. He began this project at a propitious moment, when the tide of history seemed to be turning against him even as he maintained high office. The attempted mutiny in Trinidad in 1970 and the steps he then felt compelled to take to bolster national security led him to become a contemned figure in some circles. This challenge was made worse by the rise of the local Black Power movement, in which he should have been an untouchable figure by almost any fair accounting. In response, Williams then embraced the challenge of a massive historical project that to some extent filled the void left by disappointment and dismay.

This book is the result of that effort. Williams here underscores his passion to reject white supremacy of all sorts – British, European, American, Australian, Canadian, what-have-you. *The Blackest Thing in Slavery* is structured to lead the reader from the earliest weaponizing of white supremacy as a doctrine down to its ramifications in the twentieth century. Williams delves into a wide array of sources to not only excoriate but also severely authenticate this historical racism. If most of his digging is in so-called "secondary" sources, he mines mainly not the opinions of other scholars but their original material – letters, proclamations, analyses, economic data and the like – that serve to keep his own strict intellectual purpose on course.

With precision he documents the pervasiveness of white racism in virtually every major aspect of white culture – in art (especially literature), religion, philosophy, history, education, philanthropy and diplomacy, as well as other infected areas. The idea of white supremacy dominated the cultures of Spain, Portugal, Britain and the rest of Europe, almost without exception, as well as those of the New World in North, Central and South America. It wreaked havoc everywhere despite the hallowed Declaration of Independence with its historic and unquestionably inspired assertion that "all men are created equal" and possess "unalienable Rights" to enjoy "Life, Liberty and the pursuit of Happiness". Wantonly and callously destroying the Inca, Aztec and other Amerindian empires, white supremacy devalued accomplished peoples into slaves and serfs.

Williams's prose not only crackles with the open fire of indignation but also remains poised and entertaining; the inherent tension of the book is relieved by a keen narrative sense and also by humour that ranges from the "donnish" to Trinidadian *picong*, or fondness for humorous insult. Williams moves nimbly from country to country and age to age as he documents the viral infection of the world. But he also acknowledges the major historical and social phenomena that challenged his own capacity to understand the past and present. These centre in two special areas.

The first is the relative failure of his continued reaching out as a political leader to Indians in Trinidad and Tobago. This lack of broad success came in the face of his record of consistently honouring Indian culture, Hindu, Muslim and Christian. Although he enjoyed some support among all three groups, rumours and allegations, distressing to Williams, circulated that he disliked Indians. The record shows, however, that he repeatedly affirmed his high regard for the Indian heritage, as in lecturing publicly (and separately) on Nehru, Gandhi and Tagore. In 2006, the visiting vice president of India hailed him as "a great statesman and a visionary" and "a friend of India". Nevertheless, always seeking after a finer understanding of the past and the world, Williams takes upon himself here the task of looking afresh at the record of India and its diaspora in their intersection with white supremacy, as well as in their almost unrivalled variety and complexity.

The other special area of concern, perhaps even more vexing personally to some extent, was Williams's difficulties with the local Black Power movement, which he had done much to nurture and substantiate. This international movement had been nourished by other Caribbean personalities such as Marcus Garvey, Aimé Césaire, Frantz Fanon and the young Trinidadian-born American activist Stokely Carmichael, who had become its premier popular champion. Surely no one who knew Williams's record could justify excluding him from the pantheon of individuals who had contributed seminally to the idea of Black Power. Nevertheless, in the heat of ideological antagonisms, he found himself challenged on this score. Williams was not bitter in response. Understanding the complaints of the young and impatient, he was determined to address them. Nevertheless, to some extent the infamous "whirligig of time" had poignantly brought in its revenges.

This book ends in the late 1970s. It closes, necessarily, with Williams apparently wandering (in the famous words of Matthew Arnold), "on a darkling plain / Swept with confused alarms of struggle and flight, / Where ignorant armies clash by night".

It could hardly be otherwise. Dying in 1981, Williams could not have anticipated certain major events that would further vex his great subject of white supremacy and the resistance of non-white peoples. These events include the fall of the Berlin Wall in 1989 and of the Union of Soviet Socialist Republics in 1991; the collapse of apartheid and the election in

1994 of Nelson Mandela as president of South Africa; the wildly successful embrace of capitalism by communist China (in the wake of economic reforms starting in 1978); the rise in might of the Arab states in the long aftermath of the founding of the Organization of the Petroleum Exporting Countries; the improbable triumph of Barack Obama in winning the US presidency in 2008 and 2012; and, to some observers, the evident revival in the United States of the idea of white supremacy in the words and actions of the American leaders who succeeded Obama.

If Williams could not foresee such events, he could look back and report and analyse with a brilliance and fervour matched by few others. *The Blackest Thing in Slavery* is a cautionary phenomenon as well as a boon to all of us who would better understand the past, especially where racism and people of colour are concerned. It is perhaps the most concise and penetrating record of the malignity and historic pervasiveness of white racism that we have, as we continue to be indebted to the vision, skills and courage of Eric Eustace Williams.

Arnold Rampersad
Sara Hart Kimball Professor Emeritus in the Humanities, Stanford University.

Introduction

The story is told of an argument among whites as to whether Columbus or Ericson was the true discoverer of America. An Amerindian listener interposed: "Discover nothing, we knew it was here all the time."[1]

Most scholars who have studied the writings of Eric Williams regard the final collection of his speeches and writings, *Forged from the Love of Liberty*, as his last legacy.[2] This book came just over a decade after his previous major work, *From Columbus to Castro*, published in 1970. What is less well known is that in 1973 he started work on what he envisaged as his last testament, namely a book that would have as its main focus the narrative of slavery and bonded labour in the European and non-European world and the emergence from servitude of African and Asian peoples. Williams hoped to trace the struggle of African, Asian and New World peoples as a means of demonstrating the invincible will of such peoples, who had by the twentieth century emerged as world leaders in diverse spheres of human activity. At the time of his death in March 1981, Williams had written thirteen chapters of the manuscript, covering just over a thousand typewritten pages, written between 1973 and 1980. In this book these have been condensed into eight chapters. The title of the manuscript was drawn from the writing of the Cuban radical José de la Luz y Caballero, who had expressed the sentiment that "the blackest thing in slavery was not the black man". Williams was clearly an admirer of Caballero, since he quoted him not only in his initial book proposal but also in the larger work.

In choosing his literary exemplars Williams showed a clear preference for philosophers who were also political activists. Caballero (1800–1862) was a Cuban scholar described by José Martí as the father of Cuban intellectualism in the nineteenth century. Among his major works, published by the University of Havana long after his death, were *La Polémica Filosófica (The Controversial Philosophy* [1946]) and *Elencos y Discursos (List of Speeches* [1950]). What pleased Williams was his vehement opposition to slavery, which existed in Cuba until 1886. Caballero was harassed by the Cuban plantocracy, and was brought to trial, but was exonerated for lack of evidence. He ended his days as director of the College of San Salvador in Cuba.

2 | THE BLACKEST THING IN SLAVERY WAS NOT THE BLACK MAN

There were other Caribbean scholar/activists whom Williams admired. José Martí (1853–1895) created the Cuban Revolutionary Party in 1892 and was killed three years later in the 1895 uprising against Spanish rule. To Williams he was the father of the Cuban revolution, whose favourite quip was that "man is more than white, more than mulatto, more than Negro". Another Caribbean hero, in Williams's view, was the Martiniquan scholar/activist Frantz Fanon (1925–1961) who had asked the question, "Can the white man live healthily with the black man or the black man live healthily with the white man?" Williams's diaries demonstrated his close familiarity with most of Fanon's books: *Black Skins, White Masks* (1958), *The Wretched of the Earth* (1961), *A Dying Colonialism* (1965) and *Toward the African Revolution* (1969). As he retreated further and further from public life from the mid-1970s, Williams relied heavily on the writings of the Guyanese historian and activist Walter Rodney (1942–1980), particularly *West Africa and the Atlantic Slave Trade* (1967), *A History of the Upper Guinea Coast* (1970), and above all, *How Europe Underdeveloped Africa* (1972). Both his diaries and the manuscript indicate his admiration for Rodney's work. At the time of Rodney's assassination in June 1980 Williams was revising his chapters on slavery.

Before embarking on an examination of the manuscript, we must pause to outline the course of its trajectory. Early in 1973, Williams submitted a paper to a conference in Puerto Rico which commemorated the 1873 abolition of slavery in that colony. The paper, bearing the title "The Blackest Thing in Slavery Was Not the Black Man", was published in the spring edition of the *Revista*.[3] In March 1973, a copy of this paper was sent to the publisher André Deutsch (who had previously published Williams's works) and Basil Davidson, who had published more than a dozen books on African themes. Among Davidson's most popular books were *Old Africa Rediscovered* (1959), *Black Mother: The Years of the African Slave Trade* (1961), and *African Genius: An Introduction to African Cultural and Social History* (1969). In a joint letter to his publisher and this eminent Africanist, Williams suggested that an extended version of the paper could be published and that he was prepared to do the necessary expansion. The expanded version of the essay, Williams wrote, would be "a synthesis of the vast amount of knowledge we now have available for particular ethnic groups in the hemisphere over particular periods of time; the aim being to demonstrate the relevance of this synthesis for race relations problems and patterns in our society". The book could be properly illustrated by pictures such as an audience given by the king of Mali or a "nude black Mexican woman seated, which would surprise the world which does not associate Mexico with black people".[4]

After consultation between Deutsch and Davidson, the publisher commissioned the book and Williams proceeded to write up the chapters. In a television interview given in 1976, Williams indicated that the first draft of the book had been completed in 1973, after which he had put the manuscript on hold for about a year, since he wanted to include "the Indian heritage which had been so neglected in some areas where Hindus and Muslims came in large numbers". He needed (after 1973) to visit Asia to understand more about that part of the world, particularly the Asiatic dimension of the non-white world's struggle for equality in the international power relations struggle.[5] In this post-1973 period, Williams made two trips to Asia as a member of a team of educational experts sponsored by the United Nations to examine the feasibility of a UN university. During these trips, he purchased the books of two philosopher-politicians whose writings were informed by their political activism. These Indian writers were Jawaharlal Nehru (1889–1964), whom Williams had met on an earlier visit, and Sri Aurobindo (1872–1950), the radical revolutionary of the Indian struggle for independence. A graduate of Cambridge University, Aurobindo returned to India in 1893 and soon fell afoul of the Indian leaders who sought freedom through prayer, petition and protest. Aurobindo told his followers that political freedom was the life and breath of the nation, without which people could never realize their destiny. In pursuance of that freedom, he stirred the Indian masses to violent subversive activity, which he secretly planned, and organized boycotts of British goods and institutions such as courts and schools. After about a decade of such protest, he retired to a life of deep contemplation, study and writing. As a devoted teacher, he founded the Aurobindo International Centre of Education, which later blossomed into Jadavpur University. Williams was very familiar with the voluminous writings of Sri Aurobindo and admired his learning, political activism and later retirement to the life of the mind.

An essential ingredient for our understanding of Williams's preparation of his manuscript is his collection of diaries, some thirty-one of them, written between 1956 and March 1981, the month of his death. These were multipurpose memoirs which covered most of his activities during the period. The diaries examined for this essay spanned the period 1978 to 1981, during which time he focused intensely on writing and rewriting chapters of *The Blackest Thing*. The diaries took various physical forms. For 1978, there is a large standard diary printed in the United States; for 1979 there is an Adjutant Te Be diary in German, as well as a *New York Times* executive diary, and for 1981 there is a British West Indian Airways desk diary. During 1978 and 1979, the years of most concentrated research

4 | THE BLACKEST THING IN SLAVERY WAS NOT THE BLACK MAN

and writing, he kept not only these desk diaries but also separate slips of paper (four by six-and-a-half inches, or ten by seventeen centimetres) in which he carefully noted the books he was reading, as well as notes to guide his actual writing; there are hundreds of these small pages in the files. On one of them, he lists Islamic achievements, derived from a Time-Life book on early Islam. On another slip he lists Arabic terms from the same source. On a further page he recorded that from 1 to 7 April 1978 he spent thirty-one-and-a-half hours in reading and annotating a long list of history texts.[6]

Being the devoted historian that he was, Williams was familiar with diaries as a source for history writing, and with the many purposes and forms of the diary. Our understanding of the term "diary" dates from the late sixteenth century, when English-speaking diarists began recording their everyday activities.[7] The Protestant revolution encouraged individualism by emphasizing that personal lives mattered independently of the teachings and edicts of the church:

> Keeping a diary provided another avenue for quiet contemplation, as well as a way of adopting to the individualism, capitalism, nationalism and industrialism that became distinguishing features of modern society.[8]

The diary could also be a repository for confidential thoughts or a haven for inner musings; this was certainly applicable in Williams's case. On 1 January 1978 he confided to his standard diary: "Press: Rubbish in *Express* about Caricom, and new start for New Year. Rubbish in *Guardian* about New Year resolutions – work ethic, cleaning up the country etc. Making oneself heard (by oneself only) and seeing oneself in print (by oneself only) are goals in themselves."[9]

The Williams diaries take the form of a first-person narrative, but he would have been familiar with other forms of diary-writing, such as Daniel Defoe's fictional *Robinson Crusoe* (1719), which was compulsory reading at Queen's Royal College in Port of Spain, where he had his secondary education. He was familiar with the diaries of John Morton reproduced in Sarah Morton's *John Morton of Trinidad* (1916) and was particularly incensed by the accounts of Anthony Trollope in his book *The West Indies and the Spanish Main* (1859). A text frequently consulted by Williams was that of James Anthony Froude, professor of modern history at Oxford, *The English in the West Indies* (1888) and Charles Kingsley's description of his West Indian sojourn, *At Last: A Christmas in the West Indies* (1871). He was infuriated by Froude's contention that West Indians were incapable of governing themselves. His critical review of these texts was published in *British Historians and the West Indies* (1962) and repeated in *The Blackest*

Thing. As a seasoned researcher, Williams might have read the diaries of colonial governors and missionaries lodged at Rhodes House, Oxford University, his alma mater. Among his most treasured books was Nehru's *Glimpses of World History* (1962), which consisted of letters written by Nehru while he was in prison.

As an inheritor of a long tradition of diary-writing, Williams took to keeping diaries with a passion. His diary became an intimate friend, a confidant, a remembrance of appointments and a bibliography of the dozens of books on all manner of subjects which he constantly read. He noted every haircut (for which he consistently paid $10), his monthly donations to charity, the times at which his housekeeper Claudia Rohim brought his meals and his excitement whenever his daughter Erica visited or wrote to him. In Erica's own words, as Eric Williams the man gave way to Eric Williams the politician, she remained the exception, the politician's Achilles's heel.[10] The visits of his main physician Dr Halsey McShine, and the dinners they shared until early 1980, are meticulously noted, as is the increase in bills for medicines, purchased for him by John O'Halloran, his cabinet minister and trusted confidant. His blood-pressure readings for 1978, taken about three times a month, are carefully recorded.

Williams's increasing disengagement from public life while holding the office of prime minister needs to be contextualized. Erica Williams noted, correctly, that from the early 1970s, her father "became increasingly disillusioned about his role as leader, some of his peers and the society in general".[11] "From that time," she adds, "he worked increasingly from his residence rather than in his office in Whitehall."

The Black Power uprising of 1970 appeared to be the beginning of his disillusionment. The "ungratefulness" of the black population, for whom he had done so much since 1956, came as a shock to the prime minister, which never left his consciousness over the next decade. In his first public address after the uprising, on 23 March 1970, he questioned why, after all that he had done, there was such widespread dissatisfaction. The government, he said, had consciously sought to promote black economic power through the creation of 1,523 black small farmers. Small business and tourism had been encouraged, free secondary education had been brought within reach of thousands of disadvantaged families, and the public service was staffed "almost entirely by nationals, mainly black".[12] At the same time, he identified himself as an advocate of Black Power and sympathized with the aspirations of the demonstrators.

From that time, Williams trod with great care. He kept his cool while those around him were in deep panic. In a letter to Erica cited by Colin

6 | THE BLACKEST THING IN SLAVERY WAS NOT THE BLACK MAN

Palmer, he indicated that he was in command. People were demanding that he should call out the regiment, but the police were in full control of the situation.[13] He was, he said, contemplating the declaration of a state of emergency. As events escalated, he did in fact call this emergency on 21 April 1970. By May 1970, he felt he had regained control once again. In another nationwide broadcast he castigated the trade unions, university lecturers and students, as well as some politicians who wanted to take over the government by "unconstitutional means and armed revolution".[14] For the rest of 1970 and 1971, he spoke regularly about the actions which were being taken to rectify issues raised in the February Revolution of 1970. However, the matter remained on his mind.

In December 1974, Williams gave a rambling eight-hour response in Parliament to the Wooding Commission's report on constitutional changes required as the nation moved towards republicanism. He could not resist commenting on a matter which weighed heavily on his mind: "They talk about the Black Power Movement. Not one word about its decline with the declining influence of Frantz Fanon – that was basic in the Black Power Movement."[15]

Later on in the same speech, he commented on the problems which had arisen in the movement. Although its advocates spoke of unconventional politics, the movement was split into factions: "The Black Power Movement in terms of the terrific fight between Black Panthers – Newton against Eldridge Cleaver and above all Stokely Carmichael who could hardly even go back to the United States."

During 1978 and 1979 he added to the manuscript of *The Blackest Thing*, with particular regard to 1970. Stokely Carmichael, he claimed, a Trinidad-born leader of the Black Power movement in the United States, could not be allowed to return home, because on a visit to Guyana in 1970, he had excluded the East Indian population from the struggle for black liberation. This position, Williams claimed, was contrary to the tendency of Trinidadians and Tobagonians to combine both races. Carmichael's presence in Trinidad at that time would have complicated race relations there. Yet the chapter in question, chapter 8, is prefaced by the slogan "black is beautiful", a phrase popularized by Carmichael (Kwame Ture). As Williams wrote and rewrote different versions of *The Blackest Thing*, the aftermath of 1970 kept recurring in his mind. He traced the causes of those disturbances to the Black Power movement of 1970 and deeply regretted the loss of life among members of the National Union of Freedom Fighters, which was a radical offshoot of the Black Power movement.[16]

There were other clear indications of Williams's alienation from mainstream society. In 1975, he complained in Parliament that public servants were burdening the House of Representatives with decisions which they themselves could have made. What he did not say was that they dared not make those decisions for fear of arousing his disapproval. The general elections of 1976 were a further source of aggravation. As the selection of candidates proceeded, he objected to five nominees whom he called "millstones", unworthy to be representatives of his People's National Movement party. After all five were endorsed by their party groups, Williams refused to sign their nomination papers, hoping that the central executive would support his position. That executive confirmed the five "millstones" and Williams retaliated by refusing to speak on their platforms. All five were elected and spent the next five years as backbenchers.[17]

The new republican constitution of 1976, largely a creation of Williams, also reflects his desire to ease the burden of governance on the prime minister. The Wooding Commission had recommended that power should be diffused through a substantial reduction of the areas of patronage at the disposal of the prime minister. In this regard the commission had recommended that office-holders such as the chief justice, the other members of the Judicial and Legal Service Commission, the chairmen and other members of the other service commissions, and the chairman of the Elections and Boundaries Commission, should be appointed by the president after consultation with the prime minister and the leader of the opposition. Previously, such office-holders were appointed by the governor general in accordance with the advice of the prime minister only. Williams fully agreed with this recommendation of presidential appointment after consultation with both, and this feature became a new departure in the 1976 constitution.[18] This was a unique, different concession in a region where "doctor politics" was firmly entrenched. Doctor politics is the concentration of authority into a sole politician. In this and other ways, Williams was relieving himself of a considerable load of responsibility, which allowed him to dedicate more time to Clio, the muse of history, burying himself deeper and deeper in intensive research and writing. He would not allow the "comesse" of the society, namely the constant squabbles, to weigh him down, as had happened before (and after) in this and other societies. In his own time Albert Gomes had been hounded into exile in England and Uriah Butler died a pauper even after he had wrought so much for the nation.

Albert Gomes (1911–1978) was a journalist, trade unionist and politician who was one of the creators of the nation. The son of Portuguese immigrants, he edited the radical literary journal, *The Beacon* from 1931 to 1933. He was elected to the Port of Spain City Council from 1938 to 1947 and to the Legislative Council from 1946 to 1956. From 1950 to 1956 he was the minister of Industry, Commerce and Labour and was generally regarded as the unofficial chief minister. In 1956 he was defeated by the PNM in the general elections but won a seat in the Federal Parliament in 1958. After the demise of the federation in 1962 he went into exile in London, England, where he wrote his biography *Through a Maze of Colour* (1974) and a novel *All Papa's Children* (1978).

Tubal Uriah Butler (1897–1977) was a Grenadian who migrated to Trinidad as a worker in the oil industry. He was a veteran of the First World War who upon his return, organized the oil workers, seeking higher wages and better working conditions. In 1937 he was one of the principal leaders of the disturbances which changed the course of our nation's history. For this activity he was imprisoned in 1938 and released in May 1939. From 1950 to 1961 he was an elected member of the Legislative Council but was defeated by the PNM in 1961. He was one of the founders of the trade union movement.

Williams retreated into a world where the slings and arrows of a turbulent society could not reach him.

While Williams was becoming increasingly disenchanted with politics and the burden of governance, the nation's calypsonians and poets, always the reflection of popular opinion, were articulating the corresponding public distancing from "the Doc". As Louis Regis points out, many allegations arose against his leading ministers: they were accused "of peculation, profiteering from inside information and flaunting wealth which was popularly thought to be ill-gotten".[19] A hue and cry was raised and Selwyn Richardson, then attorney general, was appointed to inquire into the allegations. Nothing came of this investigation and Explainer, in his kaiso "Selwyn" (1977), warned Richardson:

> If you want your job to be set
> What you have to do is to start off with Cabinet
> If the PM thief
> Is to lock up he backside too.[20]

The popular bard Shorty joined the chorus, painting a gross image of Williams by advising the nation to put out a lover who could perform no more:

> If yuh man old and falling on he face
> Get a younger fella to take his place
> Put him out.

In the year of Williams's death (1981), Derek Walcott's poem "The Spoiler's Return" reflected how many in the nation viewed the former icon:

and those hearing aids turn off the truth,
and their dark glasses let you criticize
your own presumptuous image in their eyes.
Behind dark glasses is just hollow skull,
and black still poor, though black is beautiful.

By that year (1981), there was a widespread perception that the prime minister was covering up for corruption in his government: "large numbers of people were questioning the credibility of the Prime Minister", believing that "nothing the government said or promised could be taken at face value".[21]

Williams's reaction to this mounting criticism was to retreat further and further into the haven of the academy. He felt confidently at home there, surrounded by piles of books and papers. As he withdrew from public life, he devised various ways of load-shedding so that he could return to research and writing. One way was to increase the inclusion of women in the work of governance. In his diary for 2 August 1978 he noted: "Kitchen cabinet: inaugural meeting".[22] The Kitchen Cabinet signified the emergence of women from the kitchen to leadership positions in the nation. From that time, he gave increasing audience to Marilyn Gordon (who apparently headed the "kitchen cabinet"), Muriel Donawa and Dr Marguerite Wyke, two women activists from South Trinidad. From that time too, he made increasing use of interministerial committees to deal with matters of state. The diaries show increasing dependence on such committees, and the burgeoning roles of Errol Mahabir and John O'Halloran in managing these groups. **Errol Mahabir** (1931–2015) was a key member of Eric Williams's administration for two decades. A former employee of Texaco Trinidad Oil Company he was elected to the San Fernando Borough Council in 1960 where he served first as Deputy Mayor (1960–1963) and as Mayor (1963–1966). In 1966, 1971, 1976 and 1981 he was elected as representative for San Fernando West. During this time, he served in various ministerial capacities until 1986. These included Labour and Social Security, Industry and Commerce, Petroleum and Mines and External Affairs. In 2010 he was awarded the Chaconia (Gold) National Award.

Another group of a numerically diminishing cadre of advisers consisted of technocrats advising on projects which were dear to the prime minister. Heading this list was Professor Ken Julien, who spearheaded work in the energy sector alongside Mahabir. He relied on the financial expertise of Mervyn de Souza, Philip Rochford and Victor Bruce, and would summon Frank and Isidore Rampersad at all hours of the night and day for administrative assistance. This was a small group which remained with Williams after he had fallen out with some of the major mandarins in the public service, whom he accused in 1975 of conspiring to take over the governance of the society from its elected representatives.

As Williams became more and more immersed in writing and research, he shortened the duration of cabinet meetings. On 19 January 1978 he confided to his diary, "Cabinet: too many papers. Lengthens meeting."[23] His other entries for January 1978 deal at considerable length with the manuscript, and his meetings with Mahabir and other advisors appear as interludes in the larger project. On 8 January 1978, for example, he gives a list of five major books on slavery which he was either reading or annotating. This was followed by a lengthy summary entitled: "working on original chapters on African slavery section". Then came preparation for (1) "Coolieism" (2) "Manifest Destiny" (3) "Hemispheric Migration Movements". During this time, as we have seen, Williams kept a further listing of books and notes relating to the writing. He seemed worried on days when he did not work on the book and happy when he resumed:

> 12 April 1978 work on book – none
> 13 April 1978 work on book – none
> 16 April 1978 reading Craton: *Worthy Park*
> 21 April 1978 Finished Craton

In reading these diaries one gets the impression that Williams was burning the candle at both ends and this was taking a toll on his health. Yet as his health deteriorated, he chose to confide in his diary rather than his doctor. On 17 December 1980, he writes, "feeling unwell" as the only entry in the diary and on 22, 23 and 24 December his only entries are "taking life easy". On Christmas Day 1980, he expected a visit from O'Halloran and de Souza, but notes that he was unable to see them.[24] Nevertheless, he persisted with reading and revising the manuscript, constantly adding new paragraphs as his source reading progressed.

The First Draft

The paper that Williams submitted to the *Revista Inter-Americana* in 1973 focused on seven themes which dealt with race relations and their consequences, historically and geographically. It sought to analyse the relations between the white, mainly temperate world and the non-white, mainly tropical regions, from the Columbian period to the twentieth century. Europeans created myths and stories whose purpose was to demonstrate that they were superior to all other peoples; they were therefore ordained to rule over non-Europeans. These arguments are encapsulated under seven headings, each copiously supported by examples drawn from Williams's extensive research as well as the work of other scholars. It is worth our while to summarize these seven themes:

1. **The unsuitability of white labour in the tropics.** Contrary to the claim that white settlers could not do manual labour in the tropics, Williams argued that white labourers substantially contributed to the labour force in the Caribbean (St Thomas, Barbados, Jamaica, Suriname and Puerto Rico), Northern Australia (Queensland) and Brazil. White workers adapted themselves to tropical conditions, but in a situation where black slavery existed, no white wanted to do manual labour: hence the creation of the myth.

2. **The inferiority of non-European cultures.** Proponents of this manufactured point of view, Williams maintained, had conveniently neglected to address the achievements of the Maya, Aztec or Inca civilizations of Meso- and South America. Similarly, there was no recognition of the native peoples of North America or the legacies of pre-European North African peoples. There is little mention, Williams said, of the brick palaces and forts of Zimbabwe, the Caliphate at Sokoto or the agricultural accomplishments of Dahomey. The denigration of Africa was a conscience-salving excuse for the enslavement of her children.

3. **The European association of "native races" with bestiality.** Beginning with Bartolomé de Las Casas and Sepulveda, Williams said, the Europeans constantly claimed that Africans and Amerindians were less than men. In North America, Amerindians were regarded as "game to be shot or vermin to be destroyed". The Portuguese regarded Africans as "images of a lower hemisphere". Whereas Thomas Jefferson was prepared to accept the humanity of the Amerindians, he considered Africans inferior to whites. Jefferson was prepared to admit the intermingling of whites and Indians; he was certainly not prepared for "that immovable veil of black which covers all the emotions of the other race". If Jefferson and the racist Jamaican planter Edward Long were around today, Williams wondered, how would they regard the literary work of Richard Wright and Claude McKay, and the music of Marian Anderson, Duke Ellington or Louis

12 | THE BLACKEST THING IN SLAVERY WAS NOT THE BLACK MAN

Armstrong? What would they think of the evolution of the steelband in Trinidad?

4. **Apartheid.** Williams surmised that if the African race was more "animal" than human, it followed that there should be no mixing of whites and blacks. The logical long-term consequence of that ontology was the creation of South Africa. President Jefferson was caught up in his own contradictions. He preached separation by day but integrated with his slave Sally Hemings by night. The creation of mixed-race "mulatto" people and their inferior space in society created such a furore that José Martí was moved to explain that, "Man is more than white, more than mulatto, more than Negro."

5. **Three-fifths of a man.** Williams noted that when the American nation was established, the founders espoused the concept of the equality of all men, but changed their tune when it came to the electoral representation of the enslaved African. For electoral purposes the slave was to be counted as three-fifths of a man. It was the numerical predominance of the coloured population in Trinidad and the potential of black majority rule that necessitated the imposition of Crown colony government. This was similar to what occurred in Jamaica after the Morant Bay Rebellion in 1865. This produced a reversion to Crown colony status in 1866.

6. **The ordeal of the African after emancipation.** Even after emancipation, Williams emphasized, the New World plantocracy continued to regard the African as good for nothing else but to labour on the plantations. Not all of the slave colonies abolished slavery at the same time; the Danish Virgin Islands abolished the institution in 1848, after a slave revolt. Cuba and Brazil maintained slavery up to the 1880s; and after emancipation in the British colonies, the masters sought to prevent freed blacks from acquiring land. The imperial government imposed high taxes, thereby forcing Africans to seek employment on the plantations. When the former slaves abandoned the plantations, the plantocracy looked to India for replacements for the British, French and Dutch Caribbean. The United States and Brazil imported Japanese and Chinese workers, members of "lower races". After the Second World War (1939–1945) workers from the Caribbean migrated to Europe in the wake of labour shortages that existed there. Skilled workers were the ones most likely to migrate, taking their expertise, which was sorely needed at home.

7. **Conclusion.** Williams maintained that in the eyes of Europeans, the principal function of the African was to provide labour upon

which their prosperity would be constructed. The African was perceived as being less than a man and could not govern himself. Williams observed that the hollowness of that argument can be evidenced by the contemporary existence of black-led governments in the Caribbean and in Africa. In the United States the black revolt had accelerated the movement towards civil rights at many levels. The Caribbean, in its turn, had produced a plethora of black intellectuals, politicians, freedom fighters and international activists such as Stokely Carmichael and C.L.R. James. Globally there was a re-emergence of non-white nations, pointing to fresh vistas of development. Among these were Japan, China and the Arab states of the Middle East.

This re-emerging new front of non-white peoples was creating its own problems. These included India's wars against China and Pakistan, civil war in Uganda and in the Congo, Uganda's expulsion of Indians, anti-Tamil riots in Ceylon and Malaysia, and Japanese and Indian contempt for dark-skinned people. These tended to weaken the struggle against white racism.

Despite these drawbacks, there has emerged a clear philosophy that no non-white race will accept "the political bunkum", perpetrated for four centuries, justifying European domination of the world's peoples. It was the sum of these race-led indignities, the larger ontological frame, which constituted the many "black" things in slavery. Brazil's decision in 1890 to destroy its slave archives was one of these negative events which supported Caballero's contention that the black man was not the blackest thing in slavery.

In this long article we witness the veteran historian's swan-song musings on the principal area of his life's work, namely the African diaspora from slavery to the twentieth century. The paper is intellectually intense, closely argued and reflective of a deep reading of world history. These reflections indicate not only Williams's familiarity with the British Caribbean but equally his ability to use Spanish and French archival sources and to tie these together to create a larger, pan-Caribbean panorama. His treatment of the Asian dimensions of slavery and of the Asian presence in the Americas was, as he admitted in 1976, sketchy and tangential. These were issues that he sought to address after 1973.

The 1973 Version

Eric Williams's 1973 manuscript consists of eleven chapters in the following sequence:

Chapter	Heading
1.	Slavery and Racism in Europe
2.	Europeans and Amerindians
3.	African Society and Culture before the European Penetration
4.	African Slavery in the New World
5.	European Christianity and African slavery
6.	The Black Republic of Haiti
7.	The Abolition of Slavery
8.	The Calvary of Free Blacks
9.	White Supremacy
10.	Manifest Destiny
11.	Black Is Beautiful

Most of these chapters are elaborations of the original *Revista* paper which we have already discussed. A good deal of the material was drawn from Williams's previously published works. Here he reworks them, fitting the material into the ethnic theme that informed the work. For example, chapter 2, on Europeans and Amerindians, contains a good deal of the arguments and evidence of his 1970 book *From Columbus to Castro*. Chapter 9, on white supremacy, draws heavily on *British Historians and the West Indies* (1966) and chapter 6, on the black republic of Haiti, uses materials derived from C.L.R. James's *Black Jacobins* (1938).

What, then, is new in the manuscript, besides the historian's well-known anti-imperialistic epistemology? This writer finds chapter 11, "Black Is Beautiful", most engaging and also new. It is interesting because it was written some three years after the February (1970) Revolution in Trinidad and Tobago, often called the Black Power uprising. Williams stressed that what occurred there was part of an international pattern of unrest particularly among the world's youth. Examining the details of the narrative, one notes Williams's ambivalence towards Stokely Carmichael, the Black Power advocate. On the one hand, he quotes Carmichael's "black is beautiful" slogan at the head of the chapter, and in the text he speaks proudly of his fellow-national's pioneering activism in the United States, his elevation to the rank of prime minister of the Black Panthers, his promoting of the Black Power movement in London in 1967; and on the other hand, the opposition to Carmichael by other black activists such as Eldridge Cleaver.

The chapter spends a good deal of time discussing the international situation as a background to what was happening at that time in the Caribbean. Williams highlights the disabilities of the black population in the United States and the twentieth-century struggle for equality by black activists in North America, through the efforts of Marcus Garvey in the United States and in Jamaica via the Universal Negro Improvement Association (UNIA). This organization promoted black pride and links with Mother Africa. The chapter includes a discourse on the intellectual activism of Frantz Fanon and Aimé Césaire, followed by an examination of the position of black people in the United Kingdom, Puerto Rico, Cuba and Jamaica. All of this is done to contextualize the Black Power movement in the Caribbean, to describe the international climate in which the Black Power movement in the Caribbean was born:

> Disturbances broke out in 1970 originating in protests against the trial of West Indian students in Canada who had destroyed a computer room at Sir George Williams University where they alleged racial discrimination. Black American influence was evident throughout – afro hairstyles, dashikis, attacks on the "Establishment" and the "White Power Structure", designation of the police as "fuzz" and "pigs", rejection of "conventional politics". . . . Among the more serious aspects of the unrest were demands for nationalisation of oil, sugar and the banks.[25]

This last "serious" aspect was a matter to which Williams, as prime minister, gave detailed attention after 1970. The February Revolution was immediately followed by about three years of guerrilla warfare led by the National Union of Freedom Fighters. Its youthful leaders had decided to continue the struggle because they were unhappy with the early "capitulation" of the leaders of the February Revolution. As in the case of the February Revolution, Williams, in late 1973, sought to place the guerrilla movement in an international frame. "The guerrilla has become an integral part of the international scene since World War II."[26] But those who claimed to be local guerrillas had no clear-cut ideology such as the Chinese had under Mao, the Slavs under Tito or the Vietnamese in their anti-French or anti-American struggles. He claimed that they were irrelevant in Trinidad because they had no foreign or colonial aggressor, the mass of the population had not been alienated, and there was no significant and legitimate political dissatisfaction: "The so-called Trinidad 'guerrillas' may not always lack some ideological framework which will call at least for examination. So far this is not the case, and the solution seems to be merely an extension of the international movement of crime and violence, using perhaps guerrilla tactics and techniques – hard drugs included – made available through the many books on the subject, and taking advantage of the terrain wherever possible."[27]

16 | THE BLACKEST THING IN SLAVERY WAS NOT THE BLACK MAN

In all of this Williams shows considerably less hostility to the Black Power uprising than to the subsequent continuation of protest in the guerrilla campaign led by the National Union of Freedom Fighters. As these events unfolded, the leaders of the February Revolution were released after a short detention on Nelson Island and later allowed to go their own way. The leaders of the National Union of Freedom Fighters were relentlessly pursued and most were liquidated by harsh police action. Others, deemed "inferiors", were killed by their colleagues.

The Later Manuscript: 1976–1979

> The second of the great ancient civilizations developed along the Indus in what are today modern India and Pakistan. By 2300 BC it had produced two of the great cities of the ancient world, a tribute to the capacity for planning and building of that time. These cities were Mohenjo-Daro (Place of the Dead) on the lower Indus, and later Harappa, on one of its tributaries: these two cities dominated a cultural area of nearly half a million square miles and are distinguished by their wide streets, efficient drainage and absence of military equipment and fortifications.[28]

We have already looked briefly at Williams's 1976 interview on national television, noting that he had delayed the preparation of the book in 1973 because he wanted to include the Asian dimension, particularly the Indian, which he felt had been sadly neglected. In this 1976 interview he enabled the public to gain an insight into what he had found in his post-1973 research and what new questions had arisen. Why was it that Europe, and not Asia or Africa, led the discovery of the New World? Why did Islamic civilization cease its northward journey before it reached the Americas, when Muslims had blazed an earlier trail? The Chinese had also made great strides in maritime technology and had reached as far west as Mozambique in East Africa. What impediments had prevented them from sailing southwards around the Cape of Good Hope? In his television interview Williams gave some of his answers, drawing from his now extended manuscript.

The reasons for European superiority included a better diet, which included more meat in contrast to the vegetarianism and the religiously inspired dietary taboos of certain Oriental peoples. Other factors included the taming and greater utilization of the horse, the evolution of the saddle, harness and shoeing. This had facilitated the Agricultural Revolution,

Introduction | 17

leading to more expansive use of the land and enhanced food production, "as against the stagnant and static agrarian systems in Asia". While China and India had continued with their "rickshaw civilization", Europe had developed technology, the application of inventions and a culture in which anyone and everyone could go into any type of occupation. Other societies had been hobbled by slavery and the caste system. Whereas Europe was motivated by the spirit of enquiry, producing minds such as Francis Bacon, Copernicus and Leonardo da Vinci, the Muslims were bent on promoting Islamic theological orthodoxy. It was that European energy, Williams argued, which had created the United States, which in turn had attracted no fewer than thirty-five million Europeans between 1820 and 1950, with a small number going to Canada. These immigrants were running from permanent revolution and religious intolerance in Switzerland, Scandinavia and Germany. Now they had the prospect of owning land in America and acquiring jobs which were unavailable in Europe. Released from the shackles of European medievalism, the Americans created an open society with no aristocracy, no standing armies and a different university system. They took over the whole country, while dispossessing the Amerindians.

For all of its promise, however, independence had created an America whose high-sounding rhetoric about freedom was not meant for its non-white population. Such privileges were not to be afforded to people whom they casually described as "miscellaneous scraps of humanity" or "images of a lower hemisphere". The attitude of Americans to the Chinese and Japanese who had built their railroads was typical. The United States was providing asylum for millions of Europeans, but was deporting Chinese and Japanese workers and seeking to export its own black population to Liberia. This American attitude to non-Europeans was the supreme contradiction of the Declaration of Independence.

Williams's assessment did not apply only to the Americas. Extending this analysis to the non-American world, he predicted (accurately) that once President Tito of Yugoslavia was gone, the Balkans would fall apart. In the case of South Africa, he predicted a long struggle against apartheid but felt that that system would triumph. This prediction was not accurate.

Coolieism

As mentioned before, the final chapter, "Coolieism", was written after the earlier (1973) chapters. Although he did not define the term, Williams used the word "coolieism" to mean all bonded peoples from Asia: Chinese, Japanese, Filipinos and Indians. The thrust of this chapter was the insistence of the white self-governing colonies that they should control their immigration policy, which should not be dictated by the Colonial Office. Generally, the policy of the white colonies was to use non-white labour for their development, then to exclude these workers from permanent settlement. In cases where this was not totally possible, as in South Africa or Canada, those who were allowed to remain were subjected to considerable restrictions vis-à-vis voting privileges, land ownership and access to all the amenities of their societies. Australia topped the list of colonies which insisted on a policy of keeping out non-white immigrants. The first group of settlers, English convicts, were acceptable because they were white. By 1850 no fewer than sixty-eight thousand had been sent there. When labour was short, Australia imported Kanaka natives from the Pacific, who were sent back as soon as their tasks were done. In 1839 New South Wales considered importing labourers from India, but this was strenuously opposed by the Colonial Office. James Stephen, the principal policy-maker, warned against those who "would debase by their intermixture with the nobler European race . . . They would bring with them the idolatry and debasing habits of their country".[29] Despite pleas from London that Australia, as a member of the Commonwealth, should not discriminate by using racial criteria, the country persisted with its whites-only policy, continuing to import workers from Britain, Spain, Germany, Scandinavia and Austria.

The Australian attitude set a precedent for Canada. Membership in the British Commonwealth provided no protection to Indians who wanted to emigrate to Canada. On the other hand, Italians, Jews, Swedes, Irish and Scotsmen could do so without restrictions. South Africa's labour history was similar to that of the Caribbean. After the abolition of slavery, efforts were made to import Chinese labourers from Java, then poor Europeans from Madeira and Réunion. When these failed, Indians were brought from 1860, mainly to Natal, a practice that lasted until 1911, when the government of India terminated it. During the half-century of Indian indentureship in South Africa, every effort was made to reduce the status of the Indians, to renege on white commitments and to drive them out whenever this was possible. "We want Indians," they said, "as labourers but not as free men."[30] In 1919 a South African League to combat the "Asiatic Evil" was founded to save South Africa from the presence of too many Indians. The second part of this "Coolieism" chapter explores the common problems which labourers confronted in plantation colonies such as Mauritius, Fiji and the Caribbean. Among these was the enormous sexual disparity, causing serious social problems. The preponderance of males among the Indians made the few available women the subject of keen competition.

Then there was the high suicide rate, the resentment by the Burmese and the Ceylonese of competition in business from outside, as well as religious and linguistic differences in many areas. Independent India under Nehru sought to encourage Indians abroad to become full citizens of their places of settlement and not look towards India as their home.

The final part of the chapter deals with Indian immigration to the Caribbean, which started in British Guiana in 1838 and ended throughout the empire in 1917. During this period the British were joined in this "new system of slavery", transporting "bound coolies" to the Caribbean. Williams tells of the unfairness of a system that forced blacks to indirectly subsidize Indian immigration, since one-third of the immigration costs was borne out of public revenues. A number of pages are then devoted to the conditions of indentureship, particularly the harshness of the system. "As the whip was the discipline of slavery, the jail was the discipline of indenture."[31] Illness was rampant on the estates, mortality was frightening, vagrancy was frequent and time spent in jail was a prominent feature of estate life. Looking at the scenario, the West Indian black had an expression for it, namely "slave coolie". However, all of this effort on the part of the Europeans to boost sugar production in the Caribbean, using Indian labour, paled in the face of Australian cane sugar production:

> By 1893 the blacks had been repatriated, and with the Sugar Works Guarantee Act the plantation system was replaced by a system of central factories supported by a community of farmers, all white, with the State fixing the price of cane and selling price of sugar. Sugar production in the West Indies was slave or half-slave, half-free. In white Australia it was socialism. By 1896 Queensland was producing more than the older West Indian colonies or British Guiana.[32]

In his final testament Williams tried to fill that gap, placing Indian indentureship and settlement against the larger international canvas. He does the same for other oppressed groups such as Chinese, Javanese and other Asiatic peoples who were used as hewers of wood and drawers of water in the Pacific and Atlantic worlds.

Importance of the Book

What, finally, makes this volume, originally written during the 1970s, relevant to our time? For one, it is a formidable example of a subaltern history, that is, a narrative which comes from one who arose from a society which was experiencing the stifling reality of Crown colony government. In this society white was right and upward mobility for the rest was extremely limited.

While doing research abroad, Williams watched painfully the riots and loss of life in the Caribbean during the 1930s. Later on, he wrote about them. As he matured as a historian, he was able to place that colonial condition in a larger global context which now included all victims of forced labour, wherever this existed. Into that colonized-labour frame, he fitted First Peoples (Amerindians), Africans, Japanese, Indians, Javanese and Kanakas from the South Pacific who could work but could not settle in Australia. Williams's particular way of seeing forms the backbone of his interpretation of the world. This world view has been a major influence on subsequent historians, including those whose works he used in his final testament.

The narrative and analysis which follow represent an abridged version of a tome of considerable length, over a thousand pages of intense writing. The task of choosing what to excise from the third version proved daunting. As a general rule, those sections which were drawn from previously published works by Williams have been excluded, as well as the repetitive material which reappeared in later versions of the manuscript. Williams was constantly rewriting chapters, adding new material gleaned from his most recent reading. Many of the detailed statistical tables were left out, although the essential arguments are maintained.

1.

Europe 1492

Slavery and Racism

> *From the hour of their birth, some are marked out for subjection, others for rule.*
>
> Aristotle, *Politics*

How did Europe in 1492 compare with the other great polities of the world – the Middle East, India, China, the Central Eurasian steppes? The origins of civilization are associated with great river basins. The Nile Valley produced the Egyptian civilization of the Pharaohs, the rulers believed to be divine, whose outstanding monuments remain, the Pyramids and the Sphinx – the triumph of the use of stone in architecture, with the simplest tools and without pulleys or iron, a tribute to their organization of labour with state domination of the economy, and a level of sophistication reflected in their beauty aids – rouge, hair dyes, nail polish, wigs, with their ladies at the height of fashion displaying gilded breasts with blue nipples. The valley of the Tigris and Euphrates, the land known today as Iraq and Iran, produced the Sumerian civilization, with its writing, its law (the Code of Hammurabi), and its architecture, culminating in the Ziggurat of Nebuchadnezzar, the biblical Tower of Babel.[1]

The second of the great ancient civilizations developed along the Indus in what are today modern India and Pakistan. By 2300 BC it had produced two of the great cities of the ancient world, a tribute to the capacity for planning and building of that time. These cities were Mohenjo-Daro (Place of the Dead) on the lower Indus, and later Harappa, on one of its tributaries: these two cities dominated a cultural area of nearly half a million square miles, and are distinguished by their wide streets, efficient drainage and absence of military equipment and fortifications. Their subsequent collapse has been attributed to subterranean volcanic activity which literally drowned them in mud. The Indian civilization that evolved after this was based on Aryan control.

The Aryans, building in wood or mud and having no large cities, left as their record only a wealth of literature in the *Vedas*, a sharp contrast to

Hindu culture in their eating of cows and the attitude to the Dravidians of the South, the *dasas*, or slaves, whom the *Vedas* described as short, black, noseless. The evolution of what came to be called greater India included, in the first century after Christ, Malaysia, what is today Indonesia, Cambodia, Borneo, large Indian colonies of Burma, Thailand and Indochina, in what is today Vietnam; Gupta emperors who saw the triumph of Sanskrit, the final form of the great national epics, the *Mahabharata* and *Ramayana*, and the philosophical poem the *Bhagavad Gita*, the supreme scripture of the Hindus, and India's outstanding contributions, the zero and the decimal system. Indian influence extended also to the Philippines and even to Formosa (Taiwan), which were both, for a time, part of the Hindu kingdom of Sumatra in Indonesia.

The disintegration of Europe coincided with the rise of the Arab Empire under the religion of Islam in the seventh century. Breaking out of the Arabian Peninsula one year after the death of Prophet Mohammed, within two decades the Arabs had overrun the entire Middle East: Syria in 615 AD; Iraq in 637 AD; Palestine in 640 AD; Egypt in 647 AD; the entire Persian Empire (Iran) in 650 AD. They even moved eastward to India, westward to the Atlantic and crossed the Strait of Gibraltar into Spain, Portugal and France. Their advance into Europe was halted in 732 when they were defeated near Tours. Their sphere of influence in Europe was then limited to Spain and Portugal; steadily pushed back in Spain, by the end of the thirteenth century they were limited essentially to Granada, from which they were ultimately evicted in January 1492, the very year in which Columbus discovered the New World. At its height Islam spread from the Pyrenees to the Sundaland, from Morocco to Central Asia – the entire area culturally Islamized, linguistically Arabized, with Arabic the language of everyday use from Persia to the Atlantic. Arab power was well demonstrated in the Crusades, the religious wars fought to recover for Christianity the holy places in Jerusalem. It was essentially an Arab victory, under the leadership of such commanders as Suleiman the Magnificent; the height of Muslim control of Europe was reached with the capture of Constantinople in 1453 and the liquidation of the Byzantine Empire. By the fifteenth century the leading world power was the Arab empire, not Europe or any state of Europe. It covered an area from Spain to India, exceeding even the Roman Empire in its prime. It was not until the fifteenth century that Europe made its first contact with the states of West Africa and North Africa, which had long been penetrated by the Arabs, which were Islamic in religion, and which were known to Arab scholars, travellers and geographers. The cities of Gaul and Italy had nothing to compare with the splendour of Baghdad or Córdoba. Only in south Italy, Spain and North Africa did the Western societies come into collision with Islam, and Islam, with Byzantium, exercised true economic hegemony over the West.

Arab economic supremacy was paralleled by the preeminence of Arab scholarship. For the Renaissance in Europe in the early sixteenth century, a revival of humanist interest in the ancient classics of Greece and Rome, the world must thank the Arabs, who, especially from their European stronghold in Spain and their influential contacts in Venice, made possible the translation of the original Greek manuscripts and texts into Arabic and then into Latin. One merely has to make a roll call of the names – Hunayn, the translator of Galen's medical texts (given by the Caliph gold equal to the weight of the books he translated); Ibn Sina (Avicenna); Ibn Rushd (Averroes), one of the foremost interpreters of Aristotle; the Jewish Ibn Meymun (Maimonides). Add to these Razi (Rhazes), physician, and his treatise on smallpox; the Persian medical school of Junidshapur; the pharmacies and mobile clinics of Baghdad; Islam's contribution to mathematics through the publicization, from the Hindus, of the three most basic tools – Arabic numerals, the decimal system, the concept of zero; the Arab influence on the Venetian achievement of the publication of the Greek classics pioneered by Manutius; the confluence of Arabic and Greek learning which made Salerno in Sicily the premier medical school of Latin Europe – and one can appreciate the debt of European scholarship to its Arab tutors and mentors.[2]

The high-water mark of nomad power was reached with Genghis Khan, the title signifying "Ruler of the Universe". The thirteenth-century Mongol empire included Korea, China, all central Asia, Russia and most of the Middle East, and in 1264 Kublai Khan moved his capital from Karakorum in Mongolia to Peking. The Mongols had defeated the Byzantine Empire at Manzikert in 1071, annexed the Punjab, where they slaughtered wholesale the Buddhist monks, pierced the Great Wall, captured Canton and sought to annex Korea, Burma and Vietnam. Mongol armies were operating from the Adriatic to the Sea of Japan, fighting China and Europe at the same time, five thousand miles apart. Much of their success was due to their military tactics: feigned flight, ambush, living off the countryside, surprise cavalry attacks, excellent siege weapons. The Arabs were greatly weakened by the onslaught of the nomads – first Genghis Khan, with the invasion of Persia in 1221, then the capture of Baghdad in 1251, and finally the invasion of Tamerlane from Samarkhand in 1379, leading to the capture of Baghdad in 1392 and Damascus in 1400. It would be long before the Ottoman Sultan lived down the picture of his being carried in an iron cage slung between

24 | THE BLACKEST THING IN SLAVERY WAS NOT THE BLACK MAN

two of Tamerlane's horses. When Islam asked the Christians for aid, the bishop of Winchester is alleged to have made his famous remark, "Let us leave these dogs to devour one another." Pope Honorius III, however, believed that the Mongols might become an ally and help to rescue the Holy Land; Mongol depredations notwithstanding, the mortal enemy of Christendom remained the Moslems.

The Focus on Religion

In this world, there were four major religions – Christianity, with its sideline Judaism; Hinduism, principally in India; Buddhism, an outgrowth of Hinduism, which spread to Japan and to China (in China, competing with Buddhism were the ethical concepts of Confucius and Tau); and Islam. First Hinduism, the origins of which go back four thousand years: professing belief in one god, it also has 330 million gods. The supreme objective of Hinduism is to achieve unification with God. The society was divided into higher and lower castes. There was at the top the Brahmin or priestly caste, and below them, in descending order: the warriors, merchants and labour; and at the bottom, the outcaste – not even a part of the caste system – the untouchables. These castes had four basic features in common: membership was based on characteristic employment (for example, merchants fell in the farmers' caste); the hereditary principle applied, expressed in complex marriage regulations; there were restrictions as to food, water, touch and ceremonial purity; each caste had its own *dharma* or moral code, regarding such duties as maintenance of the family unit, and prescribed ceremonies at marriage, birth and death. Hinduism's Trinity is Brahma the Creator, Vishnu the gracious Preserver and Shiva the Mighty and the Destroyer.

Buddhism arose as a challenge to Hinduism in the sixth century. Hinduism was able to absorb Buddhism to such an extent that thereafter Buddhism virtually disappeared from India. But it spread to Asia – principally to Japan and China, as well as to Burma, Thailand, Tibet, Cambodia, Laos and Ceylon, in all of which countries it is today the dominant religion. Splitting into two great schools of doctrine, one exalting individual liberty and salvation by personal example (cutting across the fundamental emphasis on family obligation in China), the other standing for salvation by faith and good works, the kernel of Buddhism is the Four Noble Truths dealing with the cause and cure of human suffering, and the Noble Eightfold Path, which is the practical technique of action by means of which salvation can be achieved. Out of these has emerged a practical code of conduct known as the Five Precepts, with emphasis on abstention from all illegal sexual pleasures and consumption of intoxicants.

Generally standing aloof from the affairs of the world (the withdrawal of monks and nuns came to be regarded in China as unnatural and antisocial), Buddhism has no overall authority, no pope and no elaborate ceremonies of reversion. But a class of monks has emerged, the three essentials for whom are poverty, inoffensiveness and celibacy; their normal diet is vegetarian, they follow strictly the Buddhist rule against harming any living thing, and they are usually the strictest of pacifists, emphasizing tolerance, nonviolence, respect for the individual, love of animals and nature, and belief in the fundamental spiritual equality of all human beings. Buddhism has stimulated the production of some of Asia's greatest art and architecture, of which there are some outstanding examples in contemporary Japan, whose Buddhist traditions tend to emphasize not philosophical detachment or discipline but compassion. A meeting of the World Buddhist Council was held in Rangoon in 1954, the first of its kind in five hundred years, which drew thousands of devout Buddhists from all over Southeast Asia, testified not only to the persistence of Buddhism but to its increasing vitality.

Islam, which encompasses nearly one-seventh of the total population of the earth, has been the great competitor, historically, of Christianity – with these differences: the belief that God's word was incompletely expressed in the earlier Hebrew and Christian Scriptures and fulfilled only in the Qu-ran; that the Qu-ran supersedes all previous revelations and merely confirms the truths of the Old and New Testaments; that Mohammed was the last and greatest prophet, while Islam reveres the biblical prophets from Abraham to Christ; that, denying the divinity of Christ, Islam has also repudiated attempts to deify Mohammed; and that Islam is not only a religion but also a social code and a system, the Qu-ran providing guidance for all phases of the life of the faithful, for manners and hygiene, marriage and divorce, commerce and politics, crime and punishment, peace and war.

Ritualistic observances of Islam are prescribed in the Five Pillars of Islam: generous alms-giving; the believer must say "There is no God but Allah; Mohammed is the Messenger of Allah"; pray five times daily facing Mecca; perform the fast of Ramadan; and make the pilgrimage to Mecca at least once in his lifetime. The profession of the same beliefs, the uttering, of the same prayers, and the turning of the eye towards the same holy city constitute one of the principal unifying forces for the diverse millions who make up Islam. The Hebrew and Christian fast was extended by Islam to cover an entire month, with fasting limited to the daylight hours; all believers must refrain between dawn and dark from taking food or drink and from any sexual act, with the result that trade and public affairs slow down markedly during the day. But the greatest binding force of millions around the world is the rule that each true believer should make a pilgrimage to Mecca at least once in his lifetime. No non-Muslim may make the pilgrimage or even enter Mecca. Thousands go annually, wearing identical seamless white garments, practising sexual abstinence, abstaining from shaving or having their hair cut, doing no harm to any living thing, animal or vegetable – in this sense of common brotherhood all barriers of race and class dissolve. The high-water mark of the pilgrimage is the Greater Pilgrimage to the Mount of Mercy in the Plain of Arafat, with the believer standing from noon to sunset.

Islam's strength in the world of today is twofold. The widely spread Moslem society, with its ethnic diversity, contrasts with the Christian prejudices on race and colour. The result is that one in three black Africans professes Islam, Islam gains ten black converts for every one who accepts Christianity, and in such a country as Nigeria, Islam is regarded as the religion of the blacks, as opposed to Christianity, the religion of the whites. Islam's assertion of the equality of all believers has exerted a powerful influence over Hindu outcastes or Hindus who escape from the ancient caste system.

As a social force the Christian church derived some of its power and respectability from its inevitable association with literacy, and above all with the international language of communication of the day, Latin. Some people, few in medieval society, could sign their name – El Cid, for example. For the rest, the majority of small or medium feudal lords were illiterates in the full sense of the word. At his own consecration in 1318, the Bishop of Durham, unable to understand or pronounce Latin, after struggling with *Metropolitanus*, gave it up, saying, "Let us take that word as read." One could well understand therefore that unflattering Jesuit portrait of sixteenth-century Corsica after its conversion by Franciscans centuries before. The Jesuits found priests who could not read or did not know Latin or grammar, and were ignorant of the form of the sacrament to be taken at the altar. Often dressed like laymen, they were peasants who worked in the fields and woods, and brought up their children in the sight and full knowledge of the whole community.

The Role of Women

With respect to the role of women in ancient societies, the Greek city states provide a useful starting point. The great historian of the history of the

Hellenistic world and the Roman Empire, Rostovtzeff, has frequently been criticized for his recognition of only two disenfranchised classes in Greece – resident aliens and slaves: there was a third, the women, whose creation was generally regarded as "a curse to mortal men". Demosthenes identified the three categories into which the Greeks divided their women: "We have mistresses for our enjoyment, concubines to serve our person, and wives for the bearing of legitimate offspring."

The "mistresses" were the *hetairae*, "companions to men". In addition to physical beauty, many had intellectual training and artistic talents. The most famous perhaps was Aspasia, foreign-born, the mistress of Pericles. Another was Phryne, the mistress of the sculptor Praxiteles; Alcibiades had his Timandra. Prostitution operated under state control. Solon established the first bawdy house, to provide an outlet for the lustiness of youth, without endangering the social order; in the famous encomium to him, he was "a true benefactor of humanity". The role and importance of the prostitute were presented in a document in which a widow speaks to her daughter: that

> At your age, you should be able to keep me. You must not restrict yourself to young men. Sleep above all with those not too old-looking, not so strong, not so well-built, for they pay the debt. Good-looking men think they are sufficient payment in themselves. Your main concern must be to get generous lovers for people to say – "There is a daughter who is so rich and so good to her mother."

Slave and Serf

The essence of the feudal organization of society was that the king ruled over all, his nobles fought for all, the church prayed for all and the peasants in the fields paid for all. The lord on the one hand should draw his well-being from the things that were provided for him "by the weariness and toil of his man." The monk and priest, on the other hand, lived by the "weariness" of other men. John of Salisbury wrote in the twelfth century, "Those are called the feet who discharge the humbler offices, and by whose services the members of the commonwealth walk upon solid earth" – the husbandmen, the workers in the mechanic arts, those in menial occupations. In China, it was the cult of the long fingernail, whether it was the slave regime in existence or the feudal system seeking to supplant slavery. The ideologist of slavery was Confucius, almost a contemporary of Aristotle and Plato, and it was Confucius who sought to maintain slavery, reviling the slaves as

28 | THE BLACKEST THING IN SLAVERY WAS NOT THE BLACK MAN

"birds and beasts", and looking down upon women in particular. Confucius upheld the three principal slave society institutions – the principalities by which the slave domain was parcelled out to lower-order slave owners; the hierarchy classifying the people into six grades – the Supreme Ruler (Son of Heaven), princes, senior officials, scholars, commoners and slaves; and the system of inheritance ensuring the transmission of titles, the nobility, land, people and political power to the eldest son of the legal wife. The vagaries of contemporary politics associated with the Great Proletarian Cultural Revolution of our time have regaled us with the resurrection of the old privileges and *fueros* defended by Confucius with all the tenacity of an Edmund Burke defending the age of chivalry – a feudal landlord building capital cities, formerly restricted to the ruler of a state, and higher than his ruler's, using horse trappings decorated with seven or nine tassels, putting on a dance ceremony with eight rows each having eight dancers, a form restricted to the supreme ruler's household – while Confucius also ardently defended the code of the nine punishments, to wit: exile, payment of ransom, whipping, flogging with rods, branding, cutting off the nose, cutting off the feet, castration and death. Behind all of this there were the huge slave revolts, with Confucius calling for the end of mild government; but as feudalism took over, there were the slogans of revolting peasants, "equalize the high and the low" and "even up the rich and the poor", in the great peasant uprising at the end of the Chen Dynasty (third century BC) and two great ones at the end of the Western and Eastern Han Dynasties. It all sounds very European to modern ears.

The Hero of Alexandria in the first century AD used steam power to construct a device that opened temple doors. Incredible investments of capital were made in pyramids and ziggurats, cathedrals and palaces, and the view has been put forward recently that the slave labour required for the Egyptian pyramids was Pharaoh's acknowledgement of his responsibility to provide work for his people. In China they still curse the emperor who built the Great Wall at a cost of over a million lives, every stone over its 1,400 miles costing a human life. Yet when an engineering technique was put to the Emperor Vespasian facilitating the erection of an obelisk, his reply was, in forbidding the use of the machine proposed: "Let me provide food for the common folk." But it did not only involve food, in the production of which, after all, some 75 per cent of the labour force was engaged. It was a question of attitude, of philosophy, as indicated in a letter of Seneca to a contemporary:

> Some things we know to have appeared only within our own memory: the use, for example, of glass windows which let in the full brilliance of day through

a transparent pane, or substructures of our baths and the pipes let into their walls to distribute heat and preserve an equal warmth above and below, or the shorthand which catches even the quickest speech, the hand keeping pace with the tongue. All these are inventions of the meanest slaves. Philosophy sits more loftily enthroned. She doesn't train the hand, but is instructress of the spirit! . . . No, she's not, I say, an artisan producing tools for the mere everyday necessities.

Thus slavery was the principal cause of the retardation of technological development. As Aristotle was quick to recognize, "if the shuttle could weave and the plectrum touch the lyre without a hand to guide them, chief workmen would not want servants, nor masters slaves." Like Aristotle, societies and cultures before the age of European overseas expansion depended on "the machine with a voice", the slave.

There was, therefore, no sharp dividing line between freedom and unfreedom. Greece could speak of debtor slaves who were free, and free slaves of the unprivileged class. There was a remarkable fluidity in the distinction. For Aristotle, the essential condition of the free man is that he does not live under the restraint of another. Roman intellectuals, at best showing only a frigid sympathy for the slaves, eschewed the Greek theories of natural inferiority. To Cicero slavery was the result of greed and ignorance, and the reduction to slavery of conquered natives was legitimate only if it involved people incapable of self-government; while Plutarch and Juvenal were merely critical of the cruelty of certain slave owners. Seneca, the most profound of the intellectuals on this subject, was content with emphasizing that slavery was "only corporal" and only the body of the slave was at the service of his master, and he eloquently defended the freedom of the slave's soul. But neither Cicero nor Seneca nor indeed the Stoics ever dreamed of advocating the abolition of slavery. Nor did the slaves, for that matter. The uprisings in Sicily were revolts, not revolutions. Eunus in Sicily wished the slaves to change places with the slave owners; his goal was to change not the social order but its beneficiaries.

The Old Testament, through Leviticus, distinguished between Hebrew bondsmen and non-Hebrew slaves. Initially, the former were to serve only six years, being freed without payment in the seventh. It was a temporary slavery. Later manumission could take place only during the year of the jubilee, which recurs every fifty years. Leviticus advised the Hebrews to go to foreign nations for their slaves as their property, slaves for life. Those holding Hebrew bondsmen were to allow their redemption by relatives, a protection not accorded to aliens. The Old Testament contains no explicit protest against slavery.

Early Christianity had the effect of reinforcing slavery, if only by its emphasis on salvation in the other world and the subordination of temporal distinctions to preparation for the imminent kingdom. Christ's kingdom was not of this world, so slavery was of no importance if the soul was turned towards God. The slave therefore should accept his lot and not seek to attain his freedom: "For he that was called in the Lord, being a bondservant, is the Lord's free man: likewise he that was called, being free, is Christ's bondservant." For St Paul, as for Seneca, slavery was only external; it does not exist in the moral and spiritual domain. But if he excludes the slave market as unjust, slavery is no less for him a legitimate institution, one of the bases of the society of the time. His aim was to Christianize the institution, not to suppress it. While Paul in his celebrated letter exhorted Philemon to take back Onesimus, whom Paul had converted to Christianity, what was involved was that Christians should treat the slaves as spiritual brethren. St Basil later saw in Paul's Epistle the only precedent for returning fugitive slaves to their masters. St John Chrysostom even advised the slave to prefer servitude to manumission. The primitive church was hardly concerned with social relations.

The early Fathers, and especially St Augustine, were all unanimous in their view that slavery, along with the secular instruments of coercion and government, was part of the punishment for man's fall from grace. All slaves deserved to be slaves; the only true slave was the slave to sin. A pious slave could well be serving a master who was a slave of vice. Kindness to slaves was a Christian duty; the church's responsibility was to ensure the security of masters in controlling their property. Thus no slave could be ordained unless he had been emancipated. Baptism had no effect on the status of the slave.

The Council of Gangres in 362 laid anathema on "anyone who under the pretence of godliness should teach a slave to despise his master, or to withdraw himself from his service". As Origen put it, a slave who disobeys his master disobeys God. The church, itself possessing slaves in a society based on the fixity of conditions, was concerned to respect the rights of the master. Only in one sense did it oppose the rights of property: where the master was a Jew and the slave a Christian. The non-Jewish slave of a Jew was to be freed if circumcised or if attempts were made to convert him to Judaism. Where the slave trade was involved and Jews concerned, the church forbade not the trade in slaves, even by Jews, but their prolonged possession of Christian slaves, and the sale of Christian slaves by Jews. It was this concept of slavery which, with the decline and fall of the Roman Empire, was transmitted to feudal and medieval Europe, modified, in the context of the breakdown of centralized law and order, to suit local conditions, from slavery to serfdom or villeinage, with the two systems coexisting for a long period.

This summarizes the position of the slave in the emergence of the feudal system in the words of one of the most distinguished scholars of feudalism. But the condition of the slaves varied from locality to locality. Some were in the lower forms of domestic service, partly in agricultural labour, maintained in the master's house or farm, regarded as human cattle, classified as movable property. A second category was the tenant slave, who owned his dwelling, provided his own subsistence by his own labour, could sell the surplus of his harvest, no longer directly dependent on the master for support; left by the master, whose own interest was in sufficient workdays, to cultivate his holding. The duties of such a tenant were fixed by the custom, scholarly authority puts it, "in a stability absolutely contrary to the very conception of slavery, of which the arbitrary authority of the master was the essential element". The caprice of the master was not the law of the serf, who was protected by the custom of the manor. The serf's attachment was to a *seigneur*, a landowner, not as the slave to a master.

It was in England that the confrontation took place, the Peasants' Revolt of 1381. Facing that oppression which had been denounced in France as the "endless greed of seigneurs" who "would take from you, if they could, even your share of daylight", the "English Revolt" fulfilled that fourteenth-century prophecy that the day was coming "when the worms of the earth will most cruelly devour the lions, leopards and wolves". They very nearly did in 1381; the Peasants' Revolt came within an ace of toppling the government. Spurred on by a third poll tax in four years, reaching out to everyone over fifteen, the fundamental grievance, as enunciated by Wat Tyler, was the bonds of villeinage and the lack of legal and political rights. The chronicler has left us a record of their thinking and murmurings: "In the beginning of the world there were no slaves and no one ought to be treated as such." They were determined to be free, and if they laboured or did any "work", they would be paid for it.

> They are clothed in velvet and rich stuffs, ornamented with ermine and other furs, while we are forced to wear poor clothing. They have wines, spices, and fine bread, while we have only rye and the refuse of straw; and when we drink, it must be water. Are we not all descended from the same parents, Adam and Eve? . . . We are called slaves, and if we do not perform our service we are beaten and we have no sovereign to whom we can complain or who would be willing to hear us.

To the king they said, "We wish you to make us free forever. We wish to be no longer called slaves, nor held in bondage." It was the vision of Piers Plowman, in the words of the poet: "mankind arises from one origin" you who know the living man, now in death, "which is the villein now and which the knight, now that "the crows have gnawed their carcasses so bare – so bare". All serve the Lord, Christians, Jews and heathens: "God has all creation in his care." The revolt was defeated by fraud and not by force: cynical revocation of all the charters of freedom issued personally by a young king, on the ground, as stated by his parliament of landowners, that they were issued under duress. The young king went one better: he said to a delegation of the rebels, "Villeins ye are, and villeins ye shall remain."

Special attention was paid to the competition of slaves with free white workers; slaves were not to follow in the Balearic Islands any trade for which there existed a guild organization. In Genoa, from fear of poisoning, Tartar and Turkic slaves were not to be taught the art of compounding potions. In Barcelona certain trades were banned to slaves. The guild regulation of the brakemen of 1373 decreed that the obligation to attend the funeral of a colleague was not to extend to slaves whom some masters allowed to perform the tasks; nor could the funeral flag of the guild be spread over the bodies of these captives. By this time, black slavery was not a novelty in southern Europe, though the Sudanese slaves brought by Moslems along the caravan routes had become the norm rather than the exception with the Portuguese conquest of Guinea, after which blacks were introduced directly into Spain and Portugal by the maritime route, which eliminated the Moslem intermediary and the long continental haul by caravan. In the years 1441 to 1448, at least 927 black slaves were sent to Portugal. Statistics for later years were: from Guinea to Lisbon, 1480–1493, 3,587 slaves (532 a year); to Lagos, 1490–1498, 739; making a combined annual average of 883 slaves. In 1551 there was one slave in Lisbon for every freeman. In 1620 Lisbon alone had 10,470 slaves.[3] The slave trade had become a royal monopoly requiring a licence; when the Portuguese Cortes in 1472 protested against the export of Guinea slaves as restricting the development of new lands, the king disagreed, taking the commercial point of view rather than the agrarian. In earlier years burial of slaves was not allowed in cemeteries; one got rid of what there was in whatever way. By 1515 the king intervened and ordered black corpses to be thrown into a common ditch, *Pozo dos Negros*. Black slaves were so numerous in Seville that a special judge was appointed for blacks and mulattoes, slave and free – a black formerly attached to the royal court. The blacks had their own religious fraternities in Barcelona (from 1455), in Valencia and in Seville.

Europe 1492 | 33

With the black slave, the slave trade and slavery assumed a new dimension. Azurara's striking paragraph in his narrative of The *Discovery and Conquest of Guinea* tells the whole story – cruelty, filthy lucre, naive proselytism, sombre despair of the victims, whose ethnic diversity was clearly emphasized. The whole world associated with the transaction, expressing the surprise, mixed with indignation, of the Portuguese population. Verlinden interprets

> that if the bourgeois of Lagos or the peasants of Algarve wept or cried at this spectacle, it was because something new had been born, the horror of which exceeded what they had known: the modern trade, mass phenomenon, anonymous misfortune, crushing backward colonial populations with the blind fatality of a force which was beyond them. This was produced by the sudden amplification of the technique of transport in the white world, as well as the needs of manpower of a universe on the threshold of economic transformation.[4]

By then Europe had achieved two other elements in the necessary infrastructure. Having got the trade, Portugal immediately established a House of Trade in Lisbon, which came to control all three sections – India, Guinea and the slave trade, Lisbon ultimately representing the concentration of the African, Asian and Brazilian trades. From 1481, at the insistence of the Portuguese Cortes, the monarchy moved to forbid foreigners, especially Genoese and Florentines, to settle in Portugal because they stole the "royal secrets as to Africa and the islands". Foreigners were officially excluded at all times from direct participation in the African trade in either slaves or commodities. Further, this was not just academic or theoretical. An early Belgian notice on the value of the slave trade emanating from Tournai in 1480 stressed how one could buy on the Slave Coast, for a barber's basin, a woman and child, who could be sold for a respectable weight of gold dust at Elmina. Having got the labour supply, Spain also had the appropriate crop – the sugarcane, grown in Sicily in 1462.

Slavery developed as a concrete economic institution in Mediterranean and Atlantic islands in the fifteenth century, producing sugar, beginning with Crete, Sicily, Cyprus, and, on the mainland, in Spain and Portugal, Valencia, Malaga and the Algarve, and spreading to the Atlantic – Madeira, Canaries and São Tomé. The original labour supply came from the Black Sea area and sub-Saharan Africa, constituting a mixture of free men from Europe, a few local serfs and some slaves captured in Levantine wars under planters of European origins from Venice, Catalonia, France and Genoa. It was Cyprus that first laid the foundation of a sugar industry directed by Europeans, utilizing slave labour brought from south Russia, to be marketed in Europe.

34 | THE BLACKEST THING IN SLAVERY WAS NOT THE BLACK MAN

Long before the discovery of America, a new sugar press invented in Sicily spread to the Iberian Peninsula and Atlantic islands, and a sugar industry using Sicilian technology and technicians, Genoese capital and Portuguese maritime expertise spread to Madeira and the Canary Islands, supplying sugar to Europe and West Africa. It was in the Canary Islands that the sugar industry scored its first achievement: the disappearance of the aborigines, the Guanches, under the brutality of the conquerors, while Madeira's timber supplies vanished under the aggression of sugarcane monoculture. We are not far from that later prohibition in Portugal of participation by non-Portuguese subjects in the sugar trade, or that threat of reprisals in Venice against the persons or possessions of any workers or master craftsmen refiners who left the city to exercise their trade elsewhere. If Columbus or Cabral or someone else had not discovered America around 1492/1500, Europe (at least south Europe) might well have become one vast slave plantation and/or factory, utilizing black African labour. Atlantic colonial slavery merely supplemented and then supplanted European slave production.

One further point arises in respect of the new lease of life for the slave system in the Iberian Peninsula. We shall examine later the claim made for the Iberian slave system as being superior to the Anglo-Saxon in respect of the treatment of slaves, owing to religious influence, ease of manumission, better treatment and less race prejudice. All this was based on the codification of Spanish slave law of Alfonso the Wise in 1260, known as *Las Siete Partidas*. But this was valid for Castile only; the Catalonia-Aragon complex had its own code, the Code of Tortosa, of 1272, which remained in full force up to the seventeenth century, as important for Mediterranean Spain as *Las Siete Partidas* was, "above all a theatrical work, aiming to create an ideal law, largely Roman and canonical in inspiration". Its chief characteristic was the difference it posed between captives of the same religion and slaves of another belief, leading to its conclusion that the condition of the latter is "the greatest misfortune which can befall men in this world". So what? After the 1260 *Las Siete Partidas*, all slavery involved slaves of another belief – ultimately of another race and colour. *Las Siete Partidas* gave the master complete authority over his slave, with the right to kill in certain circumstances; decreed that the profits of slaves belonged to the master; provided for manumission but required the manumitted slave to love, honour and obey the master who manumitted him; asserted the master's right of property over fugitive slaves unless the fugitive escaped to Moslem territory; provided for slave marriage even against the will of the master; and prohibited the separation of families. The *Partidas* will be elaborated presently.

Daily Life

When Columbus discovered the New World in 1492, Europe was essentially a poor continent frequently subject to famine and epidemics. There were recurrent outbreaks of plague, of which the most devastating was the Black Death in 1348, commemorated in Boccaccio's *Decameron*, which is a series of conversations and narratives in a villa near Florence at the time of the Black Death. Spread by the small medieval black rat and facilitated by the wooden houses of the day, bubonic plague took two forms: it infected the bloodstream, caused external bleeding and was spread by contact; in its more virulent form, it infected the lungs and was spread by respiratory infection.

Behind the laconic and casual comment of Froissart – "a third of the world died" – lay a picture of an almost incredible devastation. A French physician said that it seemed as if one sick person would infect the whole world. The pope reported a death toll of twenty-four million. A ghost ship with a cargo of wool and a dead crew drifted offshore of Norway until it ran aground near Bergen. A single graveyard received eleven thousand corpses in six weeks. A bishop in England gave permission to laymen to make confessions to one another, as was done by the Apostles: "if no man is present, then even to a woman". The platitude of the day was: "This is the end of the world." Someone recorded, "In those days was burying without sorrow and wedding without friendship." Siena's projected cathedral, planned to be the largest in the world, was abandoned; half the city's population had died. Most cities ordained the silencing of funeral bells and of the crier's announcement of death. Siena imposed a fine on the wearing of mourning clothes by all except widows. Three archbishops of Canterbury died within a year.

Was malaria in the Pontine Marshes one of the causes of the decadence of the Roman Empire? They were notorious fever-breeders for centuries, and malaria was often called by the English "Roman fever". The French called it *paludisme*, from the Latin for "swamp", signifying a sickness of wetlands. Varro and Vetruvius warned of the diseases bred in swamps; Columella urged farmers not to build near a swamp "which breeds insects armed with annoying stings". Since the days of ancient Rome, malaria had been notoriously the prime cause of the land's desolation. Then there was syphilis, "a new and strange malady – unknown to the ancients", as it was described in 1575. The controversy it produced is not yet settled. Was it an indigenous European export to the New World, or was it the New World's reciprocal gift to the Old for its smallpox and measles? Did the Bible

36 | THE BLACKEST THING IN SLAVERY WAS NOT THE BLACK MAN

identify syphilis when the Lord "smote Job with sore boils from the sole of his feet unto his crown"? Or in David's lament that "my wounds stink and are corrupt. My loins are filled with a loathsome disease; and there is no soundness in my flesh"? Or in the Second Commandment in Exodus describing God, "a jealous God, visiting the iniquity of the fathers upon the children unto the third and fourth generation" (though we now know that congenital syphilis is transmissible only to the second generation)? Or in Jeremiah's prediction that "the fathers have eaten a sour grape, and the children's teeth are set on edge"? Or in Numbers with the woman who is like the dead man "of whom the flesh is half consumed when he cometh out of his mother's womb"? Or in Deuteronomy's description of the stages of syphilis: scab, itch, madness, blindness? On the other hand, is the present knowledge of the epidemiology of syphilis consistent with the suggestion that Columbus's small crew could have launched such an epidemic as seems first to be recorded by the French army before Naples in 1494?

The Europeans were victims not only of plague but also famine, which goes far back into European history. The European society, behind all the pomp and power, chivalry and the glitter of the church, was miserably poor, comprising in all countries a mass of underemployed and destitute vagrants and vagabonds, a huge proletariat which constituted a structural feature of medieval life. They could not have lived without the soup distributed at the doors of monasteries, while huge numbers were employed by the *hidalgos* as domestic servants. *Viva la povertà*, "long live poverty", was the slogan of the revolt of the *straccioni* at Lucca in 1531, the revolt of the ragged men. Marseilles in 1566 proceeded to expel all undesirables; but to expel from one place was merely to drive them to another. The English Poor Law drove the poor off the streets, but they remained destitute, and when the Black Death disrupted society by drastically reducing the number in the labour force, governments stepped in to force wages back to pre-plague levels. The English Statute of Labourers of 1350 presented idleness of the workers as a crime against society. Wrote the Venetian envoy to England, "There is no country where there are so many thieves and robbers as in England, insomuch that few venture to go in the country excepting in the middle of the day, and fewer still in the towns at night, and least of all in London."

The *Mendigos*, the brotherhood of the poor, constituted a state within a state, with its own festivals and gatherings of the dregs of society branded as thieves, bandits, tramps, debtors fleeing from creditors, husbands fleeing from wives – and all collected in Seville, seeking to emigrate to the New World. One of the great medieval scholars has left us a graphic picture of the

Europe 1492 | 37

polarization of society – a rich and vigorous nobility of powerful dynasties owning vast properties; and the poor and disinherited, the *picardía*. The world of the black market was above all of poverty. At the heart of that society lay bitter despair. The Estates General of France bewailed in 1484, "As for the little people, one could not imagine the persecution, poverty and misery they have suffered and still suffer in many ways." Vives advocated the relief of the poor in 1526. What relief? "Let no one among, the poor be idle," he wrote, quoting St Paul: if any would not work, neither should he eat. For wasters and spendthrifts, "Give irksome trades and smaller rations. They must not die of hunger, but they must feel its pangs."

Life was not only rough, it was cheap. "None goeth unarmed in public," it was said of the Netherlands, and in fourteenth-century Italy, one was warned against going out at night. A Bellini painting shows an attack by mercenaries on travellers on the highway; in the background woodcutters continued calmly at their jobs, accustomed to such assaults. Italian football was played with the heads of executed prisoners of war. A new attitude to death emerged: formerly the dominant idea of death was the spiritual journey of the soul; now the rotting of the body seemed more significant. The emphasis was on worms and putrefaction and gruesome physical details. The tomb of Harsigny, the great physician, demonstrated the striking change: his body lay naked, with all the extreme thinness of very old age, hands crossed over the genitals, a stark confession of the nothingness of mortal life. Madness became familiar in the Middle Ages in all its varieties.

If European nations enjoyed no obvious political superiority over other major countries, no more than Christianity had any obvious religious or social superiority over other major religions, it was unquestionable that Europe enjoyed – whether over China, India, Arabia – three indisputable advantages: superior technology, superior diet and an intellectual outlook, whether on scholasticism, technology and the dignity of labour, that was dynamic and not rooted in the past. China, indeed, had led the way in technology: in the production of silk and the machinery required for its manufacture; in the production of delicate porcelains whose translucent blue and white ware the best Italian craftsmen were unable to duplicate; in gunpowder; in the compass described in an eleventh-century Chinese work; in printing, perhaps (though this has raised a controversy as to whether it was cultural diffusion or independent discovery. The westward flow of techniques is impressive).[5]

But Europe had the enormous advantage of the crank, second in importance only to the wheel; the crank was unknown to the Greeks and

Romans. Antiquity also suffered the disability of inefficient use of animal power. It was ignorant of the horseshoe and knew only the yoke system of harness – good for the ox but not for the horse – a mechanically defective harness which did not allow for one animal to be harnessed in front of another. The faulty arrangement of breast and girth bands in ancient harnesses exerted a choking pressure on the horse's windpipe. Thus all great weights had to be drawn by gangs of slaves, since animal power was not technically available in sufficient quantity.

By the tenth century, three major and decisive inventions appeared virtually simultaneously in Europe: the modern horse collar, the tandem harness and the horseshoe. The combined result of these three inventions was to give Europe a new supply of non-human power, with no increase in costs or labour; so much so that it has been said that these inventions did for the eleventh and twelfth centuries what the steam engine did for the nineteenth. The new harness made the horse available for agricultural labour. But the horse feeds on grain, the ox on hay. Grain was more expensive. The substitution of the three-field for the two-field system, allowing more acres in crops each year with less ploughing, was combined with the heavy wheeled plough to achieve more efficient and productive use of land and labour. The horse in the three-field system as against the ox in the two-field system provided a decisive economic advantage for northern Europe over the Mediterranean area and still more over non-European systems. If the ox saved food, the horse saved man-hours. Furthermore, Europe was able to achieve what China failed to achieve with its horizontally turned mills: the transformation of the windmill into a wheel fitted vertically, as the Romans had done centuries before in respect of watermills. The Middle Ages saw also the beginnings of mechanization in the textile industry – a home industry in the classical societies – first, fulling; secondly, weaving; thirdly, spinning. The European technological lead has been summed up by one scholar as follows:

> The cumulative effect of the newly available animal, water, and wind power was the rapid replacement from the twelfth century of human by non-human energy. The chief glory of the later Middle Ages was not its cathedrals or its spires or scholasticism; it was the building for the first time in history of a complex civilisation which rested not on the backs of sweating slaves or coolies but primarily on non-human power.

Europe's second indisputable advantage in the race for world dominion was its superior diet: a diet of meat as against a vegetarian diet in other parts of the world. Someone has said, "Tell me what you eat, and I will tell you who you are." Hindu India, where the cow was a religious obsession, not only did not eat meat; the dung was dried and used as fuel. The Islamic world regarded pork as an abomination; by the mid-sixteenth century it was observed in France that pork was the habitual food of poor people. Proportionately speaking, there were ten oxen in France over every one in China; China remained ignorant of milk, cheese and butter. By contrast Europe was a carnivorous continent, and cheese was one of the staple foods, thus remaining squarely in the ancient Mediterranean agrarian pattern of corn, olives, vines and stockraising established well before the Homeric legends; broken, however, by the fact that the Roman ate little meat.

Between five and six centuries after the technological revolution for which Europe has been lauded for its shift from manpower to mechanical power, the Jesuits in China were holding up as an example the Chinese custom of accomplishing "all sorts of mechanical work with many fewer instruments than we use", and, going even further in their encomium, justifying this by asking, "What use would machine and working animals be there?" Europe's increasing independence of slavery and "coolieism" on European soil strengthened and extended the boundaries of unfree labour in the rest of the world which Europe moved to dominate.

Europe's most decisive advantage was its intellectual dynamism. By the fourteenth century Europe was in intellectual ferment, with its increasing universities – Bologna, Paris and Oxford in the twelfth century: Oxford with its scholars of Merton College, Paris with its Terminists – all concentrating on science, so that one of Galileo's major contributions to mechanics is at least three centuries older; Padua, Naples, Salamanca in the thirteenth; Prague, Cracow, Vienna in the fourteenth. One of the popes has left us a picture, from 1458, of student life in Vienna:

> Students largely devote themselves to pleasure, and are avid for food . . . and wine; few come out with any learning, nor are they restrained by any discipline. Day and night they roam about . . . their wits are completely addled by the shamelessness of the women. . . . This is a ragged, boorish lot, and there is a very great number of whores. Rare is the woman who is content with one husband. The nobles, when they come to visit the citizens, draw their wives off to secret meetings; when the husbands leave home, full of wine, their wives yield to the nobles.

The Islamic madrassas – clearly in the lead up to the thirteenth century, with Islamic scholarship at its best; the great Islamic doctors, the translation centres of Baghdad and Toledo – dropped behind, enthroning scholasticism and suppressing the spirit of enquiry, preferring the rote memorization

40 | THE BLACKEST THING IN SLAVERY WAS NOT THE BLACK MAN

of authoritative texts, conservative theologians rejecting all scientific and philosophical speculation as leading to heresy and atheism. Islam made theology the queen of the sciences at the very period when European intellectualism was challenging the theory and practice of scholasticism. Consider the twelfth-century controversy in the Islamic world between Al-Ghazzali, the foremost theologian of Islam, and Ibn Rushd (of Córdoba in Spain), the foremost Moslem Aristotelian philosopher better known as Averroes. Al-Ghazzali, in his *Incoherence of Philosophy*, attacked the whole secular school, and saw in divine revelation the ultimate source of truth. Averroes, counterattacking with his *Incoherence of the Incoherence*, called for subjection of knowledge to the test of reason and denied that philosophy was inimical to the faith. The educated classes rejected Averroes, whom they suspected of atheism. Less than a century before Columbus's voyage the distinguished historian Ibn Khaldun, often acclaimed as the father of sociology, was rejecting philosophy and science as useless and dangerous, pontificating:

> It should be known that the opinion the philosophers hold is wrong in all its aspects. . . . The problems of physics are of no importance in our religious affairs or our livelihoods. Therefore, we must leave them alone. . . . Whoever studies it (logic) should do so only after he is saturated with the religious law and has studied the interpretation of the Koran and jurisprudence. No one who has no knowledge of the Moslem religious sciences should apply himself to it. Without that knowledge he can hardly be safe from its pernicious aspects.

Europe's intellectual dynamism was manifested also in the attitude to labour and to technology. The monks and friars of Europe not only preached, they practised the dignity of labour. To work was not only to pray, it was to dignify the worker, to break down the alienation of the philosopher and intellectual from the artisan, it was to combine sweat with brain. It was a friar of the thirteenth century, Roger Bacon, with his experimentation and his interest in optics, who foresaw many of the technological achievements of the future:

> Machines may be made by which the largest. ships, with only one man steering them, will move faster than if they were filled with rowers; waggons may be built which will move with unbelievable speed and without aid of beasts; flying machines can be constructed in which a man may beat the air with mechanical wings like a bird . . . machines will make it possible for men to go to the bottom of seas and rivers.

The outstanding development was the floating magnetic compass, the most momentous invention to promote ocean voyages. Known from the twelfth century, its introduction was delayed by such stories as that of the magnetic mountain towards which all ships bearing a compass and iron nails would be drawn to be destroyed. Less than a century after the discovery of the New World, an Elizabethan courtier, Raleigh, man of the New Age, gave vent to the new dynamism: "I shall never be persuaded that God hath shut up all the light of learning within the lanthorn of Aristotle's brains."

The Inequality of the Races

Europeans by 1492 had developed the theory and the practice of racism with four groups in particular – Jews, Irish, Arabs and black Africans. The foundations of anti-Semitism were laid by the early church fathers, especially the tirades of St John Chrysostom, Priest of Antioch, who denounced the Jews as Christ-killers. In 1205, Pope Innocent III propounded the doctrine that for this reason the Jews were doomed to perpetual servitude. The charge was made of ritual murder of Christian victims – blood libel; first raised in London in 1144 and in Europe, at Blois, in 1171. Pope Gregory X, in 1272, following one of his predecessors twenty-five years before, attacked the ritual murder charge, which he called "a silly pretext" and "a miserable pretext", accusing "the parents of these children, or some other Christian enemies of these Jews" of secretly hiding the children in order to blame the Jews and extort money from them. In 1240, there took place in Paris the famous trial of the Talmud for heresy and blasphemy ending in preordained conviction and burning of twenty-four cartloads of Talmudic works. The church multiplied its decrees designed to isolate Jews from Christian society: Jews were not to employ Christians as servants, nor to serve as doctors to Christians, to intermarry, to sell flour, bread, wine, oil, shoes or any article of clothing to Christians, to build new synagogues. The occupations barred to Jews by the guilds included weaving, metal working, mining, tailoring, shoemaking, goldsmithing, baking, milling and carpentry. Pope Innocent III at the Fourth Lateran Council of 1215 decreed the wearing of the Jewish badge which came to be known as the Badge of Shame.

As spelled out in England, every Jew at all times, in the city or outside it, walking or riding, had to wear upon his outer garment a piece of cloth or parchment, prescribed a few years before both sexes, as a badge two fingers wide and four long, of a different colour from the rest of the garment. The Jewish Statute of 1275 amended this to read: a badge of yellow taffeta, six fingers long and three broad, to be worn by every Jew over seven. The Council of Vienna (1267) prescribed the pointed Jewish hat. The

42 | THE BLACKEST THING IN SLAVERY WAS NOT THE BLACK MAN

superficial resemblance of Jews to the Christian population, the difficulty of recognizing them anthropologically, must have been considerable to justify these discriminatory measures. No one knew this better than the Nazis, who, having recourse also to special badges, had in addition to adopt religious criteria to determine who were Jews. They came up with the answer: those persons were considered as of the Jewish race whose ancestry included a prescribed number of practising Jews.[6]

Three principal disabilities developed over the centuries. *Las Siete Partidas* prohibited the ownership of Christian slaves by Jews. Florence prohibited sexual intercourse between Jew and Christian, and any Christian prostitute who "leased her body" to a Jew was whipped before being sent to prison, being marched off with a placard reading "For whoredom" hanging over her breasts. The third concerned justice. As early as 419, a church council had forbidden Jews to bear witness against Christians. In 1292, Pope Gregory X, in accordance with the medieval legal principle that every man has the right to be judged by his peers, insisted that Jews could only be condemned if there were Jewish as well as Christian witnesses against them. Nonetheless the scales were weighted against the Jews. Before initiating judicial proceedings, a Jew had to pay a sum three times the sum imposed on a Christian; if the Jews got a writ of recovery, one-tenth went automatically to the exchequer.[7]

"Hath not a Jew eyes?" Shylock was to ask in *The Merchant of Venice*. Where racism directed against the Jews was a European phenomenon, the experience with the Irish was specifically English. Beginning with the Anglo-Norman invasion of 1169, the medieval conquest was never complete, though it established an English colony and an English administration on Irish soil with the claim of England's king to lordship over the whole island. In the long attempt to establish Anglo-Saxon domination over Celtic Ireland, the English developed an experience and fashioned a philosophy which was to be transferred wholesale to their overseas colonial settlements in Virginia against the Amerindians in particular, at the very time the Spaniards were developing their own philosophy on the Amerindians inspired by their special familiarity with the Arab and African question.

One has merely to read in the second half of the sixteenth century of the "wild, unreasonable beasts", "naked rogues" whom the English compared to wolves and foxes; the Irish leader at court with his yellow surplices dyed with saffron or stale human urine, at whom the English gazed as they did later at the people of China. The poet Spenser saw his "Faerie Queene" ruling over Irish who scarcely knew the purpose of clothing, reminiscent of the ancient Scythians in their barbarism and aimless marching, a starving people who "looked like descriptions of the Irish anatomies of death, they spake like ghosts crying out of their graves". Spenser led the imperialist call for help in "reducing of that savage nation to better government and civility", advocating specifically the policy of anglicization and justifying the savagery of English military operations. In the devastation of Munster in the 1580 rebellion, over thirty thousand Irish were killed or died of starvation; in Spenser's words, "In short space there were none almost left and a most populous and plentiful country suddenly left void of man or beast." Only a little longer, and but for the distraction of Virginia and New England, and the English would have arrived at the conclusion that the only good wild Irishman was a dead wild Irishman.[8]

Rich's *The Irish Hubbub* of 1617 emphasized the role of Ireland over many years as "the receptacle for our English runagates, that for their misled lives in England do come running over into Ireland". The considered conclusion of a popular British historian cannot be seriously challenged: "It has been said that the Elizabethan eagles flew to the Spanish Main while the vultures swooped down on Ireland, but they, were in many cases one and the same bird." Specifically, England's Irish experience sufficed to transplant the following practices and prejudices to the New World:

1. The establishment of a new race in the conquered territory, a strong British colony in a province hitherto a Gaelic stronghold, drawing on the Scots Presbyterians for their Ulster plantations, which represented the confiscation of six counties predominantly Catholic – Nova Scotia, someone sneeringly nicknamed the new creation. Thought was given to the total removal of the indigenous population and the substitution of a more docile people. But it was agreed that no state would be able to spare so many people for the "new inhabitants"! Therefore the contemplated genocide was abandoned as "'a marvellous sumptuous charge", and English laws gravely announced that it was not the intention to extirpate "the entire nation".

2. A massive revolutionary transfer of land from the Catholic conquered to the Protestant conquerors, where Catholic land ownership was reduced to about 14 per cent of the total by the end of the seventeenth century; Protestants, constituting one-quarter of the whole population, were distinctively the landowning class, while Catholics, three in four of the population, were as distinctively the tenant class. Gaelic polity, with its property rights belonging to lineage groups rather than to individuals, the land being redistributed

THE BLACKEST THING IN SLAVERY WAS NOT THE BLACK MAN

among members at intervals determined by custom, was replaced by a system of individual ownership developed in native Irish areas, and associated with a steady reduction in the number of native landholders.

3. The *Herrenvolk* set out to "civilize" the churls; with two cultures clearly evident, the English set out to make the island's population "one body". First, the Irish must speak English: "The speech being Irish, the heart must needs be Irish," averred Spenser. "It hath been ever the case of the conqueror to despise the language of the conquered and to force him by all means to learn his." As someone else put it: "Now put the case that the Irish tongue were as sacred as the Hebrew, as learned as the Greek, as fluent as the Latin, as amorous as the Italian, as courteous as the Spanish, as courteous as the French, yet truly I see, not but it may be very well spared in the English Pale." Then the Irish must dress like the English and "wear clothing of the English fashion". Then they must live like the English, not in their "nasty, brutish condition" in cabins without "chimneys or windows, on a staple diet of milk and potatoes looking for all the World so rough and barbarous and miserable that many of them are little better in their ways than the most remote Indians". Above all they must "qualify their houses so that English women may be content to be their wives"; in the English view, a house that could be built in three days was "in itself an affront to a work-loving nation". Above all, they must live in towns, which alone could be associated with a "civilized" existence.

This was what English observers meant when, after "the war that finished Ireland", the reconquest by Cromwell, they conclude that Ireland was "almost a blank sheet on which the English commonwealth could write what it wished". It has taken them a long time to do their writing, notwithstanding their scorched-earth policy and effort to starve the Irish into submission; but as they moved off to Virginia and elsewhere, with Irish soldiers, students and rebels going into exile to practise their Catholicism, they could not see so far into the future.

European racism towards Arabs begins with the decisive fact that the relations between the two ethnic groups in respect of Spain and Portugal were based on a simple fact of life – for eight centuries the Arabs were the lords and masters, not the Christians; the dark, and not the blond. To Brazil the Portuguese took their obsession with the Moorish princess, that practical experience of women of another race (the Spaniards took the dark eyes of Andalusia, where the Arabs were centred) which Gilberto Freyre had seen as the outstanding contribution to their miscibility – of the Portuguese to human relations, and which explains, to a very large degree, some of the differences between Anglo-Saxon and Iberian attitudes to Amerindian women.[9] The Portuguese in Brazil were of the view that the Amerindian women could rival the choicest white women. Diego Alvarez took his Amerindian princess to France; not so John Smith and Pocahontas in Virginia. The reconquest in Spain was spread over centuries – from Toledo in 1055 (whatever its importance in Spanish Christian eyes, it was never more than an outpost in the centre of the peninsula from the point of view of Islam) through Saragossa, Córdoba, Valencia, Seville, down to the capture of Granada in 1492. But the Arabs remained in Spain, the Spaniards now being the overlords. By 1566 the Spanish monarchy had decided to act, the goal being to eliminate all traces of Islam. Morisco peasants were sent in chains from Aragon into exile in Castile, with old Christian families from Galicia and Asturia, Castilians moved into the deserted villages of Granada. The Arabs were forbidden to wear Arab dress (no veils for women in the street), to close their houses in Moorish fashion (they must keep open house for Christians to see if they were still surreptitiously practising their faith), to patronize Moorish baths and to speak Arabic. Eventually they were totally expelled from Spain between 1609 and 1614. The Archbishop of Valencia plaintively asked, "Who will make our shoes now?" The landlords must have added, "And who will farm our lands?"[10]

Why did Spain expel the Arabs as it had previously expelled the Jews (one of the first acts after conquest of Granada in 1490, smashing up the Iberian Islam that had developed over the centuries). The answer was that the Moors were unassimilable: the religious and cultural enmity could not be bridged; the Moor had retained all his Moorish identity and had refused to accept Western civilization. It was not a matter, Spaniards pleaded, of annihilating a hated race; it was impossible to maintain an irreducible core of Islam right in the heart of Spain. Spain opted for the most radical of all solutions – deportation, the uprooting of a civilization from its native soil, after more than seven hundred years. The crucial issue of race relations at once emerged. Jeremiah had, in the Old Testament, raised the rhetorical question, can the Ethiopian change his skin, the leopard his spots? And the Old Testament presents the first image of the black man as a slave. Petronius, for the Romans, answered Jeremiah's question in relation to sailors seeking to escape from a ship when the proposal was made that they should deceive their captors by dyeing themselves with black cork to look "like Ethiopian slaves". The ringleader counters, "Oh yes! and please circumcise us so that we look like Jews and bore our ears to imitate Arabians, and chalk our faces till Gaul takes us for her own sons, as if this colour alone could alter our shapes . . . tell me, can we also make our lips swell to a hideous thickness? Or transform our hair with curling-tongs?"

In one of the Hellenistic romances, *Daphnis and Chloe*, the Ethiopian queen gives birth to a white daughter. She explained the reason for "a complexion alien to the native Ethiopian tint": "When I consorted with my husband I was looking at the picture which represented Andromeda." The husband, in the best cuckold tradition, asks querulously, "How could we two, both Ethiopians, produce a white child?" As Louis XIV recognized when allegedly faced with a mulatto child of the queen, who explained, "she had looked at the black dwarf before she conceived, 'That must have been a very penetrating look'."

And Shakespeare is full of the conventional racism that his audience would understand – the repulsive Caliban, a play on "cannibalism"; Othello mounted on the white Desdemona, a "black ram tupping your white ewe", as Iago incites her father with his own sexual jealousy of the Moor; Launcelot sleeping with the black woman and getting her pregnant; Aaron the Moor in *Titus Andronicus*. An audience would understand all the implications of this racism (which carried with it no suggestion or implication of slavery, but merely of blackness coupled with the sexual prowess of the black man, in the phrase of Jobson, one of the first of the slave traders, "furnished with such members as are often a sort burdensome unto them", though there was or would be no shortage of white females ready to share the black man's burden). For that audience knew of the multiplicity of domestic servants in Elizabethan England, and of governmental directions to get rid of the large number of blacks in the country; "those kind of people may well be spared in this realm", as was stated in 1596, and England "to be served by their own countrymen [rather] than those kind of people".

Westward Ho!

> *The story is told of an argument among whites as to whether Columbus or Ericson was the true discoverer of America. An Amerindian listener interposed: "Discover nothing! We knew it was here all the time."*

The traditional explanation is that the indigenous inhabitants of America, Mongoloid in origin, migrated during the more temperate period in the great Ice Age, about 25,000 BC, from eastern Siberia across the Bering Strait, whence they moved to populate the entire continent. As has frequently been pointed out, this argument required us to accept the most difficult and impossible migration route while rejecting, the possibility of transpacific and transatlantic crossings by boat. The daredevil stunts in recent years, such as the famous *Ra I* and *Ra II* expeditions of Thor Heyerdahl, using such perishable materials as papyrus, remind us that the smallest of Columbus's vessels was forty tons, that Drake's *Golden Hind* was seventy-five feet in length, that Frobisher's twenty-ton *Gabriel* crossed the North Atlantic.[11]

In his *City of God*, St Augustine devoted a chapter to the question of whether the descendants of Adam or of the sons of Noah produced monstrous races of men. The travel literature of the Middle Ages was dominated by the belief in wild men. The Spanish Conquistadors left on their voyages of discovery convinced that they would encounter all kinds of mythical beings and monsters – humans with tails, women with beards, headless creatures, giants, pigmies, griffins, humans with doglike faces; and lands of gold and the fabulous wealth of El Dorado, the kingdom of Prester John, the Fountain of Youth, a tribe out of ancient Wales, a tribe of Amazonian women who lived without men except for brief periods each for conception, children of the lost Atlantis, the Lost Tribe of Israel, the Seven Enchanted Cities. Columbus reported that he had sighted mermaids. One of the earliest descriptions of the New World spoke of its inhabitants as being "blue in colour" and with square heads. Who were these "squares"?

A formidable mass of evidence has accumulated to show the close contact of Old World civilizations with the New World, thousands of years before Columbus (or Ericson) and the presence in the New World, with their artistic and cultural survival, of African peoples, Semitic peoples, Mongol races from China, Japan, Indonesia, Melanesia and the South Pacific, and even peoples of Celtic origin.

The migrations dating from 2300 BC to 586 AD were transatlantic migrations ending in Mexico, Guatemala and El Salvador. More than once the view has been expressed that the mythical voyage of the Irish monk St Brendan to America is more than mere rumour. Discoveries in America of elements of Asian art associated with Buddhism, and of Chinese artefacts and Japanese-like pottery in Peru and Ecuador, lend confirmation to the thesis of Japanese participation in the evolution of pre-Columbian America and the report of a mission of Buddhist priests from Japan to the kingdom of Fu-Sang (either Mexico or Guatemala). The persistence of the belief in the lost tribes of Israel, and that the Amerindian was their descendant, was strengthened by the observation of William Penn that when he looked at the Amerindians, "I imagined myself in the Jewish quarter of London."

Not much imagination is required where the Africans are concerned. Unless they dropped from heaven, the colossal Olmec heads that have emerged in such profusion in Central America can only be the product of Afro-American contact over the centuries.

When one sees the scarification, tattooing and the African hairstyle of the terracotta head in the National Museum of Mexico City; or the figure of the circumcised black in the National Palace of Costa Rica; or the evidence of the fine gold jewellery with the protective deity of jewellers as late as the Aztec period, black and with kinky hair, the most formidable of the many monumental Olmec Negro heads, Monument F, found at Tres Zapotes – one is prepared for those contemporary Spanish accounts of fierce African tribes in remote areas – the precursors of Brazil's Palmares republic or Suriname's Bush Negroes – in Panama, in the explorations of Vasco Núñez de Balboa. Of these blacks Peter Martyr writes as follows:

> There they met Negro slaves from a region only two days in distance from Caruaca, where nothing else but Negroes are bred, who are ferocious and extraordinary cruel. They (the explorers) believe that in former times Negroes who were out for robbery navigated from Ethiopia and, being shipwrecked, established themselves in those Mountains. The inhabitants of Caruaca have internal fights full of hatred with these Negroes. They enslave each other mutually or just kill each other.

Whether or not one is prepared to admit that extensive Afro-American contacts preceded the European discovery by several centuries, the fact is that all over Mexico archaeological evidence has been unearthed in profusion relating to the presence of black people. This holds true also for such other areas such as Panama, Colombia, Ecuador and Peru. The conservative explanation of one of Mexico's leading archaeologists with possibly the least bias to such heresy is as follows:

> Kinky hair, broad chubby noses, thick lips and other less definable corporeal features belong to the ethnic group of Negroes, alien to Amerindian man. It is possible that at the end of the pre-classic period a small group of Negroes arrived on the Atlantic shores of America, though they could not perpetuate their biological inheritance, on account of their small numbers. Memory, legend and myth would surely deify them or endow them with the character of cultural heroes depicted in terracotta figurines and who were immortalized in monumental stone sculptures.[12]

This is clearly unacceptable in the light of all that we know of the close economic and cultural relations between Africa and the New World before the discovery; Columbus's obsession with the reports of Marco Polo and his misunderstanding of his Amerindian hosts; reports of earlier Old World contacts with America, excluding the Europeans in Scandinavia.

The Discovery of America

Columbus is our authority for the statement that King Don Juan (of Portugal) had told him that canoes had been found which started from the coast of Guinea and navigated to the West with merchandise. It was Columbus who reported that the Amerindians of Hispaniola had told him of black people coming from the south and southeast who brought the spearpoint of the alloy called *guanín* which he himself received in the island. A Mexican scholar, Orozco y Berra, on the discovery of the first colossal granite head of a Negro, at once suspected the African influence in Mexican civilization and concluded from the finds that the past relations had existed between Mexicans and black Africans.[13]

King John had also affirmed to Columbus his belief in the existence of populous lands to the southwest of Africa and his intention to send an expedition to explore. A Portuguese scholar stressed the large number of Portuguese voyages in the Atlantic before Columbus and the persistent belief that an "authentic island" had been there sighted in 1448 which formed the basis of Portugal's official expedition of 1498. He wrote that this conviction of land to the southwest explains Portugal's acceptance of the Treaty of Tordesillas, with its allocation to Brazil of lands 370 leagues west of the Cape Verde islands, as against the one hundred allocated by the Papal Bull. While it is true that Brazil was discovered in 1500, when Cabral's expedition to India was blown off course, Batalha Reis emphasizes that "the north-east corner of South America had been seen before 1448, although this cannot be confirmed, with the same historical certainty with which we can affirm that, in 1492 Columbus landed on some of the Antilles". It follows from this that, with these peoples from Africa, China and Japan, and Semitic and Celtic peoples, ancient America must be included, with Egypt and India, as one of the world's major areas of intense racial mixtures.

One curious story relative to these early contacts between the Old World and the New concerns the appearance of elephants in some of the drawings and sculptures in the New World. The traditionalists were furious: elephants in South America? Impossible; what looked like an elephant was merely a very rare bird. So, then, what was the elephant discovered in Mexico four feet underground after Tepexpan Man was found, allowing the Mexicans to say that it was then, on 13 March 1953, that ancient man in Mexico was officially a fact and no longer a fancy?

50 | THE BLACKEST THING IN SLAVERY WAS NOT THE BLACK MAN

This brings us to the question of medieval geography, which allowed a fifteenth-century pamphleteer in Florence to describe a giraffe he had seen as "almost like an ostrich save that its chest has no feathers but has very fine white wool . . . it has horse's feet and bird's legs . . . it has horns like a ram". Not to be outdone, a, sixteenth-century Italian chronicler of Magellan's round-the-world voyage described penguins and seals in the Straits of Magellan in terms of geese and wolves.

Medieval geography saw the world in the Christian tradition, with Jerusalem at its centre, Asia the home of the Magi, as in the Bible, and Africa as the legendary source of King Solomon's wealth. In the riot of their imaginations, there was a river of gold in Africa, lands with sheep as large as oxen, women with eyes made of precious stones, men with feet so huge that they served as parasols. The Atlantic was "the green sea of darkness"; an unnavigable swamp full of monsters reported by Arab geographers. Medieval literature in respect of Africa and Asia is full of recurrent warning – "here be dragons". One must not go too close to the equator, where men turned permanently black and no life could be sustained. Columbus acted on Toscanelli's estimate that China was 3,550 miles distant from Europe; the real distance is 11,776 miles. A bay in Haiti was placed by Columbus a thousand miles to the north, in the latitude of Wilmington in North Carolina, and Columbus's return plans, northeast by east, would have brought him to the Arctic. The direction for sailing from Europe to the West Indies was simplicity itself: south till the butter melts, and then due west. The popular theory of the day, in relation to what ultimately became known as Australia, was that far to the south there must be a land mass large enough to balance the weight of the northern continents and thus prevent the world from turning upside down.

If the Moslem Empire was not able to prevent the rise and expansion of Europe, what then of China? Its monumental Great Wall had helped materially to protect the country from invasions and to establish some sort of control over the feudal warlords. Thereafter, China led the way in naval technology in the world. The four- and seven-masted ships of the third century evolved into the great seagoing junks of the medieval period, coinciding with the magnetic compass. Maritime links were extended and maritime trade prospered to the point whereby in the twelfth century, the familiar bogey of the export of bullion emerged, as a memorial of 1219 put it: "Alas, that the gold and silver of the land should be flowing out in trade with savages from afar!" The drain of coin was prohibited, and efforts made to pay for imports in Chinese products – silks, brocades, porcelain, lacquer. By the early fifteenth century, Cheng Ho embarked on his seven great voyages to the far west – the first in 1405, the last in 1433 – in the course of which he reached the east coast of Africa, and the first African emissaries to China came on the scene; the first expedition, which reached Java, Ceylon and Calicut, comprised sixty-two ships and twenty-eight thousand men.

The rest was silence. The feudalists took over and concentrated on domestic issues. The expansionists were defeated. The dramatic change was reflected in the Forbidden City, the imperial palace in Peking, completed about 1420, a fabulous demonstration of the waste of public funds to gratify an absolute monarchy. The palace is incredible: 720,000 square metres, with over nine thousand rooms, with the Hall of Supreme Harmony, the Hall of Heavenly Purity, the Hall of Union, the Palace of Earthly Tranquility, the Hall of Royal Peace, the Hall of Mental Cultivation, the Emperor's Bedroom; and a fabulous number of sandalwood screens, which, it is said, required a thousand artisans working for ten years to complete.

China and Japan adopted another alternative to total seclusion. Both countries were closed to European contact, economic and missionary. By fiat of the emperor of China, overseas voyages were forbidden, the big ships burned. An edict of 1712 forbade Chinese to trade and reside in Southeast Asia; another edict of 1729 fixed a date after which overseas Chinese would not be allowed to return. Japan prohibited emigration on pain of death and summoned its nationals back home. As the Chinese emperor stated in 1793 in reply to a message from King George III of England regarding diplomatic and commercial relations: "Swaying the wide world, I have but one aim in view, namely to maintain perfect governance and to fulfil the duties of the State: strange and costly objects do not interest me. . . . As your Ambassador can see for himself, we possess all things. I set no value on objects strange or ingenious, and have no use for your country's manufactures."

It was clear that China did not possess one thing – a powerful merchant class. It was ruled by its scholars, as Japan was ruled by its soldiers. The merchant class that was emerging in Britain, Holland and Italy, with its political ambitions, had no place in India, China or Arabia as the Europeans turned with economic vigour, technical proficiency and social dynamism to overseas expansion. And yet one gets more than an impression that overseas expansion was only an appendage to a Europe that continued to dominate men's minds, thoughts, actions and activities. Spain continued in its Mediterranean fixation and its European obsession, taking over Portugal in 1580 in its continued domestic squabbles, wasting its substance on Italian conquests, refusing to rule over heretics in the

Netherlands, bogged down in the morass of the Holy Roman Empire that would be challenged by Voltaire in his famous question: "In what respects, Monsieur, was it, Holy? Or Roman? Or an empire? or a Nation and which everyone knew had no political cohesion, no capital city, no common law, no common finances, no common officials, but was nothing but the relic of a dead ideal."

Nor did the Arabs, the Saracens or Turkey understand the future role of Europe and the Mediterranean. From its fifteenth-century triumph, ending with the conquest of Constantinople, there had emerged a second Islam, a second Islamic Order, linked to the land, the horseman, the soldier, a northern Islam thrust deep into Europe through the Balkans. But though the Turks developed Algiers as one of the great cities they failed to dig a Suez Canal. They suspected that the ocean connected the Atlantic and India, but did not bother to find out. Developing in Algiers, one of the great cities of the fifteenth and sixteenth centuries, it was no more than a pirate port, a slave mart, a corsair capital, and the most it could achieve was that it should rain "Christians in Algiers". As Spain swung to Portugal and the Atlantic, as Portugal swung to India, Turkey plunged into Persia and the depths of Asia: the Caucasus, the Caspian, Armenia, and only later the Indian Ocean. The new focus of Turkish ambition was the Caspian Sea, having moved from the Mediterranean.

The modern trend is also to criticize the option chosen by Western Europe in the age of discovery. It opted for America, rather than the Orient. In choosing the New World, the Old World had to create all the necessary facilities. In the Far East the facilities existed; the wealth was more accessible. It was as if the discoveries meant no more than the transfer of the control of the spice trade from the Moslems to Portugal and its seat from Venice to Antwerp; and Spain's policy in respect of the discovery was to be attacked in 1555 for neglecting the conflict against the Moslems and concentrating instead on the Amerindians: "And why? It is because in these lands there are simple, guileless creatures from which rich booty may be taken without the cost of a single wound. For these expeditions religion supplies the pretext and gold the motive."

What golden age could there be when Portugal was about to excoriate Indian culture? It destroyed systematically the Hindu temples of Goa, faced a severe attack from the Indian population against the diversion of tax revenues "to the support of the Christian establishment", against state interference with inheritance practices, against the expulsion of Brahmins, and against all the Portuguese absurdities designed by baptism, European dress and jobs. This was to get Hindus to desert the customs of their fathers and take up foreign Christian practices – as Spain would do in America. It encouraged Hindus in their opposition to cut into Portuguese revenues by flooding their rice paddies with salt water and shutting down their food and silk stores – the Portuguese retaliating by destroying temples, killing cows and polluting watering places.

What age of gold when Portuguese Jesuits lumped Indians and Africans together as inferior races and saw in the Japanese alone any hope for Christian progress, as "the best who have yet been discovered"? Many European intellectuals saw the rediscovery of Plato in the fifteenth century, after the revival of Aristotle in the thirteenth century, as something more thrilling and important than Portuguese discoveries and conquests in Africa. What age of gold when Europe's white-supremacy doctrine was never more blatantly demonstrated than when, in 1499, Cardinal Ximenes, later regent, ordered eighty thousand Arabic books to be publicly burned in Granada, denounced Arabic – with Latin, Greek and Hebrew, one of the four official languages of many centuries – as "the language of a heretical and despised race"? This was the Spanish verdict on a civilization that had given the world the great mosques of Cairo and Damascus, masterpieces of architecture, famous capitals in Medina, Damascus, Baghdad and Samarra, arabesque and calligraphy, Persia's miniatures and Palermo's Muslim textile workers, Baghdad's House of Wisdom and Al-Azhar University in Cairo, the Dome of the Rock in Jerusalem and the Alhambra in Granada, and in literature the *Rubaiyat* and *Arabian Nights*.

The only sign of a golden age was the artistic revolt against church asceticism. The Renaissance in art was an open revolt against the fulminations of the Council of Trent in 1545 directed at representation of the nude in religious art. The portrayal of naked breasts was the order of the day – mighty breasts, with female bottoms mightier still. All the great artists participated – Velasquez and Rembrandt, Titian and Giorgione, Goya and Manet, above all Boucher and Courbet, with their nudes and posteriors and representations of whores, lesbians, royal mistresses and brothel scenes. Donatello, a notorious homosexual, outraged Florence society by his portrayal of David, so longingly, realistically and sexually, with such obvious delight. Renoir spoke for all his colleagues in art: "If women had no breasts or behinds, I would never have become a painter." The men's clothing completed the anti-ascetic revolution, the penis-purse of the age provocative, serving to emphasize what would in other days have been concealed, best exemplified, as so often, by Rabelais, whose Panurge had a purse three feet long, and square, not round. Women's turn would come, in due course, with the brassiere.

It was left for the Spanish Conquistadors themselves to capture and express the spirit of the new age of westward expansion, which was to become the dominant note in North America as colonists moved west from the Atlantic seaboard. It was Cabeza de Vaca, hero of the long march from Florida to Arizona, who summed up the age of discovery: "We ever held it certain that going toward the sunset we could find what we desired." The sheer vastness of the land space was intimidating and beckoning:

> Thames and all the rivers of the kings
> Ran into Mississippi and were drowned.

2.

The European Exodus

Better fifty years of Europe than a cycle of Cathay.
Alfred, Lord Tennyson, "Locksley Hall"

Give me your tired, your poor,
Your huddled masses yearning to breathe free
The wretched refuse of your teeming shore,
Send these, the homeless, tempest-tost to me,
I lift my lamp beside the golden door!
Emma Lazarus, "The New Colossus"

These monumental lines of Emma Lazarus, inscribed on the Statue of Liberty, a paean to the United States of America, "her name/Mother of Exiles", commemorate the vast European exodus over nearly five hundred years to the New World. The first phase of the European migration covers the colonial period. The European discovery of the New World immediately raised two fundamental questions. The first was whether the white man could live and work in the tropics. If white labour was increasingly excluded from tropical agriculture, the explanation must be found not in the tropical climate but in three purely economic and social considerations. The first is the limited population of the European countries, particularly marked in Spain and Portugal, though the disturbed conditions of such hopelessly disunited countries as Germany and Italy made them valuable reservoirs; witness the objections of Benjamin Franklin to the growing number of Germans in Pennsylvania and the indignant denial of the Sulzburgers in Georgia that rice cultivation was harmful to them. The second explanation is the emergence of the plantation system, which, especially in respect of sugar and tobacco, involved a discipline and a coercion of the labour force which white workers would not accept and which it was easier to impose on non-whites ignorant of the dominant language. The third and most decisive consideration was that the very fact of slavery of men of a different colour associated with work of a particularly laborious type encouraged white workers – of the same colour as the owners of plantations – to avoid all labour altogether and "to seek deliberately to place the white man above the kaffir".

The fundamental issue was whether Europe could supply the population necessary for the development of the resources of the New World. Departures from Spain in the sixteenth century averaged about a thousand a year, taking into account all the prohibitions on infidels, heretics and Moslems. A mere thirty years after Columbus's discovery, a chronicler was writing about Seville: "So many people have left for the Indies that the town is scarcely populated and almost in the hands of women." Immediately after the discovery of the West Indies the Spanish Government, on the recommendation of Columbus, sought to encourage white settlers, and a scheme of state-aided immigration was worked out in 1497. These included convicts, even murderers, but excluded conviction for heresy, treason, counterfeiting, sodomy or theft of precious metals.

Cartier's goal in Canada was establishment of a "rewarding home for the poor of the overflowing cities and towns of France". But the French colonial minister, Colbert, brought all the visionaries back to reality. To send out five hundred settlers a year, as was proposed for Canada, would in time "unpeople France". To the authorities in the Antilles demanding that he should send every year to Martinique a number of young lads of fourteen and girls of ten from the hospitals of France, Colbert retorted: "Be persuaded that it is not in the king's power, however powerful, to populate by force." To another he added, "His Majesty does not wish you to think that you have only to write to send from France workers in quantity, *engagés* and other things of this quality which are not practicable."

With an emigration of a hundred thousand from Spain in the sixteenth century, Vivero warned that Spain would soon be depopulated. But there were only thirty-two thousand Spanish households in the New World in 1574, while the streets of Madrid were full of idlers and vagabonds, numbering 150,000 in the whole of Spain at the beginning of the seventeenth century. The principal sources of the European emigrants were the convicts, vagrants, poor and religious dissenters. Women constituted, so to speak, a separate class by themselves.

The other European countries in their time followed the Spanish example, and a system of indentured servitude, with white people contracting to serve for three or four years in return for their passage and upkeep. *Engagés*, as they were called in France, emerged in the British, French and Danish Caribbean colonies and in North America, to the point where Barbados was described in about the mid-seventeenth century as England's "dunghill full of whores and rogues", Virginia "a sink to drain England of her filth and scum", and London the place for "the transporting of their overflowing multitude". It has been estimated that more than a quarter of a million people were of this class during the colonial period in the British North American colonies; the Germans were perhaps 8 per cent and Scotch-Irish perhaps 10 per cent of the population by the time of the revolution. From the beginning, Englishmen had seen in their New World possessions an opportunity to make use of people who were useless at home. Concern with the unemployed, the vagrants, the poor, dominated England in the fifteenth and sixteenth centuries.

Three major developments in Britain's parliamentary history deserve some attention. The first relates to the laws on villeinage, the old feudal system of organizing labour. In 1537, the House of Lords rejected a bill for the manumission of villeins. In 1574, Queen Elizabeth appointed a commission to take steps for the manumission of English slaves. The ancient villeinage laws formed the basis subsequently of the slave laws of Barbados and Jamaica; as a Jamaican propagandist put it, "They copied thence the principles which ruled, and the severity which characterized, the feudal system under the Saxon government." Along with this went the statute against vagabonds, with the branding of runaways and an iron ring around the neck of the "slave"; the word "slave" was used thirty-eight times in the law. Continued the Jamaican propagandist, "Such remained the effective law of England in the year 1553." One of the outstanding analysts of North American social and agricultural development before the Civil War concludes that "it appears probable that colonial lawyers seeking precedent for their legislation found it in this statute as well as in other vagrancy laws".

The second British statute relevant to the history of the British colonies in North America was the Statute of Artificers of 1563 (still in effect when Virginia was founded), re-enacting similar provisions from the Statute of Labourers of 1495. By this statute, labourers were required to work from 5 a.m. to 7 or 8 p.m. from mid-March to mid-September, and during the remaining months of the year from daybreak to night; time off for eating, drinking and rest was not to exceed two hours a day. "Gentlemen" were exempt, "idle almost by definition"; but they kept many persons "in slothful and parasitic personal service". The workers, unable to call, after the Reformation, on the feast days and holy days of Catholicism, substituted "Saint Monday" to take care of their weekend hangovers.

The third British statute was the law of 1576 providing for the building of "houses of correction" in which beggars could be put to work, "the great confinement", as one writer has put it, of the sick, the criminal and poor, designed not only to get them out of the way but also to make them contribute to the national wealth. The workhouse became the great school for the poor and the children of the poor, where they would learn habits of work. Sir William Temple wanted the teaching to start at the age of four; John Locke, expert as he was on human understanding, went one better and wished to start at age three. This fitted the ideology of the age, which saw, through Bernard Mandeville, regular schooling as only another form of idleness for the poor; and, through Governor Berkeley of Virginia, an end to Puritan specialties such as schools and books, for which he thanked God, "For learning has brought disobedience, and heresy and sects into the world, and printing has developed them, and libels against the best government. God keep us from both." As Arthur Young summed up the mood a century later, "Everyone but an idiot knows that the lower classes must be kept poor or they will never be industrious."

It was the tip of the iceberg. In 1670 a motion was presented to Parliament calling for the introduction of black slaves in order to "make servants more tractable". The motion was not discussed. But Bishop Berkeley, with Locke the outstanding philosopher of the period, proposed that "sturdy beggars . . . be seized and made slaves to the public for a term of years". The moral philosopher Francis Hutcheson advocated perpetual slavery as the ordinary punishment of idle vagrants who could not support themselves and their families by useful labour. One of Scotland's prominent figures of the Enlightenment, Andrew Fletcher, attacked the church for abolishing slavery, turning the freedmen loose on society, and enabling them to live without work by their hospitals and almshouses. Hence the two hundred thousand idle vagrants in Scotland. Fletcher's solution was that they should all be made slaves to men of property. In the meantime, an act of Parliament of 1697 required recipients of poor relief to wear a prominent red or blue "P" on the right shoulder, and strengthened existing provisions for segregating them, along with insane, diseased or impotent people, within the walls of the workhouses, hospitals, prisons and asylums – the ghettoes constructed to enclose them. Britons never, never, never shall be slaves?

The rights of Englishmen were one thing in England and quite another in Virginia. Virginian servitude became steadily more degrading than servitude in England. English laws and customs governing hiring of workers gave the servant some control over his own life, such as three months' notice if he intended to leave at the end of his term. Contracts were renewed or new ones made in court, with the constables recording the transaction. Not so in Virginia, where the servant was liable to physical abuse that would not have been tolerated in England. When a servant could complain that her servitude was not different from the slavery of the Amerindians from whom she had been ransomed for two pounds of

The European Exodus | 59

beads, and had already served ten months since the ransom, when a servant apprentice complained that his master had sold him for £150 sterling "like a damned slave", it was obvious that Virginia was moving towards a system of labour that treated men as things, and that slavery was slowly broadening down from precedent to precedent. The first move was to lengthen, by hook or by crook, servants' terms for running away, idleness, pregnancy, whatever. Laws were passed altering the term of servitude to five years for those nineteen or over, and to age twenty-four for those under nineteen (the average age of these arriving being sixteen). A maidservant who had a child served two years extra; a servant killing three hogs served six years extra. The old entitlement of freedom dues, fifty acres of land after one's term of service, was drastically altered by the big planters buying the lands in advance, so that the servant, on the expiration of his term, had to rent land or renew his contract of service.

Thus the time arrived when the servant found he might never make it out of the ranks for the mainland colonies. It is estimated that eight out of ten failed to make the grade. By the end of the century the planter aristocracy had estates of five thousand acres each at the very least; one alone possessed fifty thousand acres, and there were fifty to a hundred whose estates were valued at £50,000 at the least. Someone bought immigrants and was entitled under law to a thousand acres for his trouble; it was easy to add another zero. Another acquired eighty-five thousand acres, according to official sources, "by means not always above question", including about half under a "borrowed name". One landowner secured land in the name of his cows: after all, had not a Roman emperor threatened to make his horse a consul? The treasurer of the colony, who was also speaker of the assembly, circulated paper money he was legally required to burn. That was the climate of the age, in which no conflict of interest was recognized, and no separation of powers, no checks and balances. The Virginian planters, it has been said, converted to slavery simply by buying slaves instead of servants. In this way the annual increment of freed servants was effectively stopped. Thereafter it was only a question of ensuring that the white man was kept above the kaffir. For example, a law of 1705 specifically forbade masters to whip a Christian white servant naked, while prescribing the dismemberment of unruly black slaves, and protected the property of servants while confiscating what belonged to slaves and applying it to the use of the parish poor whites.

As for the French territories, it was equally clear that the *engagé* system meant the dregs of the urban population for the most part; in 1665 the viceroy was authorized to "utilize vagabonds of towns and fields and deport them at least for five years to populate the towns of America". It must lead to property ownership and not only to furnish unskilled wage labour. As soon as the *engagés* could no longer hope to obtain freedom from the concessions whereby clearing was possible by one man alone, or two associates, the system ended.

As far as the British colonial empire was concerned, Cromwell was the principal recruiting agent of white labour, exiling hundreds of his political victims in his Scotch-Irish wars; especially after Drogheda and Dunbar, in what have been described as organized slave-hunts. After months in prison, 1,300 royalists were shipped from Worcester to Barbados and from thence to Virginia. A person could be deported to the "tobacco islands", which became a conventional seventeenth-century phrase. Irish people shipped there after Drogheda (where every tenth man was killed), when they became free, could return – but not to Ireland. By 1669 there were twelve thousand Irish in the Caribbean.

Apart from the indentured servants and Cromwell's political exiles, there were also British convicts. Transportation to the colonies became the regular punishment for a variety of crimes, as a governor of Jamaica saw it: a choice between transportation or hanging, between Jamaica or Tyburn. Virginia became "a mere hell upon earth, another Siberia, only fit for the reception of malefactors". Between 1719 and 1772 the number of convicts transported from London and the home circuit alone to Britain's New World colonies was 17,470, in 190 shiploads. Francis Bacon might remonstrate that it was a shameful thing to take up the scum of the population and start a colony with it. Hakluyt had urged resort to condemned English men and women in whom there might be found hope of amendment. But the spirit of the age is best reflected in the seventeenth-century sugar planter: "For if Newgate or Bridewell should spew out their spawn into these islands, it would meet with no less encouragement; for no gaol-bird can be so incorrigible, but there is hope of his conformity here, as well as of his preferment, which some have happily experimented; insomuch that all sorts of men are welcome to the public, as well as the private, interests of the island."

No price was too high, apparently. In the same Nevis the same planter negotiated in 1684 the transportation of two batches of convicts from London jails. The first batch of twenty-eight "threw off their clothes overboard and came as bare to the island as if they had no clothes". The second lot of thirty-eight were marched from prison to the ship, manacled and guarded by thirty men to prevent them running away, but still they committed several thefts from people in the crowd. One of the principal sources of white emigrants from Europe was religious dissent – Protestants

The European Exodus | 61

fleeing from Catholics, Catholics from Protestants, Protestants from one another, Jews from everybody. The words of Edmund Burke in the 1770s were pertinent in his analysis of American society:

> The people are Protestants; and of that kind which is the most adverse to all implicit submission of mind and opinion. This is a persuasion not only favourable to liberty, but built upon it. . . . All Protestantism, even the most cold and passive, is a sort of dissent. But the religion most prevalent in our Northern Colonies is a refinement on the principle of resistance; it is the dissidence of dissent and the Protestantism of the Protestant religion.

A Puritan clergyman concocted the excuse: "God sifted a whole nation that he might bring choice grain over into this wilderness." How choice was the grain? The Presbyterians, Scotch-Irish for the most part, were generally poor. A description of some new arrivals in North Carolina reads, "The clothes of the people consist of deerskins. Their food of Johnny cakes, deer and bear meat. All kind of white people are found here, who live like savages. Hunting is their chief occupation."

Maryland was a haven for British Catholics, who in America and the West Indies (the Irish) gained civil rights long before they did in England. The Huguenots of France, running from Catholic discrimination, found refuge in the French territories and in North America. The German Pietist sects were welcomed – Moravians, Mennonites, particularly in Suriname and later in the Danish Virgin Islands. In the Catholic areas of America, the best example of the attitude of tolerance was displayed by Père Labat in the French West Indies. In charge of the sugar refinery of the Dominican order in Martinique, he expressed his willingness to hire a Lutheran: "It is indifferent to me whether his sugar is Lutheran or Catholic provided it is good and white."

And so to the Jews. Very prominent in Suriname from the inception of the colony, they constituted between a third and half of the white population. They were also prominent in Curaçao, testimony to the religious tolerance of the Dutch. In Barbados they were more ostracized than Quakers; they lived a separate ghetto existence, on Jew Street and Synagogue Street, and were taxed separately and very heavily. Jamaica too had its mini-ghetto of Sephardic Jews on Jew Street, who were subject to a special Jew tax.

Cartier's new venture in May 1541 emphasized the unwillingness of artisans to take part. His sorry lot of emigrants was made up almost exclusively of convicts. They arrived in gangs chained together and under armed guard, an assortment of social misfits and dishonest rabble from the stews of the great cities. The arrivals in Martinique in 1680 from Marseilles landed without even the precaution of removing their uniform as galley slaves. They were described as sick people, sexagenarians, decrepit, cripples, all condemned to live. The Danish convicts were described in St Thomas as lazy, shiftless, louts, vagabonds, idlers, uncountable fellows whom neither the workhouse nor the penitentiary in Copenhagen could improve.

And then there were the women. Spain required its emigrants to send for their wives within two years, on pain of being forced to return to Spain, but it was easy to evade this law in days when money could buy anything. The ledgers of colonial treasurers were full of *penas de casados*, penalties of the married men, which constituted a fairly regular item of income. Cortés required every settler to bring over a wife from Spain within eighteen months on pain of forfeiture of his estate. "Send white women to Brazil," urged Fr Manuel da Nóbrega, "even though they be wayward, for all would make a marriage". The girls never had it so good. In the French West Indies, as the saying went, *aussitôt arrivées, aussitôt épousées*, hardly had they arrived than they were married, thrown into the arms of those who came first.

The evidence is enormous as to the whites' refusal to work in the colonies. The viceroy of Peru said the Spaniards "would rather die than put hoes in their hands"; another report spoke of them as "always idle . . . very delicate and fit for little manual labour". According to the governor of Rio de Janeiro, though the Portuguese were reared with hoe in hand, "on setting foot in Brazil not one of them wants to work". The artisans turned to the crafts and the farmers to the soil only if they failed to find gold mines. The dominant and the ideal image was that of the conquistador, the man of good family not reared behind the plough, with his trinity of motives: God, gold, glory. The desire of all was to follow to the letter the oath exacted of them by the kingdom: "I swear that I will perform no manual labour so long as I can get a single slave to work for me by the Grace of God and the King of Portugal." Peter Martyr describes the Spaniards in Hispaniola as not moving a step from the houses on foot, but being carried about on the shoulders of the natives as though they were dignitaries of the state. Perhaps that was why the Spanish authorities once induced six thousand Bavarians who wished to go to the Indies to stay in Spain and found thirteen new communities in the Sierra Nevada to teach new industrial processes and settle on the land. A Portuguese account of Brazil at the end of the eighteenth century stressed the refusal of white servants to compete with blacks and their pleas for their masters to find them some public employment not open to blacks: soldiers, notaries, clerks, court officials. Otherwise the servants left their jobs, preferring to be vagabonds. Even the white serving women preferred

The European Exodus | 63

to take to the streets rather than compete with the black girls. The account continued:

> Is it not obvious that the inactivity of the whites is the reason for the laziness of the blacks? Why should a man not dig the ground in Brazil who in in Portugal lived solely by his hoe? Why should one not labour here who in Portugal knew nothing more than to put one hand to the plough handle and another to the goad?
>
> Why should a man go about here with his body upright who came here bent with labour? Why should he who was always plebeian strut about with the air of a noble?
>
> How plentifully would those blessed lands produce . . . if they were cultivated by other hands than those of savage Negroes, who do no more than scratch their surface?

Struggle for the New World

It was one thing for Europe, all Europe, to agree that Europeans should dominate and organize the New World. It was a horse of a different colour as to who in Europe should do the dominating and organizing.

Spain claimed the New World by papal donation, fortified by treaty with Portugal (the Treaty of Tordesillas, 1494), as well as by first discovery and right of conquest. It must be remembered that the empire then included Italy (and the Greek islands associated with Italy), including Sicily, Milan, Genoa and Flanders, in association with Italy. But even to Portugal, recognizing the papal donation, this did not solve the problem either in America or in Asia. If America fell within the Spanish sphere of influence, making allowance for Portuguese Brazil, this did not settle the question of Amazonia. By the Treaty of Tordesillas, the whole Amazon valley belonged to Spain. This claim was fortified by the astonishing expedition by Orellana, who, leaving Quito in 1541, made the remarkable journey of more than three thousand miles down the Amazon and then by sea to the Venezuelan coast. But Portuguese initiative on the coast of Brazil northwest to the mouth of the Orinoco resulted in the mouth of the Amazon becoming Portuguese, by virtue of prior colonization. In the interior, the struggle between Spain and Portugal, conducted through Jesuit missions on either side, resulted in the heart of the Amazon valley falling to the Portuguese, with the Spaniards confined to only the upper drainage; this was confirmed by the Treaty of San Ildefonso in 1777 between Portugal and Spain.

The non-Catholic states of Europe recognized no donation from the pope. Dr Johnson in England gave vent to the anti-Spanish jealousy in Europe:

64 | THE BLACKEST THING IN SLAVERY WAS NOT THE BLACK MAN

Has Heaven reserved, in pity to the poor,
No pathless waste, or undiscovered shore?
No secret island in the boundless main?
No peaceful desert yet unclaimed by Spain?

The first challenge came from Holland, which in 1566 revolted against the Hapsburg domination centred in Spain; when Spain and Portugal united briefly in 1580, the Dutch challenge was extended from the New World in the west to the territories of Spain and Portugal in the east.[1] The Dutch revolt was not only the first modern colonial revolt against imperialism, it was also a rebellion of the highly sophisticated Dutch capitalist economy against the more backward, semi-capitalist economy of Spain. The result was the temporary Dutch occupation of Portuguese Brazil and the Portuguese slave-trading post of Elmina on the west coast of Africa; the occupation of commercial entrepots like Curaçao and St Eustatius in the Caribbean; threats to the eastern colonies, to the point where Spain almost abandoned the Philippines; and the lifeline of the Manila-Acapulco galleons facilitating the exchange of Mexican silver for Chinese silks faced a serious challenge. But Piet Heyn's capture of the Spanish silver fleet in Matanzas in Cuba in 1628, after an audacious blow at the Dutch sugar fleet in Bahía in 1626, signalled a daring Dutch challenge to the Pacific coast of the Spanish colonial empire. The stupendous achievement of the dream of the century was thus described by the Heren XIX of the Dutch West India Company to Heyn: "This is the fleet which brings to Europe the golden rod which chastises the whole of Christianity and discourages it." The transfer of the booty took eight days. Heyn received an enormous welcome back home, with a treasure estimated at 11.5 million guilders. To the pope, who was anti-Spanish, Heyn's victory was as appetizing as the gospel itself.

The Dutch challenge to Spain, in Europe, America and Asia, cutting the king's veins, as the saying went, and stimulating a search for a Dutch naval base in the Caribbean, whether Puerto Rico or Santiago de Cuba or Jamaica, coincided with the English attacks on Spanish colonies and treasure fleets led by Drake. Drake was what one would call today a hijacker; they called him "pirate" in the sixteenth century, one who did not hesitate to use *cimarrones* – runaway African slaves – against Spain. Drake said to his crew, as they faced the Spanish city of Nombre de Dios, that he had brought them to the mouth of the Lola River. The Treasure of the World: if they would want it, they might henceforth blame nobody but themselves. Raleigh, in one discussion of his plans for New World colonialism, indicated that his strategy would be to take the whole Spanish fleet on the high seas. Asked whether that meant he would have been a pirate, Raleigh made the memorable reply, "Did you ever know of any that were pirates for millions? They only that that risk for small things are pirates." Drake was a pirate for millions. The buccaneers of all nationalities were a menace to peaceful trade, and from their principal centre in Tortuga, they harassed all settlements; they were men of all nationalities, even women at times, as the advanced pregnancy of one captive revealed on one occasion. The most successful of the buccaneers was Henry Morgan, who was knighted by the British Government and made deputy governor of Jamaica. As a governor of Jamaica put it, "None ever thought it possible his Majesty should send the Admiral of the Privateers to govern this island." Alleged to have begun his Caribbean existence as an indentured servant in Barbados, Morgan became one of the key figures in that fraternity of Brethren of the Coast who, between 1655 and 1671, sacked eighteen cities, four towns and more than thirty-five Spanish villages, some of them eight times, Porto Bello once, Panama twice, San Francisco de Campeche three times.

The monarchies were directly involved in these New World challenges. The Spanish empire belonged not to Spain but to the king; the New World provinces were linked to Spain through personal union with the king. The Danish monarchy had a majority interest in the plantation shareholding in St Croix when that island became Danish, though the Danish citizens at home showed no such interest in the Denmark lottery, with lots in St Croix as prizes, as the Dutch burghers showed in the shares of the West India Company. The scramble for the New World – anticipating the scramble for Africa nearly four centuries later – has been commemorated in the English phrase, "No peace beyond the line". Whatever the state of Europe, peace or war, whatever the alliances or misalliances, life in the New World went on, every man against every man, every nation for itself, and the devil take the hindmost.

Of the commodities most sought after, the precious metals – gold and silver – had pride of place. On Pizarro's overthrow of Inca Atahualpa, the Inca, in the best tradition of the feudal system of ransom, promised to fill the room in which he stood, seventeen feet by twelve, with gold to the highest stretch of his uplifted hand, in two months. For more than a month a squadron of Amerindian goldsmiths were compelled to labour at melting down and casting into gold and silver bars of equal weight a vast quantity of plate, vessels, artistic objects, the handiwork of their own craft; the value of the booty was 1.3 million pesos. Cortés's first instalment of Aztec treasure sent to the Spanish emperor from Vera Cruz was intercepted by a French privateer and went to enrich King Francis I. The king of Spain remonstrated and claimed the treasure. Francis replied: "Show me the testament of our father, Adam, wherein all these lands are assigned to your Majesty."

European needs, met until then by German mines and miners in particular, were satisfied from Peru and later Mexico after the discovery of Potosí in 1545. The Mexican supply developed in the seventeenth century – silver at the Mexican mint doubling from five million pesos a year between 1700 and 1770 to ten or eleven million and doubling again to over twenty million by 1800. Between 1690 and 1822, over 11.5 billion pesos in silver were minted in Mexico and some sixty million in gold. During the reign of Charles III, 1759–1788, imports of bullion and coin from the American colonies into Spain were nearly five hundred million pesos.

Another of the important commodities associated with the New World conquest was spices: oriental herbs and spices which Vasco da Gama had told his questioners in India that he sought. In endeavouring to avoid the increases and delays involved with the middlemen from China, India, Moslem states and the Italian cities of Venice and Genoa, the Portuguese had sought the direct route to India, and the Spaniards sought spices in America. Europeans were forced to slaughter most of their livestock every autumn because of the shortage of winter fodder. They needed preservatives that made ageing meat palatable – pepper, cinnamon, nutmeg and mace, ginger and cloves. The only one they produced locally was salt.

That is to say, Europe with the exception of Holland; and in any case the increasing use of fish required salt in large quantities as well as stimulating the discovery of new fishing grounds. It was in particular relation to the herring industry, which they made into a national priority, that the Dutch overseas expansion placed salt at the head of the list. The average Dutch salt carrier was three hundred tons; there were thirty thousand tons of shipping in the salt trade. This was the basis of the "salt congress" held in 1602 at Hoorn in West Frisia. The Venezuelan salt was 30 per cent better than that of the Iberian Peninsula; the Araya pan was so fertile it could freight a thousand ships at a time, increasing so fast that it could freight another thousand ships every 213 days. Because of the heat, the sun, the glare, the salt operations had to be done at night; as the salt ate away leather, the crews had to work in wooden shoes. The Spaniards were furious. They considered four solutions to this challenge to their monopoly: poison the lagoon; inundate it; dam up the lake and cut off communication with the sea; and construct a fort manned with a permanent garrison. Eventually the Dutch were forced to surrender their stronghold and to look for other salt pans in Curaçao, Bonaire, Aruba, St Maarten, and reached an agreement with Spain in 1670, limiting their fleets to ten at a time, maximum size fifty tons – ships licensed by the Spanish ambassador in the Hague for one trip only, with the licence not transferable; ships not to anchor or take in additional cargo besides salt in any other Caribbean port beside Araya.

The Dutch salt saga notwithstanding, the commodities most highly prized in the New World colonies were sugar and tobacco, but the European countries showed also a great interest in naval stores, especially with the increasing trend towards a timber crisis in Europe. It was an age of small states and of island economies – Cyprus, Sicily, Madeira, Canaries, etc. Small islands were favoured over large ones in the establishment of plantations because of the high ratio of coastline to land, direct access to seagoing vessels; the climate was less enervating, and, with adequate military protection, security to life and property was greater than in continental settlements. So the conquest of the New World initiated a furious struggle, which seems almost incredible today, among the European countries for their small islands, which Voltaire described in 1753 "as specks of dust", which produced so astonishing an annual circulation of goods in France.

Consider the case of Tobago. The Dutch and French fought bitterly over it and when, in 1677, the French succeeded in driving out the Dutch, the French struck a medal with the image of *Le Roi Soleil* and an inscription: *Incense Batavorum Classe ad Insulam Tobagi*, "The fleet of the Batavians burnt at the Island of Tobago". The Duke of Courland wanted it; the duke, priding himself on the predicament of being too poor for a king and too rich for a duke, developed the expedient of turning to Tobago, which he claimed as a grant from James I of England against English rivals, into a centre for the slave trade to provide a thousand slaves a year to the Spanish colonies. We could hardly believe today, in the face of the size of Tobago, that the island, named New Courland, could provide eligible colonists with at least 630 acres as private property to be free of taxes for the first three years. However, Zeelanders (from the Netherlands) arrived a year later and settled on the opposite side of the island, which remained divided until a settlement was reached in 1659 with the surrender of the Courlanders to the Dutch. Under Dutch protection a French colony was begun not far from the Courland settlement, and Tobago was reborn as a French barony, the Dutchman Lampsins being elevated to the French aristocracy as Baron of Tobago; Tobago was awarded to Lampsins by the Zeeland Chamber as a hereditary fief until he sold out to the Provincial States of Holland, which placed Tobago under the direction of the Admiralty Board of Amsterdam. And how did Europe dispose of the real Tobagonians, the Amerindians, reputed to be Caribs? The Caribs were banished to St Vincent. To complete the international vicissitudes of Tobago, in 1733 Marshal Saxe demanded the sovereignty of Madagascar, to populate it with German families; he was satisfied to accept Tobago in exchange.

These were the West Indian islands of the seventeenth and eighteenth centuries. France ceded St Bartholomew to Sweden in 1784 in exchange for imports into Gothenburg for re-export without payment of taxes. The previous attempt of the Dutch West India Company to acquire Swedish participation and create a sixth chamber for capital in Sweden. The Dutch colonial enthusiast, Usselinx, tried to develop Suriname for poor Europeans. He failed to get the support he looked for in Sweden, to which he had migrated after being ignored by the Dutch West India Company.

St Kitts became the richest British colony in the Caribbean on the eve of the American Revolution. A hundred years before that, in 1676, Nevis represented two-thirds of the total wealth of the Leeward Islands. Take St Croix as another example of the incredible value attached to these West Indian possessions. It was one island the Spaniards dismissed as "useless". Arising out of the Anglo-French Wars, those two very Christian Majesties Louis XIV and James III considered a settlement whereby, as offered by the French, St Croix would go to England in return for the English half of St Kitts. The British refused. St Croix had a population of 1,125, half African slaves. The French in 1695 ordered the removal of this population to the French half of Hispaniola, St Domingue. The colonials protested. They had no choice. The metropolitan order was explicit: burn the houses, the public buildings and the canefields; and spoil the harbours. Eventually, in 1733, Denmark and France agreed on the sale of the island for 750,000 livres. The Danes were not to resell without the approval of France, and France could instead have an option of repurchase; in any war between France and Denmark, St Croix must maintain the "most exacting neutrality".

The political confusion in the New World engendered by European state rivalries was further compounded by the insular and colonial psychology. Listen to Zeeland's appeal to the Heren XIX of the West India Company, "to determine that no colonists nor other persons would be allowed to sail to the Wild Coast than by this Chamber". Zeeland's "monopoly" was further promoted in 1654, when Zeeland ventured again to colonize the Guianas only on the express condition that "colonists buy all their supplies from and ship all their products to Zeeland". But the quintessence of insular jealousy emanated from Barbados. To the general amazement, their planters refused to spend 20 per cent of the Barbados budget to save the Leeward Islands and Jamaica from impending attack. The dons of Barbados were accused in 1663 as the sworn enemies of Suriname's development. They "wished these (Leeward) islands sunk" to forestall further settlement. The old joke of the First World War that Barbados cabled the British Government to go ahead because Barbados was behind it became, in the altered conditions of the Second World War, the joke of a message from Hitler on hearing that Barbados was still behind England: "If you stay out, we will give you Trinidad." The Turks and Caicos Islands in our day rejected a plan for closer communication with Bahamas, fearing relegation to the status of "farthest out of the out islands", demanding instead "a national identity". The secession of Anguilla from St Kitts-Nevis led to the impounding of mail, money and medicine in St Kitts and the threat from St Kitts to "turn Anguilla into a desert. They will find salt in their coffee, bones in their rice, and sand in their sugar. . . . They will have to suck each other's bones". A century and a half before, Anguilla had objected to the transfer of its legislative powers to St Kitts, which would mean "laws enacted . . . for this community . . . by a body of men living in a distant and remote island, possessing no property of any kind here and having no connexion or relation whatever" were unlikely "to be made with much regard for Anguilla". Fifty years later Anguilla petitioned the Colonial Office, describing the people of St Kitts as "utter strangers to us, ignorant of the community, careless of their wants, and therefore unequal to discharge the important duties of legislation for us".

European Society in the New World

The Trinidad novelist V.S. Naipaul has written as follows of the West Indies: "This place, I tell you, is nowhere. It doesn't exist. People are just born here. They all want to go away." From the beginning the West Indians were transients. Moreau de Saint-Méry, with his unrivalled first-hand knowledge of the French West Indies, emphasized that most colonists were alien to the land where they were born: "Our aversion toward our birthplace and the boredom . . . makes us see ourselves only as transients in, a country where we are sometimes forced to stay our whole life. Hence our unconcern for the well-being and prosperity of a country from which we expect only the means of living elsewhere." The governor of Martinique, a century before this, in 1669, in the very first generation of the settlement, had described the colonists as men who "thought continually of their return to France, and kept everything in readiness to leave at a moment's notice". For the British islands, "except for a few regular Creoles, everyone regards the colony as a temporary lodging place, where they must sojourn in sugar and molasses till their mortgages let them live elsewhere". Lord Brougham was later to sum it all up: people emigrated to the West Indies "not to live, but to gain, not to enjoy, but to save, not to subsist in the colonies, but to prepare for shining in the mother country".

Here is the established West Indian tradition of absenteeism, always dominant among the bigshots, steadily percolating down to the poor whites, from whom it spread to the poorer blacks. Modyford, who migrated from Barbados to become governor of Jamaica, made it clear he would never set his face towards Britain before sugar planting earned him £100,000 sterling. Drax, another of the big Barbados sugar planters, with a mere £300 in 1627, declared twenty years later he would not return to England until he could purchase an estate of £10,000 yearly. These were the days of the large sugar grants. Modyford had urged Charles II to be prodigal in granting the first million acres in Jamaica and to issue special tax concessions; he hoped to persuade many of the leading Barbados planters to join him in removing to Jamaica. In his seven years in office he issued about eighteen hundred land patents, over three hundred thousand acres (triple the acreage of Barbados), his own family collecting in all over twenty-one thousand acres. But the Barbados planters preferred South Carolina. Of the twenty-three governors of South Carolina from 1669 to 1737, eleven had lived in the West Indies or were the sons of West Indian planters; seven early Carolina governors had a Barbados background; four were from big planter families. As someone said, they had built up Barbados but had made their tropical paradise almost uninhabitable; Barbados had become, in human terms, the least successful colony in North America. In the first flush of imperialist enthusiasm Cromwell had wished to transfer the settlers in New England to Jamaica, reversing the Barbados-South Carolina process; by 1679 the mistake had become obvious, and the powerful propaganda in favour of the southern states had begun: "It were well hereafter we planted no more behither Jamaica, but settled and removed, if possible, rather our Northern Colonies more forward." The West Indian planters had already begun to be identified with huge debts, partly a result of their ostentatious living and conspicuous consumption. A stock description of the big planters was of "carbuncled faces, slender legs and thighs, and large prominent bellies", of slaves, "over-disciplined and underfed, their masters underdisciplined and overfed." By the middle of the eighteenth century, for example, twenty-three Barbadian planters owed £85,000 to one English merchant, the total debt to him being £120,000; and among the plantations of Jamaica, twenty-four of the largest had claims against them aggregating £526,000.

But the emigration fever was especially high among the poor whites. It was they who, unable to get their freedom dues of land in Barbados, Jamaica and the smaller islands, found opportunities in North America, and "now begin to disrelish the West Indies . . . and turn their faces towards New England". As was said of Barbados, the recipient of some twelve thousand prisoners of war and servants between 1649 and 1655, it "was now so filled that they vomit other superfluities into other places". Most hard hit were the Irish: forbidden to return to Ireland after their term of servitude or jail, "shackled by their faith, a tell-tale brogue and their general reputation". What a society this was, these poor whites! Jamaica had become a bad joke even in England. A popular book which ran through seven editions by 1700 described it as "the Dunghill of the Universe", populated exclusively by prostitutes, convicts and drunks. Its Port Royal was known as the Sodom of the Indies; when it was obliterated by earthquake, the popular verdict was the "amazing severity of God towards Jamaica". A description of the town, the buccaneers' capital, spoke of the common people walking about barefoot, pipes clenched in their teeth, satin hats jammed over their eyes, "and thus they trampouse about their streets, in their warlike posture", ready to booze a cup of punch with anyone. It was asked in Barbados in 1630, "If all whoremasters were taken off the Bench, what would the governor do for a Council?" The big planters dominated the electorate, the assembly, the council, the militia; in 1636 these men protested against the governor's appointment to the council of a man of "servile condition, personal abilities, and other scandalous circumstances". Assistant judges who were minors sat on the bench in Barbados. Repeated charges of sodomy were made, especially in Antigua. A standing commission in Barbados for punishing adultery and fornication rarely exercised its powers. Among the women servants were many suspected whores, who, it was alleged, never lacked custom on the Sabbath. In 1656 over four hundred loose women from London's brothels had arrived "in order that by their breeding they should replenish the white population".

Two striking features of white society in the Caribbean emerge from the early centuries. The first is of their houses. They blindly followed the English style, building up rather than out, several storeys high, with low-ceilinged rooms on each storey. They were like stoves or heated ovens, in face of the European superstition that too much ventilation was unhealthy. They were also fortresses, the big whites on guard against servants and slaves, as if they lived under a state of siege. The houses were built with bulwarks and bastions from which the occupants could pour scalding water upon attacking servants and slaves.

The second was sanitation, in general, with particular reference to burials. Barbados in the 1690s was tossing the corpses of yellow-fever victims into the swamp next to the capital city, infecting the drinking water. Military commanders were famous for putting barracks adjacent to swamps. Heavy rains in Barbados in 1668 caused a deep gully in the churchyard where about fifteen hundred people had been buried over thirty years; as the account goes, floating coffins striking on each side of the banks of the beach were washed out to the ocean, "not waiting for the Resurrection".

The white servants were very badly treated. They could not marry without the master's consent; on their death they were thrown into unmarked holes like dogs. Early engravings show them at work in the sugar mills. Ligon was scandalized at the beatings of servants on the slightest provocation in Barbados, which he described as a hell for the working class. "I have seen such cruelty there done to servants as I did not think one Christian would have done to another." A slave dealer in Charleston said that he had never seen an instance of cruelty to black slaves equal to the cruelty exercised upon Irish servants. Between 1750 and 1755, the bodies of two hundred white servants were tossed into New York harbour. The applications for compensation for plunder by the French in St Kitts showed one in every two claims for less than £100; 70 per cent of the applications under £100 were sworn to by men and women who could not sign their names and had to scratch their mark.

Pacte Colonial

The consensus was that the European emigrants went out to the colonies to serve the interest of their respective metropolitan countries. As it developed into a formal policy, known generally by its French name, the *Exclusif* – the English knew it as the Navigation Acts, the laws of trade and navigation – trade with the colonial areas was the exclusive privilege of the "mother" country, from whom the colonies had to buy their imports, to whom the colonies had to send their principal exports, both imports and exports being carried by ships built in the metropolitan country (or its colonies), with the majority of sailors from the metropolitan country (or its colonies). Spain went further still. In her will, in a codicil, Queen Isabella ordered that the Aragonese were to be excluded from America. Spain designated the port (Seville) from which outward cargoes could leave or inward cargoes return, and the ports in the colonies to which they would sail (Vera Cruz in New Spain, Cartagena in New Granada, Nombre de Dios or Porto Bello in Panama), both inward and outward cargoes being conducted under convoy sailing at fixed times of the year. If, in between, the colonies ran short, it was too bad; they must await supplies, and were emphatically forbidden to trade with heretical foreigners – especially heretical foreign nations. Perish the colonies, said Spanish officialdom, rather than sacrifice the principle. Baracoa, centre of Cuban smuggling, was to be depopulated and its inhabitants relocated to Cumana in Venezuela, to stop smuggling, and the galleons were put on police duty to stop the Dutch salt ships. For ten years tobacco cultivation was prohibited in Venezuela to stop Dutch traders. We have piteous stories of Spanish colonials insisting on early mass so that their nakedness could not be seen, and of a Spanish governor reporting to the effect that he could not report because he lacked stationery.

The fundamental weakness of the Spanish colonial regime was that it lacked the capacity to produce the requirements of the colonies. Gone was any excuse about papal donation or exclusive. The Spanish foreign minister spoke as follows to the British ambassador in Madrid: "God has committed the Indies to the trust of the Spaniards that all natives might partake of the riches of the new world; it is even necessary that all Europe should contribute towards supplying . . . that vast empire with their manufactures and merchandises." Perfidious Albion! There was the enemy. Britain became the greatest smuggler in the New World. Of all the people called to propagandize British claims was John Milton, just after his blazing sonnet for vengeance in Italy against "the triple tyrant" and "the Babylonian woe". Milton was charged to justify before world opinion the American policy of Cromwell. He did it in a manifesto of October 1655, *Scriptum Domini Protectoris Contra Hispanos,* advancing the following reasons: cruelty of the Spanish authorities, civil and ecclesiastical, against England; inhuman treatment and extermination of the aborigines; unjustified Spanish claims to possession of all America; natural and contractual rights of England to traffic in Spanish seas. The British sought to establish through their Darien Company an American Venice, which they proposed to call New Caledonia.

On the other hand, the exclusive had necessarily to be modified to allow for colonial production where the metropolitan supply was inadequate. The doctrine forbade colonial competition with the metropolitan country, and specifically required the colonies to concentrate on raw materials and eschew industrial development. No sugar refineries in the French West Indies, ruled Colbert. No textile industry in Jamaica, Britain decreed. Even the Dutch, champions of free trade, enemy of mercantilism, at first required, through their West India Company, that all their trade with the colonies should be done in company ships, and that colonists were to do no weaving, so as to protect the industry in the Netherlands. Not a nail, not a horseshoe was to be manufactured in the British North American colonies, where the British were unsuccessful in their effort to stop a rum distillery in New England. No further planting of vineyards and olives was to be allowed in the Spanish colonies, ruled Philip II; production of wine and olive oil, at first permitted, threatened metropolitan production in perhaps the two most sensitive areas of Mediterranean economy. But both the Spanish and British colonies allowed the development of shipbuilding and the emergence of a colonial marine, especially for the development of the fishery resources.

But colonial interests could not indefinitely be sacrificed to metropolitan. After the British defeat of France in the Seven Years War, the Exclusive underwent fundamental changes. France, under Choiseul, saw the basis of national revival in colonial trade. It surrendered Canada to Britain, and developed a commercial empire in the Caribbean but required India for its textiles (to clothe the slaves and purchase them in Africa) and Newfoundland for its codfish (to feed the slaves). Hence Choiseul's famous attempt to "mitigate" the Exclusive in his instructions to the colonial governments in 1765: "There can be circumstances in which the wealth and the prohibition which must jointly be found in the colonies nonetheless can be in a state of incompatibility. Then the law of prohibition, for all its essential nature, nonetheless must yield. It is necessary to create and to protect before one can enjoy; what is first in intent, can but follow in the execution."

Hence France's experiments with free ports in St Lucia and in St Domingue and its relaxation of the prohibition on foreign codfish. Hence Choiseul's ill-fated plan to develop a white plantation colony in Guiana to replace Canada as a source of food for the West Indies: fourteen thousand died. But the French port lobby was too powerful for Choiseul. The Spaniards too officially modified the Exclusive. The *Cédula de Gracias* of 1815 permitted trade with the United States and allowed foreigners to settle in the colonies – the beginnings of the vast development of Cuba, with its sugar, of Puerto Rico, with its European immigrants.

Colonial Independence

The English colonial system in America represented a persistent struggle against France in Canada and down the Mississippi to Louisiana, against the Dutch New Amsterdam until it was surrendered to Britain in exchange for Suriname, and even against Sweden, whose meteoric rise to a brief military preeminence in Europe was associated with colonialist expansion in West Africa, the Caribbean (the small colony of St Bartholomew, shared with France) and in North America on the Delaware River. In North America the British came up against the Spaniards in Florida and Louisiana, and the independent United States inherited this antagonism. The basic problem was that Spain in Florida claimed land it could not develop, supervised Amerindian tribes it could not control and regulated vital waterways that reached into the territory of the independent United States, at a time when Spain had opened up New Orleans to US produce, and the US flag dominated both the harbour of New Orleans and the city's flour market, while Spanish products were exported on US vessels.

In the colonial period the European emigrants were not slow in seeking to weaken or remove the control of the metropolitan country, especially in matters of trade. The British colonials, carrying even to America the parliamentary traditions of England and the successful efforts of Parliament to control the executive in the seventeenth century, were quick to demonstrate that, as has been said of colonial Virginia, "English freedom" meant to be as free as possible from interference by England. The New England colonies, for example, with Massachusetts in the lead, formed a confederation called the United Colonies of New England, which was denounced by a royal commission as a "usurped authority" which "took more power than was ever given, or intended them". The New England Puritans observed no such restraint and Massachusetts refused even its own freemen the right of appeal to the Crown.

In Virginia, burgesses and council carried on a perpetual fight with the royal governor, shipping one back to England in 1635. With their control of the legislature they were also tax collectors. The council not only advised the governor, including his veto on legislative measures, but served as the upper house of the colonial legislature as well as the supreme court of the colony. If the seventeenth-century danger was a sinister absolute monarchy in England seeking to subordinate the legislative power to the executive, Virginia showed the other side of the coin: a handful of men in an elected house removing the separation between legislative, executive and judicial powers, as well as the bureaucracy, through the multiple office-holding permitted. It was, characteristically, the Virginia legislature which led the campaign in America against the Stamp Act. In the Caribbean, with the enormous sugar monoculture developing, it was Barbados which took the initiative in opposing the British commercial system and laws of trade, the Navigation Acts, restricting colonial produce to British ports in British-built ships manned predominantly by British crews. Barbados passed a "Declaration of Independence" in 1651 making the colony a free state.

The bitterness of the Spanish-born Spaniards towards the creoles, tinged with contempt, was one of the principal causes of the independence movement in the Spanish colonies. The pronounced antagonisms among those from Spain – between Castilians, Basques, Andalusians,

76 | THE BLACKEST THING IN SLAVERY WAS NOT THE BLACK MAN

Extremeños – culminating not infrequently in bloody street disputes in America and arising out of the Crown's attempt to impose political unity on the peninsula, were assuaged only by the common contempt felt by all the groups for the creoles. Of 170 viceroys appointed between 1535 and 1813, only four were born in the New World. Of the 705 bishops appointed in those three centuries, only 105, or 15 per cent, were born in the Americas. The University of Mexico faculty in 1777 blamed the king for excluding creoles from high office in respect of his royal appointments. According to the representations of the Ayuntamiento between 1771 and 1792, no mitre in New Spain was worn by a creole; in 1808 only one episcopal see was occupied by one born in America. Franciscans in particular were accused of maintaining "a foreign partiality".

The creoles were infuriated by the contempt of the Abbé de Pauw – the American continent, being only recently formed, had scarcely finished drying out; in places the land was still a deep swamp. Therefore, the meagre vegetation, the scentless plants, feeble animals and short-bodied men, hairless and discouragingly impotent in the marriage bed. "We have come to the point of fearlessly asserting that the creoles of the fourth and fifth generations have less talent, less capacity for learning than the true Europeans." Had not the great naturalist himself, Buffon, declared American animals to be inferior, owing to the meagre native grasses, which were not nearly as large and succulent those of Europe? It was said that dogs ceased to bark after breathing American air.

In this context it was the height of irrelevance for the viceroy of Mexico to say in 1810: "A Gachupín Spaniard born in Europe or *criollo* is a Spaniard born in America; Gachupín is the father of the *criollo*; the *criollo* is the son of the Gachupín; the Gachupín is the husband of the daughter of the *criollo*; the *criollo* is the grandfather of the sons of the Gachupín. What more?" The British friar Thomas Gage had exploded this myth long before, in a communication to Cromwell: the two sections of whites were more opposed to each other than in Europe are French and Spaniards. It was, said Juan and Ulloa in the early nineteenth century, "sufficient to be born in the Indies to abhor the European. It was very common to hear some repeat that if they could remove from their veins the blood of the Spaniard which they have from their fathers, they would do it, because it would not be mixed with what they acquired from their mothers".

The Anglo-Spanish warfare of the eighteenth century suggested that neither nation gave a thought to the effect on their white colonial; and Spain's support of the struggle for independence of the British colonials in North America caused general apprehensions in Spanish political circles. As early as 1741 Admiral Vernon had proposed British aid for the emancipation (not annexation) of the Spanish colonies, and the Spanish colonials had worked out twenty-five years later proposals to be put to the British Government for a republican system in Spanish America, the opening of its ports to all nations, and the cession to Britain of Vera Cruz and San Juan de Ulúa, which would assure them of the trade of Mexico. The French, however, proposed the transformation of Louisiana (then still Spanish) into a republic under the protection of Spain and the guarantee of France. Chatham, in his turn, put forward to France and Spain a treaty by which the three powers would agree to cooperate in the defence of their American possessions, and, in order to strengthen the ties between colonies and metropolis: he proposed in 1762 to establish various kingdoms in North America confederated with Britain. This was the substance of Aranda's secret report of 1783, to establish three kingdoms in Spanish America: Mexico, Peru and Costa Firme – confederated with Spain, with the king of Spain as emperor. Mexico would pay its annual dues as a feudal fief in silver, Peru in gold, Costa Firme in colonial products, especially tobacco. The new creation would constitute an intimate union between the four crowns.

To Simón Bolívar, in the midst of the struggle for independence, the Europeans residing among them in Spanish America were "our eternal enemies", as he claimed in his memorial to the Citizens of New Granada in an anonymous pamphlet published in 1813. Complaining further to the British governor of Curaçao in that year about "the fierce Spaniard", Bolívar continued: "He signalized his entrance into the New World by death and destruction. He annihilated the original inhabitants, and, when his raging fury found no others left to destroy, he turned upon his own sons whom he had brought forth in the land that he had usurped." Bolívar proceeded to define and defend the creole Spaniard in a letter of 1815 written while he was in Jamaica:

We scarcely retain a vestige of what once was; we are, moreover, neither Indian nor European, but a species midway between the legitimate proprietors of this country and the Spanish usurpers. In short, though Americans by birth we derive our rights from Europe. . . . The role of the inhabitants of the American Hemisphere has for centuries been purely passive. Politically they were nonexistent. We are still in a position lower than slavery. . . . Satraps of Persia are Persians, pashas of the Grand Turk are Turks, and sultans of Tartary are Tartars. Chinese mandarins are not from Genghis Khan. America received everything from Spain, who, in effect deprived her of the experience that she would have gained from the exercise of an active tyranny by not allowing her to take part in her own domestic affairs and administration.[2]

Bolívar turned to Great Britain for assistance in the struggle for independence. The quid pro quo he was prepared to offer Britain was trade and commercial hegemony

> the provinces of Panama and Nicaragua will be turned over to the British government for the latter to make of them the centre of commerce by building canals which, after the dikes guarding both oceans have been broken, will reduce all distances, however long, and permanently establish British commercial supremacy. . . . These extensive benefits can be obtained with the most insignificant means: twenty or thirty thousand rifles, a million pounds sterling, fifteen or twenty men-of-war, munitions, several envoys, and any volunteers who may wish to fight under the flags of America. This is all that is needed to bring liberty to half of the earth and set the world in balance.

It was back to colonialism. Set an imperialist to catch an imperialist! Bolívar would call the Old World into existence to redress the balance of the New. Why? Fourteen years later, from Quito, in his panoramic view of Spanish America, Bolívar lugubriously explained:

> From one end to the other, the New World is an abyss of abominations. . . . There is no good faith in America, or among the nations of America. Treaties are scraps of paper; constitutions printed matter; elections, battles, freedom, anarchy, and life, a torment. . . . Enough then of twenty years of hostilities, misery, and death. We yearn for a stable government, fitted to the actual state of our affairs, compatible with the character of our people, and capable especially of rescuing us from that hydra, from that bloody master, unfettered anarchy, that feeds upon the best of this Republic . . . Colombians . . . the second man to lead the Republic assassinated the first; the Third Division invaded the south; Pasto rebelled against the Republic; Peru laid waste to her benefactors' territories and there is hardly a province that has not exceeded its powers and prerogatives. Throughout this ill-fated period there has been nothing but blood, disorder, and destruction.

Bolívar concluded, "We have ploughed the sea."[3]

Cuba had not joined, or been allowed to join, the revolt in Spanish America against colonialism. Instead it continued throughout the nineteenth century a Spanish colony vainly struggling for independence, between the devil of Spanish colonialism and the deep blue sea of American annexation, a vast sugar plantation with a large black population kept in slavery until virtually the end of the century, living on the volcano of a potential race war. As some creoles continued to press for autonomy, they associated their political reforms with the increase of the white population, envisaging white factory workers in the refineries and small free white farmers, *colonos*, cultivating the cane. They looked to the Canary Islands; imported, under army law,

The European Exodus | 79

Galicians, pauperized by hunger and *latifundia*; workers from Vizcaya, one of Spain's poorest provinces; Catalans – all lumped together under the name "colonization", representing the substitution of wage slavery for the race slavery of the Africans.

The metropolitan countries were ever alive to the danger of colonial rebellions. The Spanish in particular feared a recrudescence of European bred feudalism, especially in the Peruvian civil wars, and when powerful men in Honduras battled one another for all the world as if they were in Europe. Above all, Spain was very sensitive to the fact that the wealth of Peru could finance a separate independent state. Little Barbados in 1651 declared itself a free state, but, inevitably, it did not last. Thereafter there was always the fear, as one governor put it, that a Creolian generation might "emancipate themselves". Spain feared the communes, the towns. It had defeated the rising of the Spanish *comuneros* of 1520 at Vilalar in 1521, and thereafter had taken steps to bring municipal governments under central control. But this did not prevent the uprising of the *comuneros* in New Granada in 1781, on the heels of the last great Inca uprising in that year. Spain agreed to all the demands, the agreement sanctified by the archbishop by a special religious service; but in a separate secret document Spain disavowed the agreement as obtained by force.

Then came the rebellions in Mexico and Venezuela. In Venezuela, the conspiracy of 1797 in La Guaira included the demand that all towns and harbours should be thrown open to all the nations of the world. Hidalgo's Revolt in Mexico in 1810 set the pattern for the general independence some years later. It was preceded by a series of plots and conspiracies in 1766 against exclusion of creoles from office; in 1799, the Conspiracy of the Machetes, a general uprising of creoles against Europeans – but creoles of the less privileged class: silversmiths, watchmakers, policemen, shopkeepers, described as men without wealth, ideas, connections, support or prospects, "wretched and timid people" – and for the most part they looked to British support, as in 1766 (ten years before 1776) with Britain to get Vera Cruz and San Juan de Ulúa as inalienable property, with trade with Europe in English ships. Eighty-five were executed, seventy-three whipped, 674 sentenced to life imprisonment, 117 banished from their native regions. Hidalgo, a renegade priest, declaring himself Captain General of Mexico, Generalissimo of all the Americas, attacked by the Inquisition as an apostate and heretic, sought the support of the Amerindians, the slaves and the urban poor.[4]

The British North American colonies had not been able in the colonial period, in 1754, to carve out a common policy of defence against the French and the Amerindians, despite the taunt of Franklin that if the Iroquois could form a union, why could not a dozen English colonies? But it was the South Carolina delegate to the Stamp Act Congress of 1765 who called for unity: "There ought to be no New England men, no New Yorkers, but make all of us Americans." As Americans, with help from both France and Spain, they won their independence from Britain on the battlefield, and proceeded to work out their own independence constitution, after considerable wrangling which had demonstrated the sectional rifts between slave and non-slave states; the interstate jealousies in respect of trade, navigation, river transport, tariffs, taxation; bitter jealousy between the bigger states and the smaller; the differences over the bill of rights; the conflict between a strong central government and states' rights. The British North Americans were always fearful of the threat of foreign intervention, especially one invited by the small states. They had to face this foreign intervention in the 1812 war against Great Britain, when Britain reoccupied Michigan territory, threatened to invade the United States, contemplated an attack on New Orleans by a large number of trained troops under the command of the Duke of Wellington (who declined the invitation), and was inciting Amerindian revolt on the one hand and New England secession on the other hand had not the British, in the bitterness of defeat, threatened that they would sign thirteen peace treaties with the separate independent states whose union they would not recognize. In a mammoth convention at Philadelphia in 1787, agreement was reached on the basic differences: representation by population in the lower house, equality of representation by states in the Senate; a compromise on slavery; a central government with power to tax over the tariff and to act for the general welfare. The leader of the war of independence fourteen years before became the first president of the United States, in a demonstration of colonial unity and universal respect not paralleled in any other colonial area.

The US experience was vastly different from the outcome of the revolutionary actions and sentiments elsewhere in the New World. The British Caribbean can be quickly dismissed. Towards the end of 1774 the Jamaica Assembly passed a resolution in support of the mainland colonies; so did the legislatures of Barbados, Tobago and Grenada. The dominant note in the Jamaica resolution was dependence, not independence: so much so that the Continental Congress responded, "By converting your sugar plantations into fields of grain, you can supply yourselves with the necessaries of life." Questionable economics, perhaps, suspect politics almost certainly – in the context of subsequent development of the US sugar economy. But the Americans were too busy with their war of independence to argue with a bunch of colonials such as they had ceased themselves to be. They put it tactfully: "The peculiar situation of your Island forbids your assistance. But we have your good wishes. From the good wishes of the friends of liberty and mankind, we shall always derive consolation." The Americans understood it was just another in the long historical record of resolutions on this, that and the other.

European Immigration after Independence

With the end of the colonial system in the United States, Latin America and Haiti, the migration to the New World became more truly European. The principal receptacles were the United States, Brazil, Argentina, Canada and Venezuela. Not the mania of a single generation, the movement falls into four broad phases, as follows in the case of the United States:

1830–1860 principally Celtic to United States;
1860–1890 principally English and German;
1890–1914 principally Mediterranean and Slavic;
1921 introduction of a quota system aimed principally at new groups from southern and eastern Europe.

A number of emigration schemes were organized to different parts of the New World in the nineteenth century, without success. Thus in December 1825, 260 Scotsmen went to Caracas and about 250 to Argentina. Both plans were failures, and the emigrants to Caracas were removed by the British Government to upper Canada. Over two thousand were attracted from Switzerland in 1819 by a plan to establish a new Freiburg in Brazil; two years later, only four in ten survived. A Belgian colonization project was developed for Guatemala for ten thousand colonists in three years, and fifteen ships did in fact sail. Santo Tomás in 1545, instead of a settlement of ten thousand, was a village of a dozen wooden houses and fifty straw huts, with about three hundred people. The Germans tried everything – a plan to buy the Chatham Islands off New Zealand, which was vetoed by the British Government; a Prussian dream of a colony on the Mosquito Coast; and when that emerged as a graveyard, a dream of accepting a Mexican offer to sell California; a German colony in Texas supposedly as a British bulwark against Yankee imperialism and to check the spread of slavery, but the promise made in Germany of 320 acres per family became, for those seven hundred who arrived in 1844, a half-acre in town and ten acres in the country – the US annexation of Texas in 1845 mercifully put an end to the imposture. The principal factor in this extensive migration was the desire

82 | THE BLACKEST THING IN SLAVERY WAS NOT THE BLACK MAN

to escape from European poverty, landlessness and unemployment. As the couplet had it: "Houseless near a thousand homes / And near a thousand tables pine for want of food."

The high-water mark in this respect was reached with the potato famine in Ireland in 1846, followed by the harsh conditions in Germany. Unemployment among coalminers in Wales – which gave rise to the nocturnal desperadoes who called themselves "Rebecca and her daughters". The displacement of labour by machinery among the weavers of Silesia, Osnabruck, Hanover and Oldenburg and the disruption of the traditional peasant economies in eastern Europe, reducing the peasant to the status of a propertyless day labourer, all contributed to what Dr Samuel Johnson had called "the epidemical fury of emigration". The carts piled up in long files on the road to Strasburg, carrying would-be emigrants to America. Cologne provided cheap lodgings for emigrants of limited means. Belgium forbade emigrants to enter the country who could not show funds sufficient for their support. Many communes sent their beggars and their chronic poor to America. A rumour of free transport from Rotterdam and Amsterdam in 1816 led to an invasion by thirty thousand prospective emigrants who crowded into Amsterdam tenements and squatted in the streets. It was chaos everywhere. This was the emigration fever in Ireland – seeking to be transported to any part of America; they knew not whither, in any vessel, they cared not what was provided – she bore them away from the poverty and destitution of their native land. Lord Macaulay, on seeing Ireland in 1849 at the height of the evictions, from Limerick to Killarney and thence to Cork, painted this picture of destitution:

> Hundreds of dwellings in ruins, abandoned by the late inmates, who have fled to America; the labouring people dressed literally, not rhetorically, worse than the scarecrows of England; the children of whole villages turning out to beg of every coach and car that goes by. . . . Between the poorest English peasant and the Irish peasant there is ample room for ten or twelve well-marked degrees of poverty.[5]

America was the soil on which the ageing Europe sought to rejuvenate its spirit. For the common man of Europe, America was Utopia: "To us, who have long been half-starved in England," ran one letter in 1818, "it appears like a continuous feast." Another letter read: "The poorest families adorn the table three times a day like a wedding dinner – coffee, beef, fowls, pies, eggs, pickles, good bread; and their favourite beverage is whiskey or peach brandy. Say, is it so in England?" Everybody seemed to have a rich uncle in America; letters from emigrants were read at mass meetings in European villages and hamlets. To the European, America meant no tithes for the church, freedom from heavy taxation, no compulsory military service: no "threefold pressure of standing armies, enormous taxes, and ecclesiastical domination". America also meant abundance of available land, a rate of wages so high that one day's labour could buy an acre to grow corn; perhaps most important of all, it meant the end of class distinctions – all wear the same quality clothes; "no fawning, cringing, adulation here; the squire and the mechanic converse as familiarly as do weavers in England. We call no man master here". Three days' work in Canada was better than six in England. There were no crowds of "ragged, unwashed men and women", as at the street corners in London, Manchester, Liverpool and Glasgow. Wrote the man who had lost a leg, "I could do much better here with one leg than in Crosley with two." Wrote the emigrant in upper Canada, "Were you here and seeing the improvements that are going on among us, you would not believe that we were once Glasgow weavers." The seventy-five thousand immigrants to Canada from 1812 to 1827 were in possession on the average of half a dollar a head on landing. US law did not penalize destitution; the immigrants in New York in 1856 had an average of $68 for each of the 142,342. But in twenty years the Irish fugitives from the famine remitted over £20 million to Ireland.

A.H. Everett, noted orator, said in 1835: "The poor-houses and parishes of England . . . design to transfer a part of this incumbrance to the charity of the United States. It is not sufficient that the penal colonies of Australia are open to her convicts, England, it would seem, needs also that a species of pauper colony should be opened in America for her poor." An anonymous English emigrant and naturalized citizen wrote in 1854:

> Anybody, or everybody, may come without let or hindrance. The rogues and vagabonds from London, Paris, Amsterdam, Vienna, Naples, Hamburg, Berlin, Rome, Genoa, Leghorn, Geneva, etc. may come and do come in. The outpouring of alms and work houses, and prisons and penitentiaries, may come and do come. . . . And what are the consequences? . . . That, go where you will in the United States, you find nearly all the dens of iniquity, taverns, grog-shops, beer houses, gambling places, and houses of ill fame and worse deeds, are kept by foreigners. That, at the various ports, the alms-houses and hospitals are, in the main, occupied by foreigners; and that numerous objects of poverty and destitution are to be seen crawling along the streets in every direction. That not a few become criminals, filling our prisons and putting the country to great expense.

There is nothing surprising therefore in the fact that the peak year for emigration to the United States from England was 1888 and from Germany 1882. The poverty of the Irish emigrants: their ignorance on board ship of meat and bread in preference to potatoes – so that during the famine the distribution of flour was a waste, as most households had no ovens, and most housewives did not know how to bake the loaves; their arrival in America in tatters and rags, faces gaunt with starvation – led New England residents to believe that all the misery of Ireland had been emptied on their shores. Their ubiquitous iron pot, representing their destitution, was a standing joke, serving the three purposes of tea kettle, for boiling the potatoes and for washing their tattered clothes. The iron pot was in general the sum of their movable effects. The Irish, said the attorney general of Nova Scotia in evidence before the House of Commons, did not know, before emigrating, what it was to lie on a bed.

The universal opinion in Europe was that work was abundant and wages princely in America. Where the American labourer earned seventeen cents an hour, his European counterpart earned ten in Great Britain and France, and eight in Germany. The US carpenter's thirty-six-cents-an-hour wage compared with twenty in Great Britain, fifteen in France, thirteen in Germany. The bricklayer who earned thirteen cents an hour in France and Germany and twenty-one cents in Great Britain would command fifty-five in America.

It was inevitable that, as the Royal Italian Agricultural Commission reported, emigration was spontaneous. It becomes like a contagious disease. Even the children speak of "going to America". That was why in one single year, 1906, Italy lost through emigration nearly half as many people as were employed in mines, quarries and factories. Europe was threatened with depopulation, as it was reported in northern Hungary; one official Italian report stressed the price paid for emigration: prostitution among formerly respectable women and infanticide. Some Italians came to regret Columbus's discovery of America; the emigration movement had become too large for Italy's good.

The United States had to live with the consequences. Many immigrants were assisted in their passages – this was true of Australia also, where there was an official British aid scheme. One in four Italians arrived on the basis of steamship tickets prepaid by relatives already in the United States. Jewish immigration societies facilitated emigration from eastern Europe. The US Immigration Commission of 1910 reported of Bulgarian emigrants:

> It required the continued savings of years of a score or more peasants to provide the means for one person to emigrate to the US. They have a kind of lottery by which one of the group would have the benefit of savings of all to the others and go. The lucky one would, after a few months in the US, repay, with interest, the amount advanced by his compatriots, with the result that they all would have a

The European Exodus | 85

still stronger desire to go to America, and then would fall another drawing and another emigrant.

US law required an immigrant to show $50 in cash, insurance against his becoming a public charge. Of the immigrants from 1905 to 1909, only 13 per cent fulfilled this requirement. Nearly 90 per cent showed less than $50. Of those showing cash, the per-capita figure was $30, the figure falling to as low as $11 for the Lithuanians.

The principal target of the Canadian legislation denying entry to those who might become public charges was the English. In the years 1903 to 1909, English aliens represented 2,007 of the 3,149 deportations from Canada, exclusive of 206 Scotch and eighty-one Irish. In the words of the chief medical officer of Canada's Department of Immigration in his annual report for 1908:

> Not only does the large number of people from English cities come to our large cities, but it is especially true of that class, ne'er do wells, social and moral derelicts, and ineffectives in general. They are not only physically unequal to the task, of farm life but they are further, usually incapable of enduring the quiet of rural life. Hence if sent to the country they too frequently drift back to town, and when winter comes and work fails they seek aid in those institutions set apart for the city poor and helpless.

The second general characteristic of this European immigration was that it was overwhelmingly illiterate. This illiteracy was the outstanding difference between the so-called "old" immigration from northern and eastern Europe and "new" immigration from southern and eastern Europe into the United States. Of the total immigrants between 1899 and 1900, 1,912,131 – 28.6 per cent, approximately one in four, could neither read nor write. From the "old" areas the illiteracy rate was less than 3 per cent; from the new areas it was nearly 36 per cent – being over 50 per cent for South Italians, Turks, Portuguese, Ruthenians and Syrians, and over 40 per cent for Bulgarians, Dalmatians and Lithuanians. The problem was particularly acute where the Italians were concerned, if only because of the enormous volume of the Italian immigration. A part of the general social problem in Italy, the illiteracy among immigrants reflected the illiteracy among conscripts, among couples signing the marriage register; it had led to the imposition of severe legal disabilities in 1904 on illiterates: they could not carry arms and could not operate any establishment under police administration if not in possession of a certificate of primary education. Of the Italian immigrants from 1899 to 1909 aged fourteen and over, numbering 1,829,011, over 850,000, or 47 per cent, were illiterate. The Immigration Commission commented: "If illiterates, without exception, were denied admission, Italian immigration undoubtedly would be reduced to about half its present volume." So everyone in Europe and America turned a blind eye – so long as the immigrants were white. Australia and New Zealand had already passed, following Natal, acts requiring literacy tests of all immigrants in writing or reading a passage of fifty lines in any language of Europe. But the test was never imposed on any European immigrant. When British Columbia in Canada sought to do likewise in its immigration act of 1900, the act was disallowed, as were similar acts in following years. The act specified the condition of admission as ability to "write in the characters of some language of Europe".

A third principal characteristic of this later European immigration from southern and eastern Europe was that, in the words of the Emigration Commission, it was to a considerable degree a movement of transient industrial workers rather than emigrants to "become actual settlers". A similar tendency was equally pronounced with respect to European emigration to Australia. Likewise this became one of the principal arguments against Asian immigration into the United States and Canada, that it was principally a movement of transient males.

A special note on Jewish emigration would not be inappropriate. The first major exodus began in 1881, in flight from pogroms in the Ukraine, a public protest against which was organized by a committee in Paris headed by Victor Hugo. A large number of the more than a million emigrants departing from Bremen alone between 1882 and 1902 must have been Jewish. Between 1901 and 1914, over 1.6 million Jews left Europe – almost all from Russia, Romania and Galicia. A large majority came from the slums of Europe's cities – Warsaw, Vilna and Lodz. According to one militant, they were only preparing socialists for America, like those Belgian peasants who told the *International* that "it will be difficult to build up Socialism on the soil of old Europe", so they proposed a "general emigration to America". The Jewish emigrants were described by their compatriots as "marching off to the trains with Torah in one hand and *Das Kapital* in the other".

A sympathetic account of the emigration described it as combining at least three kinds of change: first, a physical uprooting from the long-familiar setting of small-town life in eastern Europe to the wastes and possibilities of urban America; second, a severe rupture from and sometimes grave dispossession of the moral values and cultural supports of the Jewish tradition; and third, a radical shift in class composition, mostly as a sudden enforced proletarianization. Any one of these alone would have been painful; the three together made for a culture shock from which it would take many immigrants years to recover. Some never did. The account continues: "Almost all the figures of moral authority remained in the old country." Some of the most acute problems encountered were the pressure to work on the Sabbath, the awful strain of peddling, and the sweatshop, especially in the garment industry; the unbelievable conditions of the overcrowded and insanitary New York tenements (making tuberculosis, in the popular mind, "a Jewish disease"); and the ever-lengthening newspaper feature, "Gallery of Missing Husbands". The Jewish population of New York increased from 60,000 in 1870 to 82,000 in 1880 and over a million in 1910.

In Italy, the practice of selling labour was so widespread that people spoke in Italy of "birds of passage" who made Italy their home and America their workshop. At best one in three European immigrants eventually returned to Europe; many, as in 1908, after less than five years' residence; a very large proportion of those returning did not migrate again. Of aliens admitted in 1899–1910, one in eight had previously been in the United States.

Very pronounced criticisms were made from time to time of this European immigration regarding the capacity of many of the immigrants to be assimilated especially to the way of life in the New World. Particular hostility was voiced in Canada against Italians. Mr Newman, roadmaster of the Canadian Pacific Railway, stated to the Royal Commission on Chinese and Japanese immigration in 1902:

> The Hungarians and Italians that are here I do not call really white men. They are a very poor class of workmen generally. . . . Hungarians and Italians are not in favour with the British labourers here. They come here and earn money and send it home, instead of spending it in the country. Not more than one in a hundred of the Italians that come here to work on the railway take out citizen papers.

His contempt for Italians was echoed by Mr Marple of Vancouver. "I never call Italians white labour. . . . The Italians are not equal to Canadians, white men. . . . The Japanese labour in my opinion is fully equal to the Italian . . . these miserable Italians." The Emigration Commission reported contemptuously of Italian habits back home and their domestic life in their earthen-floored huts, which they shared with pigs, chickens and donkeys, and in which eight or ten people of various ages and both sexes slept in one or two beds, with the farm produce – potatoes, corn – stored under the beds. In the United States the beet sugar growers of Idaho, Colorado and California spoke disparagingly of German and Russian workers and expressed preference for the Japanese, whose productivity was much higher.

88 | THE BLACKEST THING IN SLAVERY WAS NOT THE BLACK MAN

The Latin American experience with respect to the assimilation of immigrants was even more discouraging. The un-assimilability was particularly marked with the Italians (especially in Argentina) and with the Germans (especially in Brazil and also in Venezuela). When Argentina's great patriot Sarmiento gave the country its slogan, to "Europeanize" the population and "produce a regeneration of the races", or when Alberdi, its constitutional father, urged that "to govern is to populate" – meaning a European population – little did either think that he would live to describe Argentina as a "republic of foreigners", as Sarmiento did, with its agricultural colonies, akin to foreign fortresses, in the middle of the nation. As one analysis put it, the immigrant did not easily shed his European culture: "He tried to reaffirm it, especially the Swiss and German. . . . He had staked his sights more on the consulate of his country as an agent of legality than in the formal representatives of Argentinian authority, whom he mistrusted even while being forced to accept." The government of Italy, in keeping with the principle of the *ius sanguinis*, regarded the immigrants and their descendants as Italian citizens; the immigrants almost to a man avoided or ignored the simple naturalization procedures, which conferred citizenship after two years' residence. The general view was that the immigrant did not regard the receiving country as a superior country to be imitated, nor as a new country in which to settle permanently, but as a place to get rich, return to the native village in Europe, and buy land. With some six million immigrants, half Italian, one in three Spanish, one in five Polish, Argentina was and is a European country. Two of its constitutional presidents have been second-generation Italian immigrants. In the last twenty-five years, three in four of its generals, admirals and bishops have been of immigrant origin, mostly the sons of immigrants; of the top military men, one in four has been Italian, one in three Spanish, one in six either German or French or English; half the bishops have been sons of Italian peasants. As Manuel Galvez criticized a century later, the teachings of Alberdi and Sarmiento brought from the *campagna* of Italy hordes of Italian peasants who had a tremendous influence in denationalizing Argentina. "Anyone can see that we are completely civilized now." At the moment he was writing, "to govern is to Argentinize."

Consider now the German immigrants in Brazil. They looked to Europe, not to Brazil, for their doctors, teachers, artisans, priests or pastors. They imposed their language on the surrounding areas; in Santa Catarina even the blacks spoke German, and the municipal council's records were kept in German because no one knew Portuguese. One Brazilian statesman warned in the Senate that it was "time that they learned for this is Brazil not Germany"; another raised an outcry against the Germanization of Santa

Catarina. The German statesman had warned as far back as 1860: Brazilians would have to "offer guarantees that they were resolved to respect and protect the German nationality of the immigrant; consequently, they will have to make it as easy as possible for immigrants to set up independent communities of their own and, instead of appointing administrators therefor, allow them to choose directors for themselves." Immigrant colonies – Italians in Argentina, Germans in Brazil.

Consider the Venezuelan experience. Colonia Tovar, a hundred years old in 1938, comprising pure Germans, was described as an "independent colony", which had "nothing to do with Venezuela". It was "a piece of German territory, one might say, within Venezuela's borders".

The obsession with Europe was seen in the pathetic profile of the Brazilian creole, the son of Portuguese born in Brazil, the *mazombo*. For him permanent residence in Brazil was something for the convicted criminal. The *mazombo* was spiritually a European – only European culture for him. "Only France had that. *Vive Paris*. In the world Europe; in Europe, France; in France, Paris; and Paris, Montmartre." The literary pretensions followed accordingly, with the inevitable reaction, best seen in Gonzáles Martínez' attack in Mexico on the poet Darío. Darío had eulogized the swan, symbol of beauty as an end in itself. Martínez substituted the owl, symbol of the quest for wisdom. It was his slogan that mattered – "Wring the neck of the swan. Poor Leda! She had loved not wisely but too well."

The outcry in America was predictable when, in the last decade of the nineteenth century, Italians began to arrive in droves, almost 80 per cent of the men, aged fourteen to forty-five, from southern provinces, unskilled and illiterate, seldom in America going too far from New York. Pointing to the degradation associated with immigration, one commentator exploded in 1891:

> There is no reason why every stagnant pool of European population, representing the utterest failures of civilization, the worst defect in the struggle for existence, the lowest degradation of human nature, should not be completely drained off into the United States. So long as any difference of economic conditions remains in our favour, so long as the least reason appears for the miserable, the broken, the corrupt, the abject, to think that they might be better off here than there, if not in the workshop, then in the workhouse, these Huns and Poles, and Bohemians, and Russian Jews, and South Italians will continue to come, and to come by the millions.

So enlightened a public figure as Henry George could write in 1883: "What, in a few years more, are we to do for a dumping ground? Will it make our difficulty the less that our human garbage can vote?"[6]

The closing of the open door was heralded by Madison Grant, in *The Passing of the Great Race,* in 1916. That the American was no longer a new man, and no longer acted on new principles, was made abundantly clear:

Racial nondescripts flocking West . . . European Governments took the opportunity to unload upon careless, wealthy and hospitable America the sweepings of their jails and asylums . . . hordes of the wretched, submerged populations of the Polish ghettoes; the American taxed himself to sanitate and educate these poor helots . . . they are beginning to take his women. New York is becoming a *cloaca gentium.*[7]

3.

The Amerindians

It repenteth me that I have made them.

Genesis

This is Walt Whitman's immortal tribute to the legacy of the Amerindians in respect of place names of the states, counties and countries of America.

The red aborigines!

Leaving natural breaths, sounds of rain and wind, calls of birds and animals in the woods, syllabled to us for names,

Oconee, Koosa, Ottawa, Monongahela, Sauk, Natchez, Chattahoochee, Jaqueta, Oronoco, Wabash, Miami, Saginaw, Chippewa, Oshkosh, Walla-Walla,

Leaving such to the States, they melt, they depart, charging the water and the land with names.[1]

Consider a fuller list: Alabama, Alaska, Arkansas, Arizona, Connecticut, Dakota, Idaho, Illinois, Iowa, Kansas, Kentucky, Massachusetts, Mississippi, Michigan, Minnesota, Missouri, Nebraska, Oklahoma, Tennessee, Texas, Utah, Wisconsin and Wyoming in the United States; Manitoba, Ontario, Quebec, Saskatchewan and Yukon in Canada; Mexico, Nicaragua, Managua, Guatemala, Peru, Lima, Campeche, Chile, Guiana, Panama, Uruguay and Paraguay in South and Central America.

There was a surveyor-general in New York who baptized many places with the names of ancient European cities; it is said that when his atlas gave out, he had recourse to the names of Greek and Roman poets, philosophers and statesmen, until his dictionary was exhausted. The wish has often been expressed that the project attributed to Girard had succeeded, and every American plant and creature had been baptized with an Amerindian name and commemorated Amerindian existence – like petunia, the garden flower recalling the Amerindian name for tobacco in Brazil, *pétun*; Indian corn, Indian hemp, India rubber, Indian summer, Indian file, and indeed Indiana and Indianapolis.

The Mochica pottery, the Paracas textiles, testify to the versatility of the Inca culture. The use of guano in Peru; the snow goggles and dog sled

92 | THE BLACKEST THING IN SLAVERY WAS NOT THE BLACK MAN

of the Eskimos; the game of lacrosse: two major cash crops – cotton (sea island) and tobacco; food crops – corn, the tomato with its Aztec name, paprika, soursop, pineapple, guava, sapodilla, pumpkin, squash, the potato – which, when first taken to Scotland, was prohibited as not mentioned in the Bible – avocado, peanut, popcorn, cashew, manioc (cassava) and pawpaw; with the famous Latin American cuisine – tamales, tortillas, chilli, based on the two great Amerindian staples, beans and corn; the Amerindian drugs prominent in modern pharmacology – cocaine (from the coca plant), quinine (from the cinchona bark), guaicom (once a famous remedy for syphilis), curare (used in anaesthetics), datura (pain reliever) and cascara (laxative) – all testify to the scope, vitality and virility of Amerindian civilization, which has bequeathed to us a number of household words today of which the following partial list gives some examples:

> Barbecue, buccaneer, cannibal, canoe (via Europe), caucus, chocolate, condor, hammock, hurricane, jaguar, llama, moccasin, pemmican, puma, skunk, squaw, tobacco, toboggan, tomahawk, totem, wigwam.

Chewing gum (the *chicle* of Mexico); *pulque* (the intoxicant of Mexico); *jalap* (the well-known Mexican purgative); the Amerindian origin of maple sugar and maple syrup; roucou (the Mexican dye); maize – the supreme gift of the Amerindians to civilization; the remarkable chemical process by which the Amerindians removed hydrocyanic acid from a species of cassava, which then became a staple article of diet; adobe for building; the blanket (either the serape draped over the shoulders or the poncho, two blankets sewn together with a slit left open for the head) – these are the Amerindian peoples, exemplifying Schiller's famous *mot*, "What is the greatest of nations but a fragment of humanity?"

These are the people recalled by Pocahontas, *The Last of the Mohicans*; Longfellow's epic poem *Hiawatha*, Alonso de Ercilla's epic account of Amerindian resistance to the Spaniards, *La Araucana* (begun in 1568); and the speech put by Voltaire into the mouth of the wise old cacique Colocolo, as superior to Nestor's in the first book of the *Iliad*. Europe needed America in 1492, but it was not a discovery by Columbus in the service of Spain, but an invasion by Europe. Europe discovered an inhabited land. The Europeans did not settle a virgin land. They invaded and displaced a resident population. As has been well said, Columbus did not discover a new world; he established contact between two worlds, both already old.

Who then was this new man, this American, the Amerindian? An Amerindian tribesman asked the Massachusetts missionary Eliot, in 1646, "Why do you call us Indians?" As John Locke was to put it, "In the beginning all the world was America." In depicting the continents, Europe was generally pictured as wearing a crown, armed with guns, holding orb and sceptre, and handling or surrounded by scientific instruments, books and Christian symbols; as against Asia, richly dressed. America was naked – like Africa – with feathered headdress and bow and arrow. The Amerindians presented an astonishing social and cultural diversity; there were at least two thousand cultures and more societies, a multiplicity of customs and lifestyles, a variety of values and beliefs, numerous languages mutually unintelligible. They reveal an astonishing linguistic diversity – by one estimate comprising two thousand distinct languages and 123 linguistic families, 73 of which in South America are completely different. A recent catalogue lists 260 languages in Mexico and Guatemala alone. They were not primitive in respect of their vocabulary. It has been estimated that Shakespeare used about twenty-four thousand, the King James Bible about seven thousand, the Nahuatl of Mexico twenty-seven thousand and an Amerindian tribe of Tierra del Fuego had a vocabulary of at least thirty thousand words.

The first of the commentators was, inevitably, Columbus himself, reporting on the Arawak tribes of Hispaniola: "I saw no great diversity in the appearance of the people or in their manners and language. On the contrary, they all understand one another, which is a very curious thing." Columbus did not understand the language of the Amerindians. How he ascertained the religious values and property customs which he later reported must be left to the imagination – or rather his. And so to Vespucci and his *Mundus Novus* of 1503 and his letters of 1502, describing two voyages to South America in 1499 and 1501. In the letters, after describing the fragrance of herbs and flowers, the savour of fruits and roots which led him to fancy himself "near the Terrestrial Paradise", the birds, their plumes, colours, singing, numbers and beauty, leading him to doubt if he would be believed, Vespucci continues:

> I have seen habitations 220 paces long and thirty wide, ingeniously fabricated; and in one of these houses dwelt five or six thousand persons. They sleep in nets woven out of cotton, going to bed in mid-air with no other coverture. The meat which they eat most usually is what one may call human flesh à la mode. Their marriages are not with one woman only, but they mate with whom they desire and without much ceremony. They hold no private property or sovereignty of empire and kingdoms and did not know any such thing as lust for possession. In short war is a brutal business.

In Canada, Cartier was less melodramatic, possibly awed, as were his men, by the fact that they had never seen anything to equal the blanket of snow in which the land was wrapped, disappointed no doubt that he had mistaken the high basaltic cliffs for the turrets of the castles of the Island of Seven Cities, which merely turned out to be Bacalao, Newfoundland, the island of codfish: "I did not see a cartload of good earth," he reported on his search for a North West Passage; "To be short I believe that this was the land that God allotted to Cain!" To him, the Amerindians of Gaspé Basin he encountered in 1534 "may very well and truly be called wild, because there is no poorer people in the World". Echoing Champlain, that the salvation of a single soul is worth more than the conquest of an empire, Cartier thought "it was worth more from the start to seek the road to heaven than to find the route to China", and so he took possession of Canada in the name of Jesus Christ.

It was Voltaire, Rousseau and Diderot who continued the well-established tradition by using the Noble Savage in general and the Amerindian in particular for their critical moral and political purposes. Man was born good and equal and free, but everywhere in contemporary Europe he was found chained to social conventions and artificial civilization. The life of the Amerindian offered a thoroughgoing critique of European social institutions and cultural values – whether religious beliefs and institutions, nature of education, organization of government and codes of law – organization of the economy, the general social system and social inequality. They set the pattern for others to follow in employing the Amerindians as exemplars of the possibility of human freedom inherent in the state of nature. French critics used the Amerindian as a mouthpiece for their social criticism, a weapon against the enemies of national reform. Their Noble Savage was a model of human perfection, a believer in freedom and equality; the example of what all men could become if they reformed their society. Thus Chateaubriand, "Where the Amerindian went naked or dressed in a skin, there was something grand and noble about him."

The Incas have been highly praised for the sagacity of their colonization efforts and their measures to absorb conquered tribes and provinces. A tribe long accustomed to Inca rule was moved to a newly conquered region, or newly vanquished people were moved en masse to a loyalist area whose residents would be their teachers. The places chosen were always as similar as possible to their homeland. The Inca army was divided into sections, each serving only a short time on the humid and hotter coast, then sent back to the cooler mountain altitude to recuperate. The Quechua language served as the connecting link between the sections of the empire. In the conquest of what is today Ecuador, the redoubtable Cañari tribe thereafter furnished the Inca with an elite corps which has been compared to the Swiss Guards. The Inca roads and bridges, including suspension bridges, united the empire, a network of some ten thousand miles of roads, of which 2,500 miles were coast roads that, in a society without wheeled traffic, where the only transport animal was the llama, had a standard width of four feet. This road network Métraux has attacked as a symbol of Inca prodigality and the waste of their principal wealth, the Andean peasant. But would this hold for the sixty-two-mile Maya causeway from Cobá to Yaxuna, varying in height from two to eight feet, with a width of sixty-two feet? The Inca storehouses were one of the outstanding Inca developments which had no Aztec counterpart.

Aztec and Inca societies were openly militaristic and war was a principal industry. The Aztec custom was to inform all male children soon after birth that they were born to be warriors and to die in combat. The education of the boys was essentially an education for war. Those who did not go to war, even the sons of a ruler, would enjoy none of the privileges of nobility and the warrior class – no cotton clothes, no plumes, no roses to sniff, no cocoa to drink, no fine foods to eat; they would be regarded as men of low estate, to do the same work those do, even though they were of royal blood. At the age of ten the boy's hair was cut, leaving a queue, which he was not allowed to cut off until he had managed to take a prisoner in battle. This success merely placed him a single rank ahead, and unless he did better in succeeding campaigns he was obliged to retire from soldiering. He would then have to devote himself to his piece of land and his family, a peasant, who could never wear fine clothes or jewellery. From the ranks of the warriors, by contrast, were appointed most of the tax collectors, governors, judges and councilmen. Success in war would bring grants of land; the soldier who captured four enemies could sit upon a special chair. On one occasion, to stiffen army morale, Montezuma deprived all captains of their insignia or rank, forbade them to wear cotton clothing or shoes fitting for those of high rank, and prohibited them for a year from entering any of the royal palaces. Inca Atahualpa ordered the execution of all those who balked or flinched when the Spanish horseman reined his horse abruptly within inches of them, and, apocryphal though the story may be, Inca Panchacuti ordered the execution of one of his best commanders, Yupanqui, for having exceeded (with success) the limits assigned to his expedition.

The Aztec and the Inca were at a disadvantage in their resistance to the Spaniards in respect of their method of fighting a war. True, stratagem played a major part in their order of battle, the ambush particularly. It is recorded that on one occasion one of the city states sent against an enemy squadrons of naked women. One weapon mentioned in the *Popol Vuh* of the Maya was a gourd filled with wasps, thrown down from a fortress wall on the heads of an attacking force. The Aztecs remind one of the ancient Romans, with the consul opening his toga to the enemy and saying, "I bring you peace or war, take which you will." The Aztecs eschewed similarly any suggestion of surprise. In fighting an enemy, the triple alliance of city states would send an embassy who would yell bloody murder and utter the worst threats, giving them twenty days (an Aztec month) to decide, but leaving, as they withdrew, weapons for the enemy. After twenty days there would be a second embassy with even more solemn warnings – they would give another breathing space of twenty days. And so to the third warning, after which, if ignored, the empire and its antagonist were in a state of war; but even then they had to wait for the augurs to select a favourable date for the opening of the campaign. But the greatest disaster for the Aztecs was that they fought not to kill but to take prisoners for subsequent sacrifice. One is reminded of the feudal lords in Europe obsessed with the idea of taking prisoners to hold them to ransom.

The Aztecs were clearly not fighting the total war waged by the Spaniards. And the gap between the weapons on the two sides was too wide. Leaving aside the horses and dogs of the Spaniards for the moment, the confrontation was of steel blades against swords of obsidian (much appreciated by the Mexicans, this hard black volcanic glass was the counterpart of iron in contemporary Europe), guns against arrows (even if poisoned) and spear-throwers, iron helmets against feather headdresses, the arquebus (however clumsy, cumbersome and slow) against the sling (however effective and devastating). The astonishing psychological errors of Montezuma and Atahualpa, combined with the Spanish facility, fortified by their feudal experience, for taking advantage of internal dissensions and divisions (between the city states among the Aztecs, between rival Inca brothers in the Peruvian civil wars) did the rest. Where that was not enough, there was always the Spanish infinite capacity for treachery to fall back upon.[2]

The Amerindian economy was based on agriculture, hunting and fishing, depending on the regions involved. All these raised the question of the Amerindian attitude to the land. This was to become one of the principal sources of conflict between the indigenous inhabitants and the European invaders.

The Amerindian agricultural economy was most impressive. It was the Amerindians who gave the world maize and potato, two of the most valuable food crops, and cassava constituted (whether indigenous to America or of African origin) the third of the trinity on which the vegetable food supply was based. Incaland was the home of the potato. The Spaniards, obsessed with gold and silver, never recorded the potato's origin. The plant, taken to Spain, languished for decades, until its eventual migration to Ireland, which became its stronghold, and from there it moved to the New England colonies as the "Irish potato". Growing sometimes at over sixteen thousand feet in an eighteen-degree frost in the Andes, many of the cultivated varieties bore tubers regularly at fourteen thousand feet. Without the potato, human occupancy in that area would have been impossible: "Half the Indians do not have any other bread." To such an extent was the potato the staple crop of the Andean peasant that time was measured in units equivalent to the time it took to boil a potato. Famine stalked the land in years when the potato crop failed.

But potato was a low-status food; to call a man a potato-eater was equivalent to calling him a ragged beggar. An issue of corn porridge meant more than a dish of potatoes to a conscript soldier. For maize was the prestige crop, the sacred crop. Traditionally associated with Mexico as its principal centre, where there is evidence to suggest, from the ceremonial activity lavished on it in the Andes, that for the Inca it was a state crop, the noble food was alone worthy of being offered to the gods. There is archaeological evidence that the beginnings and the eventual growth of the sub-Andean culture pattern were closely related to the cultivation of a developed form of maize. It was maize farming that made possible independence from a riverine environment and brought about the expansion of population over the flanks of the mountain systems.

In the Amazon basin, the principal crop plant is cassava, forming 80 per cent of the diet of most tribes, in the form of either gruel or cakes. It attains a harvestable size in about six months, but there are tribes which prefer to wait eighteen months before pulling it out of the ground, because at this age the tubers are considerably larger and have attained their highest proportion of starch, about 25 per cent. It is yields like this which account for the stability of location of some tribes where there are no supernatural (as against ecological) reasons for removing. Another major Amerindian plant was the maguey, a cactus plant, which thrived on dry, infertile soils. It produced fibres, one of the principal sources of cloth as well as twine in Aztec times. But it had many other uses – its leaves were used for roofing or burning; its roots to make food or sugar; its liquid to make the intoxicant *pulque* or vinegar; its thorns to make needles and nails. It is understood that more than thirty different foods and drinks can be made from the maguey, most of them rich in vitamins A and B. Perhaps most important, the maguey survived the droughts and frosts that affected maize.

98 | THE BLACKEST THING IN SLAVERY WAS NOT THE BLACK MAN

The Spaniards consumed chinampa produce but ignored chinampa agricultural methods. For them Amerindian "culture" had at least an exotic appeal. The strength of the chinampa system lay in the fact that it combined intensity of cultivation with Amerindian control over production and supply. It was this very Amerindian control which was challenged by the Spaniards. Bringing their Old World practices and priorities, the Spaniards preferred wheat cultivation, and tried to promote it among the Amerindians. The Amerindians resisted and preferred their maize, especially as maize production was not subject to the tithe as wheat was. This was one of the major justifications of the Spaniards for turning to establishing their own farms and thus accelerating their acquisition of land. The upshot was that the Spaniards not only grew wheat but became competitors with the Amerindians in respect of maize. The Spanish *hacienda* combined wheat and maize, and inevitably Spanish controls were extended to Amerindian markets, notably in maize and *pulque*, displacing Amerindian supplies and continuously reducing Amerindian agriculture.

The Amerindians particularly resented the Christian attitude to their gods and their religion. The proud Inca ruler boasted: "I will be no man's tributary. I am greater than any prince upon the earth. As for the pope of whom you speak, he must be crazy to talk of giving away countries which do not belong to him." Montezuma arrogantly repudiated Cortés's rejection of the Aztec religion:

> Could I have conjectured that you would have used such reviling language as you have just done, I would certainly not have shown you my gods. In our eyes these are good divinities; they preserve our lives, give us nourishment, water and good harvest, healthy and growing weather, and victory whenever we pray to them for it. Therefore, we offer up our prayers to them, and make them sacrifices. I earnestly beg of you not to say another word to insult the profound veneration in which we hold these gods.

This was the great divide between Amerindians and Spaniards. The Amerindians worshipped a great many gods and were willing to set up among them whatever the newcomers should bring; as Motolinía put it, the Aztecs just wanted to have a hundred and one gods, instead of a hundred. The Spaniards, however, were the votaries of a closed religion whose churches could rise only upon the ruins of the former temples.

Inca Panchacuti was of the opinion that adulterers destroying the peace and happiness of others ought to be declared thieves and condemned to death without mercy. Aztec society, forbidding a citizen to take the law into his own hands, required the husband of an unfaithful wife catching her *in*

The Amerindians | 99

flagrante delicto, to bring the case before the courts. If the case was proved, society put the adulterous pair to death, burning the man alive and hanging the woman, but, if they were both nobles, placing green feather headdresses on them and burning them; others were sentenced to be stoned to death in the town square.[3]

Amerindian society was uniformly savage in its repression of drunkenness. Few societies have set up more rigid barriers against it than the Aztec. The emperor called it the cause of all the discords and dissensions, of all revolt and troubles in cities, the root and the origin of all evil and all perdition. The cause of adultery, rape, debauching of girls, incest, theft, crime, profanity, bearing false witness, calumny, riots and brawling was *pulque*, a drink like cider, obtained by fermenting the sap of the maguey. The Aztec allowed only the aged and women to drink it, those whose active life was over; enacted ferocious laws against public drunkenness; and set up a barrier of terrible punishments against indulgence by young people or middle-aged men. The young were put to death, the middle-aged man had his head shaved, a shattering disgrace.

In his domestic life the Amerindian used hammocks instead of beds, ate without chairs or tables, used mats for sleeping, providing the basis of another important industry. Night lighting was provided by tallow candles. The loincloth was generally abandoned in favour of European trousers. The Eskimo preserved meat in shallow ponds, the low temperature of the water preventing the growth of bacteria. The normal form of transport in North America was the *travois*, dragged by dogs on poles, carrying thirty-five to fifty pounds. In Peru it was the llama, the sheep of Peru, "little camels" which positively refused to carry weights in excess of twenty-five kilograms and would only go fifteen kilometres a day; detesting the harness, it was the llama's habit to spit in the face of anyone trying to harness it. The engineering achievements of these organized Amerindian societies have never ceased to astonish, as they lacked metal tools, except copper, and were restricted to stone tools. Their only draft animal was the llama, and they did not know the wheel.

It is with these limitations that one contemplates the Inca Gateway of the Sun, one of the greatest examples of stonecutting in the world, stone fitting stone with such precision that a razor blade cannot be inserted between them at any point. Of these ruins it has been authoritatively said that it is impossible to detect an error even by the use of calipers, a millimetre rule and a draughtsman's triangle. How any human beings could have cut this hard andesite rock to such perfect angles, with such true sharp edges, and often to a depth of six or eight inches from the surface, unless they possessed steel tools and most accurate mathematical instruments, is perhaps the greatest mystery of the ruins. It has been estimated that a labour force of ten thousand over a period of ten years was used for the construction of the Aztec Pyramid of the Sun at Teotihuacan, and thirty thousand at any one time in the construction of the Inca fortress of Sacsayhuamán near Cuzco.

This was the Amerindian society encountered by the European conquerors. Such was the splendour of Mayan civilization that it was often claimed that it could only be Roman or Phoenician in origin and inspiration – as Europeans were later to claim that African culture was not African. Aztec achievements were similarly credited to European or Asiatic neighbours: the splendid courts, the temples, the works of art. One of the Conquistadors, Bernal Díaz del Castillo, has left us this picture of Montezuma's Tenochtitlan as seen by Cortés.

> When we beheld on the water and firm ground, that broad causeway, running straight and level to the city, we could compare it to nothing but the enchanted scenes we had read of in Amadis of Gaul, from the great towers and temples, and other edifices of lime and stone which seemed to rise out of the water. To many of us it appeared doubtful whether we were asleep or awake; nor is the manner in which I express myself to be wondered at, for it must be considered, that never did man see, hear, or dream of anything equal to the spectacle which appeared to our eyes on this day.[4]

Albrecht Durer's testimony is even more striking. It was written in his diary in 1520, after a visit to Brussels, where he saw an exhibition of Montezuma's gifts to Cortés:

> I saw the things they brought from the land of gold to the King: a sun made of all gold, about five feet wide, also a silver moon the same size; various rare objects in arms, weapons, and projectiles; strange clothing; and every kind of rare things for human use. It is a marvel to see how beautiful all these things are. In all my life I have never seen anything that has gladdened my heart like these things. Among them I saw amazing art objects and the subtle skills of the people in those remote lands astonished me. Truly, I cannot say enough about the things I had there before me.

European Colonization and the Organization of Labour

Consider now the European society – first Spain, feudal and Catholic, secondly England, Protestant and headed for the acquisitive capitalist society. Both invaded America with clearly defined principles of European sovereignty over American territory with emphasis on the religious sanction for conquest. The basic principles in the European consensus were papal donation, first discovery, sustained possession, voluntary self-subjection by the indigenous inhabitants and armed conquest successfully maintained. The Crusades had formally established the principle that war conducted in the interests of the Holy Church was automatically just. For both Catholics and Protestants, papal donation or not, a bad religion made its votaries bad people, enemies to God and therefore also to God's chosen people.

The Catholic states of Spain and Portugal, bolstered by the papal donation of 1493, also had specific papal sanction in the Bull *Romanus Pontifex* of 1455, two years after the Turkish conquest of Constantinople. Pope Nicholas V bestowed "suitable favours and special graces on those Catholic kings and princes, who . . . not only restrain the savage excesses of the Saracens and of other infidels . . . but also for the defence and increase of the faith vanquish them and their kingdoms and habitations, though situated in the remotest parts unknown to us". For this work the pope granted the king of Portugal "free and ample faculty . . . to invade and subdue . . . all Saracens and pagans whatsoever, and other enemies of Christ wheresoever placed . . . and to reduce their persons to perpetual slavery". England, while not recognizing the papal donation or papal sanctions, developed its own Protestant authorizations to seize "remote heathen and barbarous lands".

As Prescott lamented in narrating the conquest of Peru, "imagine making a hero out of Francisco Pizarro, a man who couldn't even read his own name". The greater pity is that the educated Spaniards could see even less than Pizarro. Busy though they were, chronicling their discoveries, while melting the Inca gold and silver art objects in order to transport them more easily, they burned the *quipu* libraries as records of heathenism, while the first Catholic bishop of Mexico made a huge bonfire out of the Aztec parchments, which were often of exquisite beauty, and the officers of the Inquisition saw in them a challenge to the establishment of Christianity. Bishop Landa of Yucatan remarked: "We found a large number of books and as they contained nothing but superstition and lies of the devil, we burned them all, which the Indians regretted to an amazing degree and which caused them great anguish."

The Spaniards were interested only in gold and silver. Dazzled by Cuzco's gold, they paid no attention to the prodigious stores in the gigantic storehouses fully stocked with cloaks, weapons, metal, cloth, shields, building materials, knives, sandals and breastplates – leading one to wonder how the Inca subjects could ever have paid such an immense tribute; the Spaniards left all of it to be plundered by the Yanaconas, their Amerindian auxiliaries. Similarly, they saw no value in the vast store of turquoise among the Navajo on the west coast, their symbol of the blue desert sky. They showed no interest in the many turquoise items at the Aztec royal regalia. The Spaniards showed irritation when the Maya kept offering them jade, which the Maya thought worth more than gold. The Amerindian nobility and priesthood chose jade particularly, possibly because its colour symbolized growing vegetation. Aztec laws demanded that anyone stealing jade ornaments be stoned: "no man of low quality might possess jade". Jade was one of the important items demanded as tribute by the Aztecs. There are many reports of Spanish mishandling of emeralds in Columbia, making the precious stones valueless. It was no wonder that Hernando Pizarro, on his release from imprisonment in the fortress of Medina del Campo in 1562, regaining his estates, bought the title of Marquis of the Conquest. It was a personal vindication of his own famous dictum, *dinero es Don Caballero*, "Money is a noble lord."

After gold, land. The Europeans wanted the land and the necessary labour to work the land. The crucial problem faced by the conquistadors – Spaniards and Portuguese – was the problem of labour. The European sovereigns, concerned with profits, took steps to organize the territorial economy by reserving their share of the gold and silver from the mines and giving out the land, in feudal fashion, to their nationals. Land and mines were valueless without labour. Columbus, who had at once envisaged the enslavement of the Amerindians, provided they were cannibals – thus introducing the differentiation between "good" and "bad" Amerindians – went further than proposed and took steps to develop an Amerindian slave trade bringing slaves from what he called "useless islands". An even greater volume of slaves was to be provided for Peru and Panama, from Nicaragua and the Bahamas, to the islands with greater potential. According to Las Casas, ships were guided solely by the trail of dead Amerindians thrown from the slave ships.

But by 1500 the Spanish monarchs banned Amerindian slavery. The Spanish dilemma was brought out in instructions from Queen Isabella to Columbus's successor in 1503. The Amerindians were to be "free and not subject to servitude". At the same time, however, the Amerindians ran away, avoided all contact with Spaniards, refused to work for wages either on farms or in mines, and "go about like vagabonds", so that they could not be reached to be converted. A consultation in the presence of the Archbishop of Seville and with his approval decided "it was consonant with human and divine law to give the Indians in *encomienda*". Most of us, like Las Casas, do not know whether to laugh or to weep at the Requirement. Even when interpreted, the Amerindians could not possibly understand it; Oviedo, the royal chronicler of the Conquest, suggested that one of the Amerindians should be put in a cage to learn it at his leisure and have it explained to him by the bishop.

Las Casas thundered his denunciation of the *encomienda*, while the colonial settlers disobeyed the laws and the colonial authorities did not enforce them or connived at their infringement. It was difficult for the remote Spanish monarchy to enforce the law against such powerful vassals as Cortés in Mexico, whose *encomienda* comprised twenty-two townships, with an estimated population of over a hundred thousand. The upshot was the New Laws of 1542, which sought essentially to prevent the formation of a feudal class, to remove the Amerindians from the grasp of the settlers, to prevent the inheritance of existing *encomiendas*, and to reduce those of excessive dimensions. The Amerindians were decreed free men, vassals of the king of Spain. The attempt to enforce the New Laws led to outright rebellion in Peru and Panama.[5]

It was a rare voice that was raised in defence of the Amerindian. One such was Cieza, who, in his account of Almagro's march from Cuzco in the Peruvian civil wars, wrote: "If this were done with moderation, I should not condemn the service of the Indians, but if a man needed a pig, he took twenty; and if he wanted four Indians, he took twelve – and there were many who brought with them their concubines, carried in hammocks by the poor Indians."

The English, whether in New England or Virginia, took the view that Amerindians were outside the law of moral obligation. Thus they fought them by means that would have been regarded as dishonourable if the war was against a country in Europe – excepting Ireland, of course. They took to America four patterns of behaviour they transferred from Scotland and Ireland: the deliberate policy of divide and rule, disregard for pledges and promises to the Amerindian, total war of extermination against some communities to terrorize others, and a highly developed programme of falsification to justify the acts and policies of the conquerors. They added to this a deliberate decision to kill the men and enslave the women and children overseas in the West Indies or to exchange for Africans. "I suppose you know very well," wrote Downing, Winthrop's brother-in-law, "how we shall maintain twenty Moors cheaper than one English servant." With the breakdown of the 1795 treaty setting the borderline, the governor of the Northwest Territory, Harrison, exploded the time bomb: "Is one of the fairest portions of the globe to remain in a state of nature, the haunt of a few wretched savages, when it seems destined by the Creator to give support to a large population and to be the seat of civilization, of science and of true religion?"

This was the political climate in which Jefferson, in his *Notes on the State of Virginia*, approached the question of the three races in America – European, Amerindian and African. The essence of Jeffersonianism was the equation of whites and Amerindians, the superiority of Amerindians to blacks, and the disparagement of blacks. He saw the Amerindian as the equal of the white, brave and manly, attached to family and friends, remarkably eloquent (Chief Logan's oration reminded him of Demosthenes and Cicero), virile and not inferior to the white in his capacity for generation of ardour for his female. Such difference as there was between white and Amerindian was due entirely to environmental circumstances, and Jefferson concluded that "we shall find that they are probably formed in mind as well as in body, on the same module with the *Homo Sapiens Europeaus*".

On the Amerindians, the father of the Declaration of Independence did not speak for his countrymen; as far as he himself was concerned, not for the first time, there was a wide gulf between his egalitarian principles and his political actions. His earliest views were that "not a foot of land will ever be taken from the Indians without their own consent", modifying this somewhat later to the view that he was "alive to the obtaining lands from the Indians by all honest and peaceable means". He understood the need "to provide an extension of territory which the rapid increase of our numbers will call for"; the Amerindians "now reduced within limits too narrow for the hunter's state, humanity enjoins us to teach them agriculture and the domestic arts". White's *Lebensraum* took precedence over Amerindian equality and security of property. Even as early as 1776 Jefferson favoured strong measures to "reduce those wretches . . . But I would not stop there. I would never cease pursuing them while one of them remained on this side of the Mississippi." The Amerindians were "a useless, expensive, ungovernable ally".

This then, was Jefferson's policy – relocation of the Amerindians east of the Mississippi from Louisiana, acquired from France: the Cherokees. By 1812 Jefferson foresaw that the Amerindians "thrown further back relapse into barbarism and misery . . . and we shall be obliged to drive them, with the beasts of the forest into the stony (Rocky) mountains". Westward ho! Jefferson set the stage – expansion slowly broadened down from president to president. Monroe followed in 1819: "The hunter state can exist only in the vast uncultivated desert. It yields to the . . . greater force of civilized population; and of right it ought to yield, for the earth was given to mankind to support the greatest number of which it is capable; and no tribe or people have a right to withhold from the wants of others more than is necessary for their support and comfort."

The Amerindians | 105

American literature had a field day, portraying the Noble Savage as safely dead and historically past. The legend of the dying Indian, portrayed by the last living member of a tribe, became a staple of American literature. The outstanding example is Cooper's *Last of the Mohicans* in 1826, while Longfellow's *Song of Hiawatha* in 1855 romanticized the safely dead Amerindian. Cooper established the Amerindian as a significant literary type in world literature; eleven of his novels featured Indians. True to his class and kind, Cooper obeyed the literary conventions of the time: no Amerindian, however noble, was allowed to marry a white. Mark Twain, in his *Roughing It,* among the Gosiute, a deprived Great Basin tribe that lived in an extremely harsh environment, described them as the most depraved and degenerate on earth, "a silent, sneaking, treacherous-looking race", who would "embezzle carrion from the buzzards and coyotes", but who did believe in a Great Spirit, "thinking whisky is referred to".

The third priority of the Europeans was the conversion of the Amerindians to Christianity. The pope having decreed in 1512 that Amerindians were true descendants of Adam and Eve, Pope Paul III in his Bull *Sublimis Deus* in 1537 found it necessary to state and to order: Amerindians were not to be treated as "dumb brutes created for our service", but "as truly men . . . capable of understanding the Catholic faith. The said Indians and all other people who may later be discovered by Christians, are by no means to be deprived of their liberty or the possession of their property, even though they may be outside the faith of Jesus Christ, nor should they in any way be enslaved". It was stated for the North American Indians by a British propagandist in 1583:

> The savages are to be brought from falsehood to truth, from darkness to light, from the highway of death to the path of life, from superstitious idolatry to sincere Christianity, from the devil to Christ, from hell to heaven. Beside the knowledge how to till and dress the ground, they shall be reduced from unseemly customs to honest manners, from disordered riotous routs and companies to a well governed commonwealth, and withal shall be taught mechanical occupations, arts, and liberal sciences.

Among the North American Indians, the trouble was the rivalry created by competing Protestant sects. When the Africans requested permission to establish a mission near the new Roman Catholic church, Chief Crowfoot denied it. Since the first church had been built, all the old women and men and children had died; if another was built, all would die. "They had too much church." Among the Eskimo, the struggle between Anglican and Catholic divided tribes, families and school children, wasted lives and money and betrayed the whole idea of the missions. As someone aptly put it, "rival missionaries eager to convert the same cannibal are apt to behave like rival cannibals stalking the same missionary". At the same time the missions interfered with the hunting routine, by their ban on Sunday work and travel and by gathering the Amerindians for baptism and services at times when they needed to collect their winter supplies. Their ideas of hygiene, sex and God were fine perhaps in a Europe where they were part of the whole way of life and worked with a settled congregation in European farm villages. To stop the drum dancing and the lip ornaments destroyed confidence and pride; to prohibit several wives meant a very hard time for the wives who were "dropped".

The Amerindian had difficulty anyhow understanding certain concepts, however much the missionaries learned the native language. In these villages the Amerindians had to accept Jesuit tutelage in every aspect of life. "Compel them to come in," they echoed St Luke, and condoned force as the only way to get them to accept the relocation, these people whom da Nóbrega denounced as "the most vile and miserable heathen in all mankind". The missions' coexistence produced a curious world of detribalized Amerindians isolated from daily colonial life and subjected to incessant religious indoctrination. The poor chiefs suffered most – one wife, no cannibalism, stop drinking, attack on the medicine man. The result, inevitably, was reaction against Christianity. Da Nóbrega laid down the law to be given to them: forbid the eating of human flesh or tribal wars; restrict them to one wife; make them wear clothes; remove their sorcerers; maintain justice between them and between them and the Christians; make them live quietly in one place, avoiding a nomadic existence.

The Jesuits, in their black robes, exercised all the functions – doctors, judges, agricultural cooperatives; they appointed chiefs for life, and annual magistrates; the children were removed from their parents, housed in colleges and segregated by sex. This was ethnocide, the complete emasculation and suppression of tribal culture, under a regimentation which provided no scope for intellectual stimulus or debate. The education of the children, sufficient for them to recite and perform religious offices, had nothing whatever to do with the Amerindian environment. Its most laudable feature, music, which became a powerful weapon for conversion, was unnatural and imported. Any expression of their culture that did not conform to Catholic morality was emasculated. The Jesuit dream, brought closer to reality by their missions, was of a continuous chain of missions, a semi-autonomous theocratic state stretching from the Bolivian Altiplano and Potosí silver mines to the Atlantic seaboard.

The trouble was that the Jesuit system of insulated, paternalistic missions may have been fine on remote frontiers, but was unworkable when surrounded by colonists. The 1596 decree of Philip II on the system of mission reservations required the Jesuits to persuade the heathen to come to communicate with the settlers, and declare to them that they were free and would live at liberty and own their property as they would in the hills. This was followed by the law of 1609 proclaiming full freedom for the Amerindians, who would not be compelled to work, and must be paid for their labour and enjoy their property freely and securely; those already enslaved were to be freed.

The community exploded; there was an anti-Jesuit rising in Bahía, and two years later the law of 1609 was cancelled and slavery reintroduced, but no one was to serve more than ten years. A century later they were required to "live in villages with behaviour public and proper to rational men", could be attacked if "they go naked, recognize neither king nor governor, and do not live in the form or manner of a republic, trample the laws of nature, make no distinction between mothers and daughters in the satisfaction of their lust, eat one another". At best, as one governor remarked, they were "rational beasts". A relentless campaign of vilification was unleashed by the settlers against the Jesuits, claiming on the one hand that the Jesuits were a power-hungry secret society intent on creating a private empire and more concerned with material wealth than spiritual mission: their missions "look more like great store houses than places of prayer"; and on the other hand, denouncing their protégés, the Amerindians, as neither noble savages nor even useful allies but subhuman beasts, "squalid barbarians, bestial and abject, like wild beasts in everything except their human appearance".

The Amerindian Resistance

So distinguished an authority as Adam Smith was later to lend the weight of his reputation to the absurd charge that the Amerindian, unlike the African, did not resist his oppressors and did not fight for his freedom. Astonishment is frequently expressed at the decisive victories achieved by a handful of Spaniards over far more formidable numbers. Pizarro advanced into the heart of the Inca Empire with sixty-two horsemen, 106 infantry, of whom twenty were crossbowmen and three musketeers. The Inca Empire fell in half an hour. Quesada subdued the rich and populous province of Bogotá with 160 men without firearms but with horses. Even the merest British fur trader in the Hudson's Bay Company could say, "We were Caesars, there being nobody to contradict us." The principal reason for this was the superior military technology of the conquistadors. To people who had never seen a horse, the sight of man on a horse, with the man in full armour, was simply terrifying. In Quesada's campaign in Bogotá it was noted that Amerindians fell on their faces to avoid even the sight of what they regarded as a new animal. In Mexico, as the Spaniards reported, the Amerindians, ignorant of the fact that the horses were "irrational beasts", offered them the same fare as their masters, turkeys, maize, cakes and meat, and when the horses ignored the food, the Amerindians begged the Spaniards "to tell the horses not to be angry with them". Prescott tells us in respect of Peru that the Amerindians never overcame their dread of horses and firearms, and never came to close quarters with Spanish steel, Montezuma was led to believe that the swords were no more dangerous than women's weaving battens, that the firearms were capable of firing only two shots, and that the horses were powerless at night. De Soto pulled up his horse at full gallop at the very feet of the Inca; attendants who sprang back were later beheaded for showing timidity before strangers.[6] Until the Amerindians of Hispaniola saw a man dismounting from his horse, they thought horse and man were one monstrous creature; the Amerindians in Peru thought the monstrous animal had broken into two parts when Pizarro was accidentally thrown from his horse.

Over and above the horse, the Spaniards had the dog – the Alaunt or feudal war dog, trained to pull down boars and bears in the forests of Central Europe. The Amerindians were terrified of the dogs. One became particularly famous, the dog Becerrillo. Ten Spaniards with Becerrillo were more feared than one hundred without him. The mastiff Leoncico received a captain's pay for his efficiency against the naked bodies of the Amerindians until they poisoned him. The story is told of the old Amerindian woman taking a letter to some Christians. When the dog was loosed upon her she sat down, showed the letter to the dog, and said in her native dialect: "*Señor perro* (Mr Dog), I am taking this letter to the Governor; do not hurt me." The dog sniffed her and left her alone.

The Spaniards also had in their favour the pronounced intertribal jealousy and feuds. Cortés played on it successfully in Mexico in enlisting the aid of the Tlaxcalas against Montezuma, and various Peruvian tribes invited Pizarro to protect them from the Inca. Never was there a more unlikely liberator. Listen to Pizarro to the Inca's son: "You must understand that I have come for no other reason than to free you from slavery to the men of Quito. Knowing the injuries they were doing to you, I wanted to come and put a stop to them and to liberate the people of Cuzco from this tyranny."

The Spaniards were powerfully aided by that prophecy so frequently encountered among the races they subjected, that their native traditions looked to the arrival of strange white men from outside of the country. Columbus claims to have heard it from a cacique in Hispaniola. It had emerged in the Spanish campaign in the Canary Islands, it was to appear to Magellan in the Moluccas, it appeared in Mexico and in Peru. Sanders calls it the trademark of the Spanish version of manifest destiny, and the consensus is that it was fabricated by the Spaniards themselves.

And the Spaniards had, as their final, potent weapon, plain simple treachery and bad faith. It was so frequently resorted to that it could only have been deliberate policy, a way of life. Narváez in Hispaniola watched impassively the slaughter at Caonao of unarmed hospitable Amerindians who had welcomed the Spaniards: Juan Alonso, a Spaniard put in command of Cacique Careta's armies in Hispaniola, and so trusted that he slept in the cacique's tent, conspired with Vasco Núñez to admit the Spaniards at night to massacre the Amerindians. The seizure of both Montezuma and Pizarro falls in this category of treachery. The accompanying priest put it straightforwardly to Pizarro in the presence of Atahualpa's attendants: "Do you not see that while we stand here wasting our breath in talking with this dog, full of pride as he is, the fields are filling with Indians? Set on, at once; I absolve you." Contrary to the Requirement, it was Spanish practice, used by Columbus, Cortés and Pizarro to make surprise attacks in the dead of night, as Cortés wrote, with a bold face, to Emperor Charles V. The Requirement was obeyed, not enforced.

The record is full of Amerindian resistance, disgust with European treachery, refusal to be vassals of the conquerors. Cacique Urracá was determined to finish with those who "do not keep faith with what they promise, neither word nor peace". In Hispaniola the Amerindians went on what Fernando Ortiz has called a collective hunger strike. Cacique Lempira arrogantly "wished to know no other lord, to have no other law, to follow no other customs than those he had". In New Galicia the Amerindians "preferred to die of hunger in their liberty than to live well fed and in peace in the service of the Spaniards".

The revolt of the Amerindian inhabitants of Chile and their war of resistance lasted over three hundred years. Formally begun in 1554, it was the first of the great Amerindian uprisings. Peace was made with the independent republic of Chile in 1881, which was called "Araucanian Flanders, or the invincible state". A strange record for an area which Valdivia, following Las Casas, had worked to acquire by peaceful conquest. The Amerindian resistance was appropriately commemorated in Ercilla's *Araucana*, the great epic begun in 1569 and completed in 1589.

Túpac Amaru II referred to himself frequently as king of Peru, Chile, Quito, Tucumán and other parts. He bitterly attacked existing abuses, especially the office of *corregidor*, which was suppressed after the rebellion which also suppressed the *mita* in the mines of Potosí. A hostile Spanish account reads as follows:

> The essence of the careful planning and perfidy of the traitor Túpac Amaru consists in this, that after speaking so often of the royal orders which authorized him to proceed against the corregidorres and other Europeans . . . he now says nothing about the order of the king and proceeds as the most distinguished Indian of the royal blood and principal line of the Incas to liberate his countrymen from the injuries, injustices, and slavery . . . he transforms himself from a royal commissioner into a redeemer from injustices and burdens . . . until they have raised him to the defunct throne of the tyrannical pagan kings of Peru, which is doubtless the goal of his contrivings . . . offers the natives freedom, not only from customs house duties but from sales taxes, tribute, and forced labour in the mines.[7]

A Spanish minister later admitted that no one knew how close Spain had come to losing not only Peru but the viceroyalty of La Plata (Buenos Aires) and even Mexico. Túpac Amaru's fundamental mistake was in not attacking Cuzco, the ancient Inca capital and the centre of Spanish power; instead he invaded, after his initial victory at Sangarará, the southern province. When he attacked Cuzco it was too late. The Spaniards were prepared; and they had Amerindian auxiliaries of their own, while Túpac Amaru's artillery was commanded by a treacherous Spaniard who systematically misdirected the fire of his pieces.

Túpac Amaru's trial took place on 15 May 1781; to his interrogators, seeking to know his accomplices, he replied: "Here the only accomplices are you and I; you as oppressor and I as liberator." The ferocity of the sentence revealed the deep fear of Spanish imperialism. Here is a description:

> Túpac was brought into the middle of the square, and there the executioner cut out his tongue. Then they broke off his chains and laid him on the ground. They tied four ropes to his hands and feet and attached the ropes to the girths of four horses, which four mestizos drove in four different directions. Cuzco had never before seen a spectacle of this kind. Either because the horses were not very strong or because the Indian was really made of iron, they simply could not tear him apart, although they tugged at him for a long time, while he dangled in the air like a spider. (Eventually the Spaniards ordered the executioner to cut off his head).[8]

The bodies of Túpac Amaru II and his wife were borne to Picchu, where they were thrown into a great bonfire, and their ashes then thrown into the sea. It was said that in the large multitude present no one gave a cry or even

The Amerindians | 111

spoke; there seemed to be no Amerindians in the multitude, or if there were, they were not in customary dress. Spanish hostility pursued him beyond the grave; the orders were that his family was to be stamped out "to the fourth generation", said the judge. "It is agreeable neither to the King or to the State that any seed or descendant remain, and every Túpac Amaru, for the noise and impression which this accursed name has produced in the natives." The viceroy decided of one of his descendants that it was "very necessary to separate Miguel Túpac Amaru from these countries and from all communication with the Indians". Others were sentenced to perpetual exile and ten years in jail. And Garcilaso de la Vega's book on Peru was proscribed because of his eulogy of the Incas.

North America had the honour roll in the Amerindian resistance movement. The Sioux attack on Custer left 265 American soldiers dead. But the astounding Amerindian revolt was that of Louis Riel, in Canada, in the rebellion of 1885. Riel was of mixed blood, a *mestizo*, a *métis*, as he was called in French. His goal was stated in the following terms: "That the North West Territory is the natural property of the Indian and Half-Breed, ought to be set apart for their exclusive use, ruled and governed by them alone".[9] In this Riel came up against a Yankee dream – a state of Minnesota, or Territory of Dakota and Montana, reaching from the Great Lakes and the Missouri River to Alaska. As stated by one of their propagandists, "The destiny of the white race in America is to destroy the red race." But Riel was up against Canada also, in its march to the Pacific via the construction of the Canadian Pacific Railroad. Riel thought he could play one white imperialist against the other. He met President Grant, who was assured by a senator that with $25,000 to the *métis* he could ensure their resistance to Canada indefinitely; he presented to the Republican Party a plan for taking Manitoba away from the Dominion of Canada, and in 1880 petitioned General Miles for a special reservation in Montana. In 1883 he became an American citizen. But he also served briefly in the Federal Parliament in Ottawa, where Prime Minister Macdonald refused to distribute, as Riel insisted, any 1.4 million acres to the *Métis* as guaranteed in the Manitoba Act. Both predatory powers agreed with the definition of the *Métis*, "a race of greasy rebels, worthless vagabonds, bloodthirsty murderers and unhung felons". Riel replied with dignity: "It is true that our savage origin is humble, but it is meet that we honour our mothers as well as our fathers. Why should we concern ourselves about what degree of mixture we possess of European or Indian blood? If we have ever so little of either gratitude or filial love, should we not be proud to say, 'We are *Métis*'?"

Riel, emphasizing the grievances of the *Métis* and the economic and political discrimination they faced and the denial to them of the enjoyment of the right of people by the Canadian Federal Government, was determined to get even with the prime minister, whom the Amerindians nicknamed "Old Tomorrow": "What is Fort Carlton? What is Prince Albert? Nothing! – We march, my braves!" He was captured and tried by jurors unfamiliar with the French language. To the end he remained determined: "If we cannot have one seventh of the lands from Canada, we will ask the people of the States, the Italians, to come and help us as immigrants. . . . I said we will invite the Italians of the States, the Irish of the States, the Bavarians . . ." Convicted – pleas for clemency came from all over the world – he appealed to President Cleveland, challenging Canada's title to the northwest and urging annexation by the United States. It was all in vain; Macdonald's mind was made up: "He shall hang though every dog in Quebec bark in his favour."

Disease

The most dreaded of the diseases was smallpox. Amerindians dreaded it more than anything: the foul odour, disfigurement, delirium (the Amerindians had an enormous fear of insanity), helplessness – all destroyed the sense of human dignity. It hastened the downfall of the Amerindian medicine man. What has been generally identified as smallpox hit Mexico in 1520. The mortality was appalling. When Cortés entered Mexico City on 13 August 1521, after stubborn defence, the Spaniards found the houses filled with corpses; nearly half the inhabitants succumbed to the infection. The mortality was general throughout New Spain; it has been estimated that nearly half the native population died in this first epidemic. The second followed in 1531. There was a third outbreak in 1545, and further visitations in 1564 and 1576. Mumps and measles followed the smallpox. It has been estimated that, in all, some 18.5 million of the total population of twenty-five million were destroyed. As has been said, this produced a "drastic psychological and cultural consequence – loss of faith in established institutions and beliefs, wholesale demoralization and simple surrender of the will to live". In Peru the death of the reigning Inca and his heir from smallpox was followed by civil war, which explains in part the triumphal march and plunder of Pizarro amid this wreckage of the Inca political structure. The Spaniards were nearly immune, from their European experience. The Amerindians, regarding epidemics as a form of divine punishment, were ripe for mass conversions. In the words of a German missionary at the end of the seventeenth century, "The Indians die so easily that the bare look and smell of a Spaniard causes them to give up the ghost." The European success was so astonishing that it has often been charged, and never denied, that they did not hesitate to resort to germ warfare, and at least one British commander in his Amerindian war did not hesitate to put out blankets infected with smallpox germs for the Amerindians. As the saying went, the best Amerindian was a dead Amerindian.

The White Man's Burden

These were the people whom the Spanish invaders encountered in the New World. They were inferior to the Europeans in technology: the disparity is vividly portrayed for us in Diego Rivera's devastating "Scene from the Conquest", in the Cortés Palace in Cuernavaca, Mexico; in which the heavily armed knights, complete with armour, visor, shield and sword, on the white horse, are set against the Amerindian on foot with his war paint, his fearful mask and his pitiful club. One thousand of them, boasted Columbus, would not stand up against three Spaniards, "so that they are good to be ordered about, to work, and sow, and do all that may be necessary, and to build towns, and they should be taught to go about clothed and to adopt our customs". Slavery, Christianity, "civilization" (clothes as against the nakedness of barbarism, urbanization as against isolated villages) – Columbus, on his very first voyage, on 16 December 1492, thus formulated Spain's "White Man's Burden". The *casus belli* soon emerged – the Caribs were cannibals.

While the demographic superiority of the Amerindians contributed to their survival on the mainland in such countries as Mexico and Peru – one of the more profound explanations is their maize-beans-squash complex – they disappeared in the Caribbean. The official verdict on their extermination has been left us by the royal chronicler, Oviedo. Admitting the ravages caused by the *encomienda* and excessive labour in the mines to satisfy the insatiable greed of the Spaniards, Oviedo concluded:

> But this was not the complete reason for the final disappearance of the Indians. God permitted it because of the sins of the immoderate Christians who enjoyed the sweat of the Indians' toil only because they did not help the Indians with his teachings in such a way that they should know God. . . . Nor did the Spaniards cease to add to this, for the divine permission which excluded the Indians from the earth, the great, heinous and enormous sins and abominations of these savage and bestial people; in regard to whom that terrible and just sentence of the Sovereign and eternal God is truly meet and just . . . it repenteth me that I have made them.

114 | THE BLACKEST THING IN SLAVERY WAS NOT THE BLACK MAN

But the Amerindians were too numerous to be exterminated in South America, in Mexico, Peru, Bolivia, Ecuador, where pro-Amerindian movements have started up – *Indianismo*, ranging from visions of a new social order based on Amerindian communal traditions to more modest efforts to raise the material and cultural level of the Amerindian by providing him with land, technical assistance and schools.

Moíses Sáenz, the Mexican scholar, to continue with the example of Peru, has stated categorically in our century, some four hundred years after Pizarro, that feudalism still exists in Peru: its dynamic expression is *Gamonalismo*. Sáenz writes:

> Nothing ever reminded me so much of the Middle Ages as this (little town of Anco) . . . contract labourers (*bracceros*) generally brought from the sierra; *Yanaconas* also serve as *pongos* (personal servants). The *yancona* works in his master's fields a certain number of days with no wages. . . . When the Indian goes to perform his service he even loses his name; he is simply called *pongo*, and he is regarded as if he were a small, inoffensive, and useful domestic animal . . . the *pongo* must wear a cap different from that worn by other Indians; with that distinctive headgear the unhappy Indian servant is subject to abuse by all in the streets and markets.

Presiding over all this is the "Society for the Protection of the Indians", accused by the Brazilian Government itself of genocide and of "practically every crime in the Brazilian penal code". The Spanish bishops had destroyed the Aztec parchments and the Inca measures. The archives of the society were destroyed by a mysterious fire in Brasilia; unlike the slavery archives, which were destroyed in 1891 on the instructions of the Minister of Finance, "under the obligation of destroying all traces of the system for the sake of the nation's reputation and to give evidence of the fraternal sentiments which we owe the mass of citizens who, by the abolition of slavery, have become members of the Brazilian community".

4.

African Slavery in the New World

The compromising expedient of the Constitution . . . which regards the slave as divested of two-fifths of the man.

James Madison, *The Federalist.*

In 1596 a Dutch privateer captured a Portuguese ship with a hundred African slaves on board; the ship, with the slaves, was taken to Middelburg, Holland. At a meeting of the Provincial States of Zeeland, the burgomaster argued that the blacks "could not be kept by anyone as slaves and sold as such, but had to be put in their natural freedom without anyone pretending (to have) rights to them as his property". The assembly unanimously agreed and the blacks were set free. The United Provinces were thus spared the necessity of creating a slave market, as had developed in Antwerp. Thereafter, when the Dutch captured a slave ship and were faced with the dilemma of the disposal of the human cargo, the ship seems to have been turned over to the blacks. Blacks, of course, were helpless and were in all probability soon recaptured and re-enslaved. If the Dutch captors wished to keep the ship, they released the blacks to the nearest land. The Dutch were soon to make up for lost time and develop their own markets for slaves or arrange for distribution to other markets. But it was an indication that the Europeans – the Portuguese apart – were somewhat slow in rising to the occasion provided by the Spanish discoveries in the New World and the Portuguese penetration of West Africa.

The Dutch were not the only European power in this predicament. In 1571, the Parliament of Bordeaux freed a cargo of blacks: "France, mother of liberty, does not permit slaves." Mother would have all the time in the world to change her values, but even in 1687, two years after the Code Noir, and with France thoroughly involved in the African slave trade, Louis XIV ordered the repatriation to Guinea of six slaves illegally transported – among the few to make the return voyage.

Hawkins, on behalf of the English, had made the first slave-trading voyage in 1563, claiming to have captured three hundred blacks; the Portuguese complained to the English government that he had taken by armed force three times that number. But as early as 1481 there had been rumours that Englishmen planned to challenge the Portuguese monopoly. On the complaint of the king of Portugal, the voyage was countermanded. A formal proposal a few years later for permission for Britain to share in the African trade was disallowed. Some years later a British expedition of three hundred vessels commanded by John Lok returned with ten black slaves, whom the British returned to their home in Guinea. On an expedition in 1620, a British trader, Jobson, was offered blacks. He replied: "We were a people who did not deal in any such commodities, neither did we buy or sell one another, or any that had our own shapes." Even then, however, Englishmen were fitting out ships "to take niggers, and carry them to foreign parts". Forty years later, Jobson's king established the Company of Royal Adventurers, trading to Africa, and gave it a monopoly on the British slave trade for a thousand years.

From Old England to New England: it was the Dutch traders, without a market of their own for slaves, who first introduced blacks to Virginia, selling twenty blacks there in 1619. By 1641 Massachusetts, in its Body of Liberties, forbade slavery unless the slaves were "lawful captives taken in just wars, and such strangers as willingly sell themselves, or are sold to us". But when in 1645 two Massachusetts citizens were accused of slave raiding in Africa on a Sunday, killing a hundred, and abducting the slaves, brought to Massachusetts to be sold, they were tried only for man-stealing. The court ordered the blacks repatriated to Guinea; neither defendant was fined or prosecuted. The slave trade became one of the key aspects of royal grandeur – Charles II took shares in the Royal African Company. In the *Asiento* of 1701 to France, the king of Spain reserved the right to one-quarter of the shares. So did the King of France. This was the height of the illustrious Louis XIV, *Le Roi Soleil, Négrier* – Louis XIV, the Sun King, Slave Trader. Queen Anne of England exulted when, at the Treaty of Utrecht in 1713, England wrested the *Asiento* from France as part of the spoils of war. King George I himself became governor of the British South Sea Company. Wrote Cardonega, the Portuguese historian: "What need have we to seek mines of gold and silver? The most real and richest of the mines is the mine of slaves where we dig quantities of pieces of Indies." French royalty concurred, "The blacks are the true mines we must seek." The Chamber of Commerce of La Rochelle voted aye, "France had no mines like Spain and Portugal; the French colonies furnished only sugar, coffee, cotton; but these products are more precious than the gold of Peru and Mexico, because they are for France the source of an immense navigation." As the Intendant General of the French Antilles summed it all up to the minister,

"The blacks are here, for the cultivation of the soil, as absolutely necessary as flour to make bread or cloths to make shirts."

The slave trade had one supreme advantage: it was carried on without the export of money. One capital investment covered no fewer than three transactions – purchase of metropolitan products which were exchanged in Africa for blacks, who were bartered in America for colonial produce, all of which was sold in the metropolitan country or exported; so large was this colonial produce that the slave ship could not carry all the merchandise, so other ships were involved. The triangular trade was supplemented in the course of time by bilateral trade in two directions – between the metropolitan country and Africa and back, and between the metropolitan and the New World and back. America, deprived of slaves, concluded the traders of Nantes, would become unproductive. White America was built up, maintained and developed on the basis of Black Africa. The slave trade was the direct cause of an enormous increase in production – industrial production in the metropolitan countries, and agricultural raw materials in the New World. The principal commodities in the trade with Africa were textiles, firearms, alcohol – especially gin, but also rum – cheap consumer goods like nails, pots and pans, kettles and the baubles that were appropriately dubbed *pacotille* – mirrors, brightly coloured beads, etcetera. Gold and ivory were the principal African products exchanged, apart from the slaves themselves.

The New World colonies supplied sugar (and its byproduct, rum), cotton, tobacco, indigo, coffee, cocoa and hardwoods. The textile industry, with the colonies supplying the cotton, was the principal beneficiary of the new markets opened up in Africa and the New World colonies for the purchase of the slaves in Africa and for clothing them in the New World plantations. But the textiles were European imitations of oriental specialties; the first copying in the transfer of technology was done by Europe. Thus we read of the *Siamoises* created in Rouen, copies of designs of the robes of Siamese ambassadors at the Court of Louis XIV, the Indian imitations machine-stamped in Europe towards 1760. The iron industry provided the agricultural implements and the sugar machinery for sugar production. Sheep-herding was enormously stimulated by the trade both with Africa and the New World. In the context of the prevailing economic doctrines restricting colonial territories to the production of agricultural raw materials – "not a nail, not a horseshoe" was to be produced in British North America – a huge sugar-refining industry developed in Europe. A petition to the British Parliament in 1659 condemned the "disorderly trade of the Plantations" and the "error" of refining sugar in Barbados, which injured thirty sugar refineries in London, and called for an act to require the sugar colonies to send only muscovado sugar to England and forbid them to refine sugar. There was, as well, a rum distillery in the New England colonies based on the importation of colonial molasses.

The metropolitan countries, as well as the European temperate colonies in New England and Canada, supplied the softwoods for house construction and large quantities of food, including fish, to allow the tropical colonies, especially the smaller Caribbean ones, to concentrate on monoculture and devote as much of their limited land space as possible to plantation crops, particularly sugar, tobacco and cotton. The African slaves, purchased with metropolitan manufactures, transported in metropolitan ships, laboured on the New World plantations with metropolitan tools and implements, clothed in metropolitan cottons, housed in barracks or shacks constructed of metropolitan materials, and fed on metropolitan foods, all to produce commodities transported in metropolitan ships to supplement and diversify the metropolitan diet and provide the raw materials for further metropolitan industrial development. Europe had never had it so good. The superstructure in Spain may have been European rather than Spanish, but the foundation was as much African as elsewhere. Seville, Lisbon, Antwerp, Amsterdam, Nantes, London, Liverpool, Bristol and Manchester – the principal streets of all (like Liverpool's) had been marked out by the chains of the African slaves, and the walls of their houses cemented by African blood; all grew on African sweat; the wealth of all, sufficient as in Seville to pave their streets with tiles of gold and silver, was the accumulation of African tears. To quote a French author, everyone lived off the slave trade. All Atlantic ports were slave ports, but to Nantes was reserved the supreme title – *la ville des négriers,* the port of the slave ships.

Europe was the Third World, after Africa and the Western Hemisphere. Europe's wars were fought for slices of the African coast and for the most insignificant of Caribbean islands. Elmina, Gorée, Cormantin, Cape Coast Castle and Christiansborg – each European country had its own headquarters in Africa; Fort Amsterdam, Fort Gross-Friedrichsburg, James Fort, Fort Orange recall the European scramble. The West Indian islands changed hands and ownership repeatedly: islands today too small were partitioned between two European claimants – St Kitts, St Martin – while the Prussians leased a single plantation from the Danes in St Thomas. De Ruyter served off the coast of Africa; Nelson, Rodney and de Grasse in the Caribbean, where El Morro in Havana and Puerto Rico and the ruins of Brimstone Hill in St Kitts are silent testimony to the European rampage. Official war was supplemented by unofficial hostilities and the raids of buccaneer outlaws and state-encouraged privateers who went about their depredations recognizing "no peace beyond the line", sacking with Drake, raiding with Esquemeling and Morgan, becoming national heroes in the process like Drake, achieving official preferment like Morgan, deputy governor of Jamaica.

The slave ships bore honoured names. Voltaire, on very good terms with the slave trader Montaudouin, thanked him in verse for having given his name to one of his ships sailing to Guinea. Turgot declined the honour. Many slave ships carried the names of the aristocracy, male and female. One slave trader of Nantes christened his ship *The Social Contract*. Honours were lavished on the slave traders, titles of nobility conferred upon them, for example, the Irishman Walsh, made a count by Louis XV. Nantes, a dirty city before the slave trade, developed an air of nobility and elegance. Chateaubriand's father was engaged in the slave trade. However, "the son forgot to indicate the name of the ship which was *Roi-de-Juda*" (Whydah). Joseph II of Austria conferred a title of nobility on a great slave trader.

The slave trade naturally had its dangers and inconveniences. A slave ship was in a sense a warship; it had to repel attacks of pirates at sea, raids of hostile natives on the coast, revolts of the slaves on board. The mortality on the vessel required a captain to carry almost half as many more men besides those needed to steer the ship, because of the necessity of controlling the blacks. Gold Coast blacks were taken on as guardians and overseers, particularly of Whydah slaves. "When we constitute a guardian, we give him a cat of nine tails as a badge of his office, which he is not a little proud of, and will exercise with great authority." Edward Long justified the chaining of the slaves because of the mutinies – "the same confinement as if they were wolves or wild boars". The slaves had to be packed closely – "not so much room as a man in his coffin either in length or breadth", said a slave trader.[1] John Newton corroborated, "Close to each other like books on a shelf. I have known them so close that the shelf would not easily contain one more." The crew too faced their tribulations: "an officer on the slave ship, a good sailor and a good trader, if he escapes shipwreck, pirates, scurvy and fever, is not massacred by his slaves, becomes rich after twenty years and a dozen voyages". Cases are recorded of seamen in rough weather, with no shelter of their own, stealing down the hatchway to sleep with the blacks in the stinking hold and begging the blacks for part of their rations.[2]

John Newton, the converted slave trader, once complained that the slave trade "renders most of those who are engaged in it too indifferent to the sufferings of their fellow creatures . . . the necessity of treating Negroes like cattle gradually brings numbness upon the heart". But he had no regrets. "During the time I was engaged in the slave trade I never had the least scruples as to its lawfulness." While waiting on the coast for a coffle to arrive, he wrote the famous hymn "How Sweet the Name of Jesus Sounds". When he was asked by the parents of the girl he wished to marry whether he could support her, he replied that he knew of only one way to make a substantial living: the slave trade.

It was said that the blacks had "a more dreadful apprehension of Barbados than we can have of hell". There was the assurance from the spokesman of South Carolina after the war of independence that "while there remained one acre of swampland un-cleared of South Carolina, I would raise my voice against restricting the importation of negroes . . . the nature of our climate . . . the flat, swampy situation of our country, obliges us to cultivate our lands with negroes, and that without them, South Carolina would soon be a desert waste". The Dutch, having acquired both forts on the West African coast and island centres of trade in the Caribbean, made up for their late start in the slave trade. A persistent item on the agenda of the Heren XIX of the West India Company was "how this trade could be maintained for the best service, of the company and to the exclusion of all foreign nations". By 1645 the Heren XIX defined the slave trade "as the soul of the company, which for the last two decades of its existence was almost exclusively a slave-trading operation. If they could only get Puerto Rico as a slave depot, it would be an inestimable treasure". They had to make do with Curaçao, that "cursed little barren island supplying slaves to the Spaniards; with its warehouse for black ebony built by 1688, it housed three thousand blacks for immediate delivery".

The ultimately decisive factor was that black slave labour was cheaper than white half-free, half-slave labour and was more permanent, notwithstanding the steady rise in the price of slaves (from fifty to over a thousand milréis in Brazil over the centuries, for example), the general planter opinion – except in the United States, with the slave farms of Virginia and Maryland (over seven hundred thousand were transferred from the border states to the lower south from 1830 to 1860) – was that it was cheaper to buy slaves than to breed them. Sheridan estimates that in Jamaica sugar plantations in the mid-1770s, the slave who laboured for twelve years yielded an annual profit of 6 per cent; fifteen years' service yielded 9 per cent; and twenty years nearly 11 per cent. As a Portuguese enthusiast wrote in 1591 about the limitless possibilities of the market for "black ivory": Angola's territory was so thickly populated that it would furnish substantial numbers of slaves "until the end of the world", the governor of Angola writing to the king of

Portugal that "the European slave trade delivers blacks from eternal death". He was echoed by the British governor of Cape Coast Castle on the Gold Coast, who exulted around 1760, "Africa not only can continue supplying the West Indies in the quantities she has hitherto, but, if necessity required it, could spare thousands, nay, millions more, and go on doing the same to the end of time."

This raises the question of the number of slaves exported from Africa by the Europeans in the nearly four and a half centuries of black slavery in the New World from the Portuguese conquest of Guinea in 1499, when the slave trade was directed essentially to Europe, until 1888, when black slavery in the Western Hemisphere was brought to an end with its abolition in Brazil, taking into account illegal importations after the Brazilian abolition of the slave trade in 1851. Estimates have been provided by a number of students of the question – about fifteen million (Davidson, Oliver and Professor J.D.Fage, Brion Davis, deriving from the earlier Kuczynski and Dunbar), twenty million (Oliveira Martins of Brazil) and twenty-five million (Rothberg). Noel Deerr, in his *History of Sugar*, estimated twelve million for the Atlantic slave trade. Philip Curtin, in his *The Atlantic Slave Trade: A Census*, reduces the estimate to 9.5 million, largely on the basis of a revision of Deerr's figures for British North America, later the United States.[3] Dr Rodney is of the opinion that the tendency to reduce the figures represents an attempt to "whitewash" the European slave trade by apologists for the capitalist system and its long record of brutality in Europe and abroad. Curtin's estimates relate for the most part to what might be called legal imports; large-scale contraband was involved throughout the entire history of the slave trade, especially in Spanish America during the period of rigid Spanish controls, and in Cuba and Brazil in the nineteenth century, with their infractions of international treaties outlawing the slave trade.[4]

It would appear therefore that one can accept Dr Rodney's figure that the average mortality over the centuries in the Middle Passage was in the vicinity of 15–20 per cent, the mortality tending to increase with the length of the voyage. This immediately brings Curtin's figure up to approximately eleven million. But, as Dr Rodney stresses, we must add to the Middle Passage the mortality on the routes from the African interior to the Slave Coast, and the casualties of the wars stimulated or generated by the slave trade. Rodney agrees that "the resultant figure would be many times the millions landed alive outside of Africa". Professor Fage goes even further, and estimates that for every African who became acclimatized to plantation slavery in the New World, at least one other African lost his life through warfare, the Middle Passage and the "seasoning" in the New World. We are by now quite close to a total depopulation in excess of twenty million, making allowance for the contraband which supplemented legal imports. The principal villains of the piece were Britain, France and Portugal. For the more than a century from 1701 to 1810, in a total export of just under 5.5 million slaves, Curtin estimates the British share at just under 2.5 million, the Portuguese at just over two million, and the French at just under one million. A more refined estimate for the period 1768–1798, involving some 3.3 million slaves, gives the British average at 51 per cent, the French at 19 per cent, the Portuguese at 18 per cent; with the Dutch and United States at 5 per cent each, and the Danes at under 2 per cent.

The Inefficiency of the Slave System of Production

In the beginning was the word, and the word was "racism". The Spanish island of Providencia (now part of Colombia), off the coast of Nicaragua, passed into British possession from 1630 to 1641, its location being ideal for the British policies of privateering and smuggling in violation of the Spanish laws of trade. Providencia became the first step on the long British road to a black slave-labour economy.

This venture was the brainchild of a few leading Puritans who were originally looking for a place of settlement and refuge for their co-religionists. One of the most active of its spirits was John Pym, and it has been repeatedly asserted that Cromwell's close friend and associate of its founders had seriously contemplated emigrating there. By the time Providencia became Puritan and British, the British had experience of blacks in the population in Bermuda and Tortuga. In Bermuda, an act had been passed in 1623 to "restrayne the insolencies of Negroes", "such vassals being forbidden to carry cudgels and other weapons in the daytime and not to be off their master's land during any undue hours in the night time". By 1633, too, a de facto separation had developed on Tortuga between whites, free and servants and blacks; the eighty-odd English had formed a council, for governing the colony and to keep in subjection the 150 blacks. The first signs had appeared, in Bermuda and Tortuga, that racial inequality had made its appearance, as was to be reflected in the Maryland law of 1639 excepting slaves from the limits fixed to the terms for servants who entered without written contracts; the basic attributes of slavery would follow in due course – lifetime servitude and inheritable status.

The British Providence Company introduced African slaves into Providencia. In 1635 they were 14 per cent of the population; in 1637, 50 per cent. It was a competition between black slave labour and the labour of white indentured servants. The servants served for three to four years; the cost of their transportation and maintenance had to be met, and they received £10 at the end of their term. In 1637, the servant was valued at £50. The black slave was purchased for £18 in 1638 (150 pounds of tobacco), which fell to £15 in 1659. One account reads: "No individual planter saw it as a responsibility to pay the premium for white labour." The company introduced a policy whereby for every black slave purchased, two white servants had to be taken on; no family could own more than six blacks, the company explained: "We well knowing that if men be left at liberty to buy as they please, no man will take off English servants." The company added, "The surplusage may be sold to the poor men who have served their apprenticeship." Thus it was in that dawn of the British plantation economy, Providencia had no plantation system of organization, and there was no demand for labour for sugar cultivation. The writing was on the wall – development in the New World was to be based on the combination of American soil, European capital and African slave labour. Amerindians would not do; the workers had to be Africans, who, Charlevoix said, were each worth six Amerindians. It did not take the Puritans long to learn the lesson of Providencia. Emmanuel Downing, brother-in-law of Winthrop, was under no illusion as to the advantages of a war against the Narragansetts: it would provide "women and children enough to exchange for Moores . . . I suppose you know very well how we shall maintain twenty Moores cheaper than one English servant".

White Europeans could well have been used in the plantation economy or in slave society. What determined their use was the question of disease and mortality. As has been well said, slavery became the dominant form of labour organization wherever the impact of disease was most critical. In the West Indies, Europeans had to survive a death rate of 75–250 per thousand per annum in the early years, especially under plantation conditions. In this situation non-Europeans from Africa were epidemiologically preferable to Europeans. They were everywhere in Cuba, working in the fields, artisans, specializing in tobacco – the small farm. Legislation in the first half of the nineteenth century in Puerto Ricco tied the free landless labourer, irrespective of colour, to the plantation economy; though the *Reglamento de Jornaleros* of 1849 of General Prim was specifically directed at compelling "free colored men, most of them parasites, who burdened the country and contributed little to its welfare, to work on the plantations so as to render unnecessary further imports of slaves".

The inefficiency of Caribbean slavery was a byword. The Swedish scientist Wadström, after his expedition to West Africa in 1787 and the publication of his findings and opinions, declared in 1794:

124 | THE BLACKEST THING IN SLAVERY WAS NOT THE BLACK MAN

> In no age or country was ever avarice more compleatly [sic] disappointed, or humanity more shockingly outraged than in the flattering but ill-judged introduction of the sugar cane into all or most of the British West Indies, especially the Ceded Islands (islands ceded to Britain by France at the peace treaty of 1763 – Dominica, St Lucia, Grenada) . . . its premature and forced cultivation has, within our own memory, swept masters and slaves, the oppressors and the oppressed, into one common grave.

The chief chore of the slaves was to dig holes some five or six inches deep with the hoe; an able field hand was expected to dig at least a hundred to a hundred and twenty of these holes in a ten-hour day. It was widely believed that there was an even more heartbreaking job on a sugar plantation – grass picking, the grass being plucked and gathered single blade by blade. "The West Indian labourers moulder away," was the lugubrious complaint of a young lawyer in St Kitts, Clement Caines, manager of several estates in his time. "This devoted race became the slaves of toil in the hands of the cultivator, the slaves of pomp in the hands of the vain, the slaves of lust in the hands of the concupiscent, and the slaves of caprice and whim in the hands of everybody." But surely the southern economy was not based on free white labour geared to the small white farmer; whoever was to blame for this, it was not the black slave. One is reminded of W.E.B. Du Bois's comment on another occasion: "Everything Negroes did was wrong. If they fought for freedom, they were beasts; if they did not fight, they were born slaves. If they cowered on the plantation, they loved slavery; if they ran away, they were lazy loafers. If they sang, they were silly; if they scowled, they were impudent . . . And they were funny, ridiculous baboons, aping men." If they were slaves, they retarded the growth of a class of white small farmers.

It was the whites themselves who imitated, developed, sustained and maintained a mode of production which grew into the closest thing to feudalism and feudal lordship imaginable in the eighteenth and nineteenth centuries, whether in slave colonies in the Caribbean or an independent republic in the southern states. Beginning with the Spanish *encomendero* in Peru, there was all the pomp and panoply of feudal lords with their commitment and dedication to localism as the highest form of liberty. One saw it in their conspicuous consumption and their entertainment. Following feudal Spain, the *encomenderos* carried over to Peru the enormous collection of servants and retainers which was reproduced on the slave plantation. Thirty and forty house servants were the norm, especially in the Big Houses in the Caribbean and Brazil; the slave taking the cushions on which the slave owners kneeled in church, the slaves driving off the

African Slavery in the New World | 125

flies and creating a breeze at the banquet table, the slave standing by to handle the master's cigar as he was being shaved, to take his shoes off, to fetch him a glass of water, to fetch the manager's pipe and tobacco lying no more than three or four paces away from him, the black girl to bring your handkerchief, the little black boy to operate your fan, the veritable squadron (in the words of Saint-Méry) to pass the dishes at the table, a double row of servants behind the chairs of their masters. The slave society's "mania for ordering people around" is well expressed in that ditty of the Old South, "Oh, that I had a million slaves, or more, / To catch the raindrops as they pour." And in that eighteenth-century print of the French Caribbean islands in which the planter's wife orders her slave, "Mimbo, tell Quasheba to tell Dido to tell Sue to come and pick up my needle" – but Quasheba has gone to market and will not be back for three hours, and Sue is scratching her master's legs for him, so the mistress laments: "Oh, dear me, one must have the patience of Job to live in this world with any comfort. Here I must wait two hours for my needle."

Conspicuous consumption everywhere. Edwards wrote of "the general plenty and magnificence" of the planters' tables in Jamaica, and a female observer commented on the family dinner which in England might reach the newspaper "had it been given by a Lord Mayor or the First Duke in the Kingdom". The planter's legacies expressed full confidence in the permanence of the slave regime and its wealth. "Money that should have been reinvested was used instead to provide property settlements for members of his family, or to support the lavish expenditure that was expected of a man of position in the West Indies." The planter was to consume, it was for the slaves to produce. Labat compared the access roads to French slave plantations to the grand avenues of Versailles. The southern planters affected the "Plantation Greek" style of architecture, frequently symbols of absenteeism, in which they lived with their mint juleps for breakfast and surrounded by their magnolia, with its large waxy blossoms and its intoxicating fragrance.[5]

The most beautiful big houses, someone said, had never acceded to the level of a good rural house in France of the same period. Another said the capital of Haiti, Port-au-Prince, resembled a Tartar camp. The capital's streets were sewers, animals wandering freely over them, circulation and passage disrupted by deliveries of sugar casks and indigo bales as well as by public chastisement of slaves; one could not drink the water in the fountains. The heat was terrible. Moreau de Saint-Méry described the climate as "six months to sweat, six months to wipe off the sweat". It was a country of transients – to quote a police memorandum in 1780, "With the exception of merchants and officials connected with the magistracy, the population is so to speak comprised of people arriving daily from Europe."

Americans Move Westwards

In the Caribbean the transients went back to the home country. In the United States they moved ever westward under the stimulus of three movements – the invention of the cotton gin, which could give fifty pounds of cotton a day, as against one a day by the old method, thus opening a vast kingdom for cotton and permitting upland cotton to be grown wherever there were two hundred frostless days a year; the acquisition of Amerindian lands by the Federal Government, such as the thirty million acres in 1803 which allowed the Georgia land lottery, and the Jackson Purchase in 1818, which opened up new areas in West Tennessee; the acquisition of new territory by the United States at the expense of Mexico, but also by purchase from France and Spain. The result was the new states admitted into the union: Louisiana (1812), Mississippi (1817), Alabama (1819), Missouri (1821), Arkansas (1836), Florida and Texas (1845). This was the quasi-feudal pattern imposed on the New World – not strictly feudal, as Frantz Fanon reminded Hegel, who had written a famous passage on lordship and bondage, master and servant. Fanon wrote: "I hope that I have shown that here (in the French islands) the master differs basically from the master described by Hegel. For Hegel there is reciprocity, here the master laughs at the consciousness of the slave. What he wants from the slave is not recognition but work."

These were the people, the planters, whom W.E.B. Du Bois described as "cursing, whoring, brawling gamblers", the so-called aristocrats of the southern states. The Brazilian Freyre has his apologies for them. He writes: "In the words of the people, There is not a Wanderley who does not drink, an Albuquerque who does not lie, a Cavalcani who does not owe. Not a Souza Leão or a Carneiro da Cunha who does not like a Negro woman." A southern propagandist defended the high personal expenditures of southerners as part of the superiority of the slave system (as no doubt it was proof of the superiority of the feudal manorial system); the point of view has been defended on the basis of that maxim enunciated by Pascal, that the habit of seeing the king and the guards, and the pomp and paraphernalia designed to command respect and inspire awe, produce those reactions when he appears alone. Another reason has been suggested: that the regular and expensive vacations in watering places, northern resorts and abroad (the West Indian planters had similarly flaunted their wealth in the watering places and resorts of the home country) were not so much evidence of household affluence or some alleged rural indifference to thrift as they were vital parts of a total social setting. The result was inevitable. The slave owner, who tied up his capital in labour, had, in the southern states, to have recourse to the sale of surplus slaves to raise the large amounts of cash needed to purchase fertilizer, improved implements and better breeds. The essence of the problem of slavery in the South was that by 1844 it was estimated that one slave in three engaged in food production could be removed from agriculture without diminishing total output. In terms of agricultural efficiency and productivity, the South could not compete with the North. Agricultural societies, state fairs, agricultural periodicals – these were for the North, not the South. The best southern agricultural journals had their subscribers in the North. The slave states could not compete with the free states in wheat cultivation. The South gave the best land to cotton and the worst to corn. Virginia wheat cultivation was shifted to land that was even worse than that used for corn.

The governor of Alabama called on planters to cooperate by building enough textile factories to absorb 20 per cent of the state's slaves as well as some poor whites. The governor of Tennessee wanted to see one-fourth of the southern slave labour diverted from the production to the manufacture of cotton in order to raise cotton prices and the better to justify cultivation. Informed opinion was that southern planters were interested in industrial development only if it involved slave labour; when the superiority of white and free labour was demonstrated, the planters lost interest.

Why the insistence on slave labour? South Carolina's textile manufacturer provided the explanation – slavery gave capital a "positive control over labour". A Natchez, Mississippi, paper commented in 1821 on Kentucky's hemp factories: "Why are slaves employed? Simply because experiment has proved that they are more docile, more constant and cheaper than free men, who are often refractory and dissipated; who waste much time by frequenting public places, attending musters, elections, etc. which the operative slave is not permitted to frequent." A big iron producer in Tennessee saw the advantage of slave factory workers in the fact that slaves did not strike and could not demand wage increases as their skill and productivity improved.

The poor whites protested against the use of slave labour in factories. In 1847 white mechanics at the Tredegar Iron Works in Richmond went on strike because the company had imported northern mechanics to teach the skilled processes to the slaves. The company president refused to abdicate his constitutional right to hire and fire at pleasure. The city's press maintained that employers should be prevented from making use of slave labour. Several petitions were sent to state legislatures urging legislation to forbid the employment of slaves in mechanic trades (as well as protesting against the use of prison labour in manufacturing, on the ground that it reduced taxation). In Salem, North Carolina, there were protests that employment in the textile mill be for whites only; it was not infrequently argued that white labour was cheaper than slave because it did not have to be fed or clothed. The basic argument, however, was that as a matter of principle, factories should be established to provide jobs for unproductive poor whites.

The New World colonies had always been dependent on their respective metropolitan countries for their imports, in return for sending their exports to them – all except the Spanish colonies of the first few decades, which were permitted to compete in consumer goods with Spain, until the metropolitan producers put pressures on the governments to protect the markets for textiles and wine. The cotton kingdom placed the South in the same colonial relationship to the North as the other remaining European colonies had been and were to their metropolitan countries. Hammond had, as spokesman for South Carolina, issued his famous toast in the Senate: "What would happen if no cotton was furnished for three years . . . England would topple headlong and carry the whole civilized world with her, save the South. No, you dare not make war on cotton. No power on earth dares to make war on it. Cotton is king."

"When in the Course of Human Events": The Rights of Man

The economic issue was crucial: was the black man superior as a worker to the white man? Was slavery as a mode of production superior to, cheaper and more efficient than free labour? But the decisive argument was the political: was the black slave a man? Could he, as man, claim the newfangled doctrines of the rights of man, the natural and inalienable rights of mankind? Chief Justice Taney, spokesman for the majority of his colleagues in the Supreme Court in 1857, denied this emphatically. "At the time of the Declaration of Independence, and when the Constitution of the United States was framed and adopted . . . (blacks) had no rights which the white man was bound to respect." No end of abuse has been heaped on Taney for this decision, which involved the Dred Scott case and the capture of and return of fugitive slaves. But Taney was not to be blamed for the racial integument of the Declaration of Independence. In the very year of this declaration, 1776, Virginia passed its bill of rights. Judge St George Tucker, one of Virginia's most famous justices, faced the question in 1806 in a case before the Court of Appeals whether Virginia's bill of rights applied to blacks. The learned judge opened as follows:

> Suppose three persons, a black or mulatto man or woman with a flat nose and a woolly head; a copper-coloured person with long jetty black, straight hair; and one with a fair complexion, brown hair, not woolly or inclining thereto, with a prominent Roman nose, were brought together before a Judge upon a writ of Habeas Corpus, on the ground of false imprisonment and detention in slavery, how must a Judge act in such case? . . He must discharge the white person and the Indian out of custody . . . and he must redeliver (into slavery) the black or mulatto person, with a flat nose and woolly hair to the person who is claiming to hold him or her as a slave, unless the black person or mulatto could . . . produce proof of his descent, in the maternal line, from a free female ancestor.

The judge emphasized that the Virginia Bill of Rights had been framed "with a cautious eye", that it was "meant to embrace the case of free citizens, or aliens only; and not by a side wind to overturn the rights of property, and give freedom to those very people whom we have been compelled from imperious circumstances to retain, generally, in the same state of bondage that they were in at the revolution, in which they had no concern, agency, or interest".

So there we have it. The Declaration of Independence was not a matter in which black slaves had any concern, agency or interest. Jefferson had tried to say precisely this in his attempt to deflect the issue of the inalienable rights of blacks, as of all men of whatever colour, by his diatribe, in his draft declaration, against the international slave trade as the climax of charges against George III, who had "prostituted his negative for suppressing every legislative attempt to prohibit or to restrain this execrable commerce". But George III – give him all the blows he deserved – had not initiated the slave trade, he had not waged "cruel war against human nature itself".

One final point will completely demolish Curtin's thesis that the large proportion which the US Afro-American population bears to the total Western Hemisphere Afro-American population testifies to the not-so-bad treatment in the United States: after all, "one measure of well-being is the ability to survive and to, multiply". In his 1950 figures for the Afro-American population, Curtin omits the migration from the Caribbean to the United States and Panama (for construction of the Panama Canal), thus inflating the figures for the United States and deflating those for the Caribbean. Between 1903 and 1924 Negroes admitted into the United States from the Caribbean excluding Cuba numbered 132,398. Of these forty-six thousand were from Jamaica alone. Jamaican emigrants to Panama numbered forty-

130 | THE BLACKEST THING IN SLAVERY WAS NOT THE BLACK MAN

five thousand. The Panama foreign-born population from the Caribbean in 1960 numbered over twelve thousand – more than half of these from Jamaica. Caribbean emigration to the United States between 1946 and 1953 numbered over thirty-five thousand. If Curtin were to bring this table up to date to the 1970 census, the proportions for the different areas would be even more distorted by the large Caribbean emigration of the last two decades. During this period:

1. Caribbean emigration to the United States totalled over 821,000 from 1945 to 1972. This includes Cuba and the Dominican Republic. Curtin gives the Cuban population of African descent at 1.5 million; this implies, from the total population for that period, a proportion about 25 per cent. But, as in all Latin America, racial labels are strongly to be suspected; one estimate of the Afro-Cuban population, made in 1964, is about two-thirds. The Dominican Republic is emphatically a mulatto country; about one-quarter of the population is non-white. Since 1950 emigration has taken approximately one million Puerto Ricans to the United States; however they might define themselves as Puerto Rican, in the United States they are regarded and treated as blacks.
2. Caribbean emigration to the United Kingdom from the British Caribbean since 1955 totals over a quarter of a million, over half from Jamaica.
3. Caribbean emigration to Canada between 1955 and 1971 totals over seventy-eight thousand. If figures for the years 1956–1963 can be accepted, 60 per cent of this emigration is black.
4. Between 1962 and 1968 some twenty-five thousand French West Indians emigrated to France.

These emigration statistics, almost certainly incomplete, represented a loss to the Caribbean region of well over two million people of whom blacks must constitute at least 60 per cent or about 1.3 million people, about one-seventh of Curtin's estimated Afro-American population of 9.8 million in 1950. Almost the entire emigration was to the United States and Canada, representing some 7 per cent of Curtin's estimated Afro-American population of fifteen million in 1950.

French visitors to and admirers of republican America were shocked to see slave quarters at Mt Vernon. "How could the father of liberty not free those poor creatures?" But, then, what would he have done with the forty-one thousand acres of frontier territory which he had acquired in the northwest? No wonder he advocated a legislative emancipation by "slow, sure and imperceptible degrees" – like New Jersey's, no doubt: so slow, so imperceptible, so conservative was its abolition law of 1804 that the state still contained slaves, euphemistically defined as apprentices, at the Civil War. Noah Webster went one better – for slavery, "an unfortunate accident, the product of the misguided policy of an unenlightened age", the solution was "the gradual elevation of serfs", whereby it would be utterly extirpated in the course of two centuries, without any extraordinary efforts to abolish it", black slaves already enjoying "many privileges of English villeins". Thus it was that Jefferson proposed to the Virginia Assembly the banishment of white women bearing mulatto children, and Jordan considers that he may have been responsible for the Virginia revision of the definition of mulatto from one-eighth to one-quarter black. Washington wrote to Lafayette in 1785 that petitions for the abolition of slavery could scarcely obtain a hearing in the Virginia legislature. Jefferson advocated the total removal of the blacks after emancipation, "beyond the reach of mixture"; he supported in general the principle of repatriation of the blacks to Africa, and thought in terms of the British African colony for freed slaves in Sierra Leone. He advocated their removal to Saint Domingue after the slave revolution in that colony. With malice prepense, he suggested that Toussaint L'Ouverture "might be willing, on many considerations, to receive over that description which would be exiled for acts deemed criminal by us, but meritorious, perhaps, by him".

It is against this background that we must consider the *cause célèbre* in which Jefferson became involved in his relationship with Sally Hemings. In 1802, in the course of Jefferson's political campaign for his second term as president, he was publicly accused, in a Virginia newspaper, by a man disappointed of his hope for federal preferment under Jefferson, of bastardy, concubinage and miscegenation with a mulatto slave, Sally Hemings, by whom Jefferson was alleged to have fathered six mulatto children. The only authenticated facts are that Jefferson seemed to have been home nine months before each birth, and that, while he never freed all of his slaves, all those freed by him were Hemings's children. Winthrop Jordan suggests the possibility that Sally and her children were the children of Jefferson's father-in-law, unknown to Jefferson's wife. Jordan adds, in commenting on Jefferson's ambivalent relations with women: "It is possible to argue that attachment with Sally represented a final happy resolution of his inner conflict. . . . Unsurprisingly, his repulsion toward Negroes would have been, all along, merely the obverse of powerful attraction. . . . One is left fully persuaded only of the known fact that any given pattern of basic personality can result in widely differing patterns of external behaviour."

132 | THE BLACKEST THING IN SLAVERY WAS NOT THE BLACK MAN

Our own generation would probably show no more concern over Sally Hemings than it did over Christine Keeler – just another opportunity for salacious gossip. So Thomas Jefferson was caught – "So what?" "Was it really true?" "Could be!" At least it was in so many other cases. Barbados of that day, we are told, was scandalized by the mulatto concubine from Tobago maintained by its governor, who enjoyed every privilege except that of publicly presiding at his table. Governor von Scholten of St Croix, who on his own initiative emancipated the slaves of the Virgin Islands, lived openly with Anna Heegard, virtually his consort, who was one-quarter coloured. When a candidate for the post of lieutenant governor in Jamaica was opposed on the ground that "he frequently lies with Black Women", there was consternation, for "the same could be said of virtually every planter on the island". One is tempted to speculate on Jefferson, the proponent of natural and inalienable rights of man, with his aversion to the colour black and his rejection of blot or mixture on the white surface, resolving his inner tensions, learning from Sally that black is beautiful, and, with the peace that passeth all understanding, saying reverently, "I believe, O Lord, help thou my unbelief."

It was in this intellectual atmosphere that three great eighteenth-century voices denounced slavery and racism and defended the blacks against the charges of intellectual inferiority. Adam Smith, in his *Theory of Moral Sentiments* of 1759, wrote his celebrated attack on the poor whites:

> There is not a Negro from the coast of Africa who does not possess a degree of magnanimity which the soul of his sordid master is too often scarce capable of conceiving. Fortune never exerted more cruelly her empire over mankind, than when she subjected those nations of heroes to the refuse of the jails of Europe, to wretches who possess the virtue neither of the countries which they came from, nor of those which they go to, and whose levity, brutality, and baseness, so justly expose them to the contempt of the vanquished.

The radical French priest the Abbé Raynal, in his *Histoire des Deux Indes*, which had the active collaboration of Diderot and other Encyclopaedists, saw slavery as the cause of the alleged inferiority of the blacks, and foresaw that only violence would bring slavery to an end. In an equally celebrated passage Raynal wrote:

> The minds of the Negroes are contracted; because slavery destroys all the springs of the soul. We have almost persuaded them that they were a singular species, born only for dependence, for subjection, for labour, and for chastisement. We have neglected nothing that might tend to degrade these unfortunate people; and we afterwards upbraid them for their meanness. . . . There are so

many indications of the impending storm, and the Negroes only want a chief, sufficiently courageous, to lead them on to vengeance and slaughter. Where is this great man, whom Nature owes to her afflicted, oppressed, and tormented children? Where is he? He will undoubtedly appear, he will show himself, he will lift up the sacred standard of liberty.[6]

The third of the great crusaders was Thomas Clarkson, the distinguished British humanitarian, the tireless agitator of the anti-slavery movement. Launching an open attack on Hume's strictures on the black man's capacity based on the black man in estate of slavery, Clarkson wrote, in his remarkable *Essay on the Slavery and the Commerce of the Human Species, Particularly the African*:

> Such then is the nature of this servitude, that we can hardly expect to find in those, who undergo it, even the glimpse of genius. For if their minds are in a continued state of depression, and if they have no expectations in life to awaken their abilities, and make them eminent, we cannot be surprised if a sullen gloomy stupidity should be the leading mark in their character, or if they should appear inferior to those, who do not only enjoy the invaluable blessings of freedom, but have every prospect before their eyes, that can allure them to exert their faculties. Now, if to these considerations we add, that the wretched Africans are torn from their country in a state of nature, and that in general, as long as their slavery continues, every obstacle is placed in the way of their improvement, we shall have a sufficient answer to any argument that may be drawn from the inferiority of their capacities.

Smith, Raynal and Clarkson were totally unrepresentative of the political thinking of the period. The political theorists of the seventeenth century had tended to emphasize the aspects of law, order and authority in the slave system. To Bossuet, anarchy was the worst of all evils, for it affected everyone, both master and slave. Grotius, attempting to construct a rational and secular defence of slavery, saw slavery as harmonious with natural justice. For Hobbes, the creator of *Leviathan*, slavery was an inevitable part of the logic of power. The dominion of the master was sanctioned by a compact which implied no reciprocal rights and obligations; the slave had no rights. Hegel, about to commit the faux pas of the century and write of Bonaparte's "world-soul" after his attempt to recapture St Domingue, was, however, able to see that "the more perfect the slave, the more enslaved becomes the master . . . the condition of omnipotent lordship becomes the reverse of what it wants to be: dependent, static, and unessential".

This was the setting in which, beginning in England and transported to America, the political philosophers raised the doctrine of natural and inalienable rights, the equality of men and the consent of the governed as the basis of all government. But John Locke, the philosopher of England's seventeenth-century revolution, simply bolted and ran when his doctrines were applied to African enslavement by Europeans. Locke wrote: "Slavery is so vile and miserable an Estate of Man, and so directly opposite to the generous Temper and Courage of our Nation; that it is hardly to be conceived, that an Englishman, much less a gentleman, should plead for it."

It was this same Locke who had helped to draw up the Fundamental Constitutions of Carolina in 1669 which provided that church membership would not affect the status of slaves, and that "every freeman of Carolina shall have absolute power and authority over his negro slaves, of what opinion or religion so ever". The only way Locke could square this with his view that a man's fundamental rights should always be protected from "the inconstant, uncertain, unknown, arbitrary will of another Man" was by denying that the black was a man. For Locke, Englishman and Gentleman, was an investor in the Royal African Company, whose very title indicated the support that slave trading commanded in the very highest political and social circles in England, further confirmed by the branding of some of the company's slaves with letters that stood for "Duke of York".

The dualism of European political thought, its ability to accommodate African slavery in its political egalitarianism, was best illustrated in America. When, in the course of human events, it became necessary for one people to dissolve the political bands which had connected them with another, the first concern of that people was to ensure the non-dissolution of the racial bands which connected them with yet another. To paraphrase Rousseau – so concerned with inequality among men – the black man was born free, but was to be everywhere in chains. The facts submitted by the American revolutionaries in respect of this reconciliation of black slavery with white liberty have been stated, with a clarity and precision that have remained impeccable, by one of the principal participants in the American constitution discussion, James Madison, in *The Federalist*, as the northern representatives argued on the case of slave representation, that if slaves were counted, why not cattle as well? Madison explained that one of their southern brethren might observe that slaves were both persons and property,

> That they partake of both these qualities; being considered by our laws, in some respects, as persons, and in other respects, as property. In being compelled to labour not for himself, but for a master; in being vendible by one master to

another master; and in being subject at all times to be restrained in his liberty, and chastised in his body, by the capricious will of another, the slave may appear to be degraded from the human ranks, and classed with those irrational animals, which fall under the legal denomination of property. In being protected on the other hand in his life and in his limbs, against the violence of all others, even the master of his labour and his liberty; and in being punishable himself for all violence committed against others; the slave is no less evidently regarded by the law as a member of the society; not as a part of the irrational creation; as a moral person, not as a mere article of property. The Federal Constitution therefore, decides with great propriety on the case of our slaves, when it views them in the mixed character of persons and of property. This is in fact their true character. . . . Let the compromising expedient of the Constitution be mutually adopted, which regards them as inhabitants, but as debased by servitude below the equal level of free inhabitants, which regards the slave as divested of two-fifths of the man.

New Hampshire blacks had appealed in 1780 "that the name of slave may not more be heard in a land gloriously contending for the sweets of freedom". But the constitutional convention of 1787 included twenty-five slave owners among its fifty-five delegates. Pinckney, of the South Carolina framers, frankly admitted that some of the framers of the Federal Constitution had opposed a bill of rights because such bills usually began by declaring "all men are by nature born free" when in fact "a large part of our property consists in men who are actually born slaves".

Three-Fifths of a Man

Slavery had ceased to be regarded as a unique moral aberration. In the words of a Puerto Rican planter on the eve of emancipation in 1873: "The only thing that makes the institution of slavery hateful is the slave himself." Pufendorf looked upon it as a highly useful instrument of social discipline which might solve the problem of Europe's "idlers, thieves, vagabonds". Hutcheson, a key figure in anti-slavery thought, was of the view that if nothing was so "effectual" as perpetual bondage in promoting industry and restraining idleness, especially in the "lower conditions" of society, slavery should be "the ordinary" punishment of such idle vagrants as, after proper admonition and trials of temporary servitude, cannot be engaged to support themselves and their families by any useful labours. Wilberforce and Buxton held up their hands in horror at the proposal to abolish or curtail the use of the whip on the slave plantation: after all, the whip was not unique to the plantation, nor was whipping unfamiliar to English children, schoolboys, wives, apprentices, sailors, malefactors and sexual perverts. As has been said, if he weeps over a prisoner, he has no desire to destroy the Bastille.

The change in the abolitionists was profound – Ramsay equated slavery with arbitrary divorce and polygamy. Wilberforce frequently attacked as unenforceable laws regulating slaves' food and clothing, hours of labour, punishment, medical care and education; it was an "inquisitorial power" which would not be tolerated where white servants were involved. Brougham opposed proposals to colonize the newly acquired Trinidad with free blacks. This was the climate in which the Declaration of Independence divested the black of 40 per cent of his humanity, buying the independence of Americans with slave labour, as has been well said.

It was not only the five states where slavery predominated; it was also New England, whose prosperity and egalitarianism were nourished by the carrying trade with the Caribbean and later with Africa. In 1777 Massachusetts had sixty distilleries producing rum. It might boast of more than five thousand blacks in its population, but ten thousand seamen were engaged in its West Indian trade. Contraband reached large proportions after abolition in 1808 – ten to twenty thousand a year after 1812 – notwithstanding the penalties, which were never enforced. As one Rhode Island legislator put it candidly, "I cannot believe that a man ought to be hung for only stealing a negro." In the excuse of a delegate to the Massachusetts Ratifying Convention, in reference to the twenty-year reprieve for the African slave trade, the trade, "although . . . not smitten by an apoplexy . . . has received a mortal wound, and will die of consumption". The leading Rhode Island opponent of slavery admitted in 1791, "An Ethiopian could as soon change his skin as a Newport merchant could be induced to change so lucrative a trade as that in slaves for the slow profits of any manufactory." Brion Davis writes: "The American colonists were not trapped in an accidental contradiction between slavery and freedom. Their rhetoric of freedom was functionally related to the existence and in many areas to the continuation of Negro slavery." The leaders of the revolution, lay and clerical, saw black slavery as "the providential means for bringing freedom and redemption to white America". They looked to ultimate deportation of the blacks, if and when freed, as Britain had deported to them its poor whites and idle vagrants. The American revolutionary presented himself to the world as an asserter of American liberties, with his Constitution in one hand and his negro lash in the other hand.

The question of slavery went much deeper than this. It has been said that the South did not repudiate the tradition of the American Revolution, but rather transformed it, "substituting for the old emphasis on the natural rights of all men a new emphasis on the rights and autonomy of communities. The South transformed the tradition in yet another fundamental way". To quote Hammond again, in a letter to Clarkson in 1845 in which he rejected the principles of the Declaration of Independence: "Slavery is the true corner-stone of our republican edifice; I repudiate as ridiculously absurd, that much lauded but nowhere accredited dogma of Mr Jefferson, that 'all men are born equal'."

So that was it. Abbé Raynal savagely attacked the Europeans: "To repopulate a part of the world you have devastated (America), corrupt and depopulate another" (Africa). Tom Paine considered it common sense, in considering the depredations of the "Men-Stealers" and the right of the true owner to reclaim his stolen and sold goods, that "the slave, who is proper owner of his freedom, has a right to reclaim it, however often sold". Robespierre thundered against the aristocrats of the skin in France, "Eh, perish your colonies if you are to preserve them at this price . . . or, if it was necessary to choose between loss of your colonies and loss of your happiness, your glory, your liberty, I would repeat: perish your colonies."

5.

European Christianity and African Slavery

Am I not a man and a brother?
Motto on seal of the Society for the Abolition of the Slave Trade

Prince Henry the Navigator, who presided over Portugal's discovery and exploitation of Guinea, initiating the African slave trade, said that slavery was not an outrageous price for Africa to pay for Christianization. In much the same vein, Père Labat is our authority for the statement that Louis XIII of France was only persuaded to promote French colonialism and support the slave trade because he was advised that "it was an infallible means, and the only one, to inspire the worship of the true God among Africans, to wean them from idolatry, and to make them persevere until death in the Christian religion which they would be forced to embrace". The Africans themselves saw it somewhat differently: "Wherever Christ is propagated, he brings with him a sword, a gun and gunpowder." But doubts persisted among some at least of the clergy. Fray Tomás de Mercado of Spain, who for his pains, had his treatise of 1587 placed on the *Index*, denounced the slave trade as fostering "two thousand falsehoods, a thousand robberies, and a thousand deceptions". In 1560 the Archbishop of Mexico City, in a communication to the king, with reference to the Spanish prohibition of enslavement of the Amerindians, wrote: "We do not know of any cause why the Negroes should be captives any more than Indians, since we are told that they received the Gospel in good will and do not make war on Christians." The Spanish monarchy salved its conscience by claiming that the black man was not originally a subject of the Crown of Castille and his enslavement had occurred prior to his entrance into the Spanish dominions and was initiated, according to the popular contemporary justification, by the heathen Africans themselves.

The question was referred to the learned churchmen of the Sorbonne in 1698. The president of the tribunal of cases of conscience was asked: "As a matter of conscience, can one sell blacks?" Going through the historical records, from papal bulls justifying the slave trade on the sole ground of evangelization to papal declarations that both Africans and Amerindians were "true men", not slaves, by nature, whose paganism did not constitute a motive for enslavement, the learned president concluded:

European Christianity and African Slavery | 139

> It follows from all this that one cannot in surety of conscience buy or sell blacks, because there is injustice in this trade. If nevertheless, all being well examined, the blacks bought are slaves by just title, and that on the part of the Negroes there is neither injustice nor deceit . . . one can even without further examination buy them, if the purpose was to convert them and make them free.

Thus did Portuguese bishops bless the slave ships and their slave cargoes on leaving Angola; thus did the almoner accompany the slave trader – "the surest way to lead the conversion of the blacks is to enslave them". But for others, "the blacks, being idolaters, have no right to liberty". Thus one refuses liberty to blacks because they are not Christians, and one makes slaves of them to make them Christians. The slave ship required prayers every morning and evening; one prayer ends, "We wish you, sir, a good journey and pray God that he keeps each and every one of you in his very Holy and Worthy care." Common prayer was inflicted on the slaves three times a day, to inspire respect due to the Supreme Being.

Some priests in the French system tried to live up to the specifications which had supposedly influenced Louis XIII. Du Tertre belaboured "the purposelessness of their work; they knew that all their sweat was for the profit of their masters, and that even if they accumulated mountains of gold, none of it would ever come to them, they would receive not one cent profit from all their labours". Père Labat condemned the food given to the slaves, their rags which passed for clothing, and the harsh toil on sugar plantations, where they worked eighteen hours a day, as against twelve a day in other occupations. The Jesuits argued that a slave could act in self-defence, even if it meant killing his aggressor in certain circumstances, to protect life and limb, property, honour, modesty and next of kin. Did this extend to attack on the white master – harsh, unjust, cruel, adulterous? Was that why the Jesuits were expelled from the French dominions? One priest was expelled for much less – he had the church bell ringing at a marriage of slaves, when he well knew that these solemnities were reserved for whites. Another was expelled for using an ambiguous or imprudent text for his sermon: "The first shall be last and the last shall be first."

The priests therefore always had their supreme justification, assuming that the slaves were presented for religious instruction. The priests argued with the *procureur* of Fort Royal in Martinique in 1842, the slaves just didn't have time. When would the instruction be given? In the mornings? But their work day starts at sunrise. After breakfast? They are allowed too little time for that anyway. During the two hours of the midday break? That would be impossible, for the slave, in these two hours, must prepare his lunch, eat it and rest after the morning labours or work in his own little garden. After evening prayers at 7 p.m.? One of the priests expostulated: "You have spent the day riding, a very hard day; if you had been working with a hoe, in the heat of the sun, would you be disposed to listen to me in the evening give religious instruction?" And so it was everywhere. Virginia was adamant – baptism did not entitle the slave to freedom; its early laws defined slaves as persons who were not Christians. Cuba, on the other hand, might by law require slave owners to send their slaves to church at the prescribed hour so that they could be taught Christian doctrine, and the church council demanded that slaves should not be made to work on holy days, on pain of fine and excommunication of the master.

The question was, who was to give the religious instruction? Here plantation and church parted company. Not the priests, said the planters. Missionaries were not appropriate to all times or places and circumstances; Cuba did not have them, nor did she need them. The *Código Negro Español* of 1789 made religious instruction mandatory, but it was suppressed in many areas in America, and Havana's bishop in 1847 could find "no trace of His Majesty's having insisted upon its execution and fulfilment". If not the priest, who then? The masters replied, the masters; the slave expects all and has all from his master. The royal officials, in support of the planters, argued that the missionaries would not know enough about "the kind of slaves we have nor of the manner in which they must be governed nor of their alimentation and habits nor of their tendencies, nor of their ignorance, nor of the complete submission in which it is absolutely necessary to keep them". The builders were decisively rejecting the stone which had been the head of the corner. The priests, argued another royal official, should confine themselves to giving religious instruction to the whites, preparing the white overseers to transmit to the slaves "the first notions of religion, industriousness and submissiveness".

The dispute as to who was to impart the religious instruction raised other issues dividing church and plantocracy. When and how? The planters objected that it was impossible to take two thousand slaves out of a mill each Sunday and march them twelve or fifteen miles to Mass; they sought therefore to reduce to ten a year the masses attended by slaves, and only four public holidays as rest days for the slaves – Christmas, New Year's Day, Annunciation and Immaculate Conception. When should the instruction be given? One priest, in a book on the subject, suggested daylight as the best time for instruction. The planters objected to the cost of the ecclesiastical establishment – a salary of four hundred pesos, plus food and animals, merely for a priest to say Mass; in addition to which he got "exorbitant fees" for burials, marriages, vigils, baptisms and "even for confessions". The planter objected to the seventh day as the day of rest and preferred it to be staggered so that it would be one "Sunday" every ten days. Their emphasis was on work, not rest: "Let them work rather than sin"; the slaves should work to win their freedom "since freedom is the most precious of all gifts". Another rumpus developed over meatless days, difficult to maintain in the context of large-scale production; reduce the meatless days to Fridays in Lent, and Christmas Eve. Then there were the cemeteries: burial in consecrated ground for mill slaves (one in ten perished annually); general processions (if four carried the corpse, the planter lost a day's work of four live people). In addition, planter barbarism warned "that carrying a female corpse by a slave might provide an opportunity for sexual excesses".

But Virginia or Cuba or St Domingue all stood shoulder to shoulder in one respect – literacy was taboo, the slave must not be taught to read and write. As the administrator of St Domingue phrased it in 1784, there was no fear or danger of revolt, "other than those of animals, surrendering to instinct alone against those who direct and control them, but to remove from this realm of possibility it is at least prudent not to teach them to read". A former slave in the United States thus described the overseer's treatment of the pregnant woman: "A woman who gives offence in the field, and is large in the family way is compelled to lie down over a hole made to receive her corpulency, and is flogged with the whip, or beat with a paddle, which had holes in it." The Portuguese church was involved in the slave trade itself. King Afonso of the Congo had requested priests from Portugal. Here is the official account of this "technical assistance":

> Afonso received the thirteen or fifteen priests with jubilant plans for educating and evangelizing his people, but a number of the fathers, succumbing to the moral and physical climate of the capital, found the buying and selling of slaves, in some cases with funds given them by Afonso, more lucrative. . . . Many took advantage of the first opportunity to be repatriated under pretext of the malignity of the climate – especially those who had dedicated themselves to commercial activities.

The Jesuits in particular were accused of taking part in slave trading and thus of affecting the Angolan economy by the volume of the depredations. The evidence indicates that the Society of Jesus even had its own ships engaged in the slave trade between Angola and Brazil. The Dominicans also, despite their vow of poverty, had great tracts of land in Zambesi operating like any entrepreneur, collecting head taxes and dealing in slaves. Portuguese documents are full of lamentations (as from Vieira in 1642,

142 | THE BLACKEST THING IN SLAVERY WAS NOT THE BLACK MAN

from Cape Verde) of a lack of missionaries to educate and evangelize, and the king of Portugal sent to São Tomé black priests whom he had had educated from childhood in Lisbon in order to deal with the problem of the Guinea slaves being baptized in batches of three hundred or four hundred or five hundred before being despatched to Brazil. In 1624, the rector of the College of Luanda, visiting the Congo, found no natives who could speak Portuguese and only one who could read.

Las Casas, to save the Amerindian, had sacrificed the African. The Spanish state adopted this as official policy. When clergymen – like Albornoz and Mercado – at the end of the sixteenth century questioned the methods by which the black slaves were acquired, Albornoz's book was placed upon the *Index*. Pombal in Brazil two centuries later had virtually done the same thing. As Caio Prado writes of Brazil in his description of the paternalism of the Jesuits with respect to the Amerindian, which, whatever its defects, did give a minimum of protection against the worst aspects of slavery:

> But there was nothing comparable for the African Negro. So zealous in upholding the freedom of the Indian, the religious orders were the first to accept and even to encourage Negro slavery to keep at bay the colonists also needed laborers and so have a free hand in the running of their missions.[1]

Where the Protestants disagreed among themselves about almost every subject under the sun, there was one on which they were agreed: the legality of the slave system. It was the bishop of London who in 1727 publicly sought to allay the fears of slave owners by ruling that "Christianity, and the embracing of the Gospel, does not make the least Alteration in Civil Property, or in any of the Duties which belong to the Civil Relations." One of his subordinates in Virginia spelled out the message to the black slaves: "Your Masters and Mistresses are God as Overseers." Whitefield in Georgia and Jonathan Edwards did not allow their religious conviction to keep them from owning slaves. The Moravians owned slaves and utilized slave labour, whether in the Danish Virgin Islands or in their quite astonishing mission in Suriname, with its successful accommodation of business and religion – surely one of the best concrete examples of religion and the age of capitalism.

Among the most successful of the religion business complex were the Quakers. Their colonial connections were very early manifested. William Penn's father captured Jamaica from the Spaniards for Cromwell; Penn himself bought and owned black slaves, and the harsh slave code of Pennsylvania was the work of a Quaker-dominated government. As late as 1780, Quaker merchants in Philadelphia were importing and selling slaves from the Caribbean. Rhode Island was at one and the same time a base of American Quakerism and the slave trade to Africa, which involved leading Quaker families. When George Fox preached in Barbados and suggested a limitation of the term of bondage to thirty years, he was well aware that Friends in Barbados and other West Indian islands owned slaves. According to a recent study, sixty-five Quakers in Barbados in 1680 owned 3,307 acres (ten over a hundred acres each) and 1,631 slaves (nine over sixty each – the definition of an important planter), as well as ninety-six Christian indentured servants contracted to work for a term of three or four years. Prominent Quaker businessmen in England, led by the Barclay family, were members of the Royal African Company; as they keyed into banking, textiles and iron, they became only more closely associated with African and Caribbean investments. Many Quaker farming families in the thirteen colonies of North America were slave owners.

It was in small West Indian islands like Anguilla and Tortola that Friends first began to question slavery, emancipate their slaves and parcel out their landowning among the slaves. Two of the earliest and most prominent were Dr Lettsom of Tortola, who founded the Medical Society of London in 1773 and was one of the original promoters of the Royal Humane Society; and Dr William Thornton, also of Tortola, the architect of the Capitol in Washington, DC, who assisted Jefferson with the plans for the University of Thornton, was one of the early advocates of repatriation of the slaves to Africa, contemplating Sierra Leone.

It was not until 1756 that the Society of Friends took any serious steps to induce slave owners to provide religious instruction for their slaves. Even then, their rigid exclusiveness prevented them from considering their converts as spiritual equals and, in Jordan's words, "They proved almost as eager to see converted Negroes enter some other church than their own." As Brion Davis has put it, "Quaker reformers could not view Negroes as even potentially autonomous beings. Most of the Negroes freed by Quaker masters were quietly dissuaded from trying to join the Society of Friends."[2]

Another example of the active association of the Christian church with the slave system is afforded by the Society for the Propagation of the Gospel (SPG), which received in 1710 a bequest from Christopher Codrington – former governor of the Leeward Islands and founder of the Codrington Library at All Souls, Oxford – of two sugar plantations in Barbados which contained over three hundred black slaves. The donor requested that missionaries be sent to live a monastic life on the plantations, and a college founded for the instruction, conversion and uplift of the blacks. The SPG saw in this bequest an opportunity to demonstrate how a community might be constructed where the different races might live together harmoniously in the light of Christian ideals. Did this involve the abandonment of sugar profits? The SPG decided against, and hired agents to manage the enterprises. When Anthony Benezet denounced the SPG for owning slaves, the results were there for all to behold. From 1717 to 1776 the SPG did not make a single convert among its slaves. The college was nearly completed in 1725, but it began to function only twenty years later. The school was restricted to white children. In 1793 only three of the SPG blacks could read. The SPG branded its slaves with the letters "S.O.C.I.E.T.Y.". Slave protests against harsh treatment and excessive labour were not unknown. The Sabbath was not recognized as a day of rest and worship. On the question of marriage, the SPG maintained a discreet silence. The SPG slave population declined by one-third in fifty years. When, in 1824, 1827 and 1821, the British Government decreed measures to ameliorate the lot of the slaves in the British West Indies, the SPG slaves, including women, still lived under the discipline of the whip, no records of punishments were kept, marriages had not yet achieved the benefit of clergy and manumission was as difficult as under secular ownership. Where the SPG had aimed at converting the "heathen" planters around, the SPG enterprise ended by conforming to local policies and usages with their goal of profits. If one could not serve both God and Mammon, the SPG put Mammon first.

It was left to John Newton to reconcile the two. A notorious slave trader, Newton had been "converted". He promptly proceeded to the Liverpool churches to thank God for the success of his last venture before his conversion and implore his blessing on his next. Twice a day he officiated personally at public worship in his slave ship, keeping a day of fasting and prayer for his crew, not for the slaves. We have his own confession: "I never knew sweeter or more so frequent hours of divine communion than in the last two voyages to Guinea." This man later publicly testified to his practical familiarity with Africans in their native villages whom he had enslaved and his experience with slavery on the sugar plantations – when he abandoned his vocation, it was on the ground of ill health, and not because he had repented. He never expressed the slightest compunction about "the line of life which Divine Providence had allotted me", and never questioned the legitimacy of his former "genteel" employment. It was merely "inattention and interest", he explained, which prevented the evil from being perceived.

In British Guiana one of the missionaries was arrested for participation in a slave revolt and sentenced by court martial; the sentence was suspended, but as luck would have it, he died in jail. British public opinion was absolutely enraged. In Trinidad a governor objected to the missionaries assuming to themselves the title of reverend. A communication from Governor Woodford to the secretary of state for the colonies, objecting to what he called "their encroachments upon the Established Churches of England and of Rome", requested permission to deny them the authority to administer the sacraments and perform the office of burial. In a further letter he claimed that the Africans had lost much faith in the Protestant form of baptism, and occasionally presented themselves at the Catholic church afterwards for the same ceremony. And when the Methodists, under the constant persecution as a result of which they had to petition the imperial government of Britain for protection, had to close their mission, the governor wrote saying that now that they had not seen anything of the Methodists for a long time; would the British Government please send out a bishop for them to help in the situation?

Thereafter the Christian church, white or black, had to compete with the secession of the blacks themselves, looking neither to America nor to Africa. The Black Muslims turned to Arabia and the Koran; the black was not African but Asian, with roots in the Prophet's Arabia rather than south of the Sahara. The Umbanda spiritual movement supposedly originated in India and made its way to Brazil, with an African theory of incarnation identified with the Indian theory of Karma. With the Ras Tafari Movement of Jamaica, with its messianic centre in Ethiopia, we come, on the surface, closer to Africa than does the Muslim church, until we learn that the blacks are in fact Jews, reincarnation of the ancient Hebrews (when the black Jews of America sought to migrate to Israel, because they doubted they would be allowed into Ethiopia, Israel refused to admit them). And so Marcus Garvey with his "back to Africa" movement, with its own Negro religion, a black God and the African Orthodox Church.

This ambivalence appears most starkly in the preachings and teachings of Joseph R. Washington. In his *Black Religion*, he advocated conversion of the blacks from their Jesusology and folk religion to mainstream Protestantism, the initiative to come from white Christians. Then in his *The Politics of God*, he underwent a radical change. No longer did he urge blacks to join the mainstream of white religion; he now pontificated that white religion is bankrupt, and pleaded for "a conscious rejection of white theological and ecclesiastical double-talk and a conscious acceptance of their black promise". Cleage, in his *Black Messiah*, proceeded to provide a "black" genealogy for Jesus, the Black Messiah, obviously using the Bible to support the religion of Black Power.

146 | THE BLACKEST THING IN SLAVERY WAS NOT THE BLACK MAN

The close identification of Christianity with slavery was clearly seen in the slave compensation claims presented to the British Government in accordance with Parliament's appropriation of £20 million for the compensation of the slave owners. The church was well represented. One clergyman in St Vincent claimed for 208 slaves; one in Tobago for 216; one in St Kitts for 126; one in Barbados for 105. In Jamaica twenty-two clergymen, individually or in partnership, owned 3,495 slaves and collected £62,335 as compensation. The list was headed by the Rt Rev H. Philpotts, Lord Bishop of Exeter. The pattern was not confined to the Caribbean. In Mauritius, which the British had taken over from the French, the Abbé Gaillardan received £16,558 in compensation for 514 slaves.

The question which the Africans had to face was, whose Jesus Christ? Whose Christianity? The rivalry between Catholic, Protestant and Muslim led to proposals for the denominational partition of Uganda and to a war of religion ended only by Lugard on behalf of the East Africa Company, establishing a British protectorate. In the Sudan, Anglo-American missionary rivalry ended in partition: the British Anglicans would educate the girls and the American Presbyterians the boys.

The first result of all this we learn from the total condemnation of missionary activity by Mary Kingsley – the gin, the absurd clothes prescribed for African women supposedly in the interests of female modesty, the absurdities of missionary education (except for the Catholics, with their priority to agriculture). Mary Kingsley ended in a rare defence of the Africans:

> I have no hesitation in saying that in the whole of West Africa, in one week, there is not one-quarter the amount of drunkenness you can see any Saturday night you choose in a couple of hours in the Vauxhall Road; and you will not find in a whole year's investigation on the Coast, one seventieth part of the evil, degradation and premature decay you can see any afternoon you choose to take a walk in the more densely populated parts of any of our towns.

The second and more enduring result was the development of an African Christianity, beginning with the installation of African catechists and clergymen (however much underpaid in comparison with the Europeans) and leading up to the first Anglican African bishop, Bishop Crowther of Nigeria. The role of the mosquito in this reorientation is not to be minimized, nor is the importance of knowledge of the African languages. But with the growth of imperialism in Africa and racism in Britain, Crowther was attacked on grounds of incompetence, and he died shortly after his declaration of the independence of the African Church. The spread of African Christian sects and movements in Nigeria, Zambia and the Congo was in line with the black churches which developed in America.

The Slave and the Law

The master was always right. That was the essence of slavery. As the French put it in later years, after the *Code Noir*, slavery required "unlimited submission and total obedience in all cases". Or, as Judge Ruffin made specific in a North Carolina case in 1829: "The power of the master must be absolute to render the submission of the slave perfect." However harsh the proposition, he expounded, "it is inherent in the relation of master and slave . . . we cannot allow the right of the master to be brought into discussion in the Courts of Justice. The slave, to remain a slave, must be made sensible that there is no appeal from his master." The French put the issue succinctly in official instructions to the colonies in 1771:

> It is only by leaving to the masters a power that is nearly absolute, that it will be possible to keep so large a number of men in that state of submission which is made necessary by their numerical superiority over the whites. If some masters abuse that power, they must be reproved in secret, so that the slaves may always be kept in the belief that the master can do no wrong in his dealing with them.

So that, whether in Virginia or in Barbados, the slave was denied any trial by jury – because of his brutish condition, as alleged in Barbados in 1688 or in Virginia in 1692. For the same reason, white courts strove to avoid decisions in respect of the murder of a slave by a white, Virginia in 1609 arguing that "it cannot be presumed that prepensed malice (which alone makes murder felony) should induce a man to destroy his own estate". It was private justice, not public. One of the leading propagandists for slavery in the southern states argued in 1853 as follows, "on our estates we dispense with the whole machinery of public, police and public courts of justice. Thus we try, decide, and execute the sentence in thousands of cases, which in other countries would go into the courts."

In the French colonies the *Code Noir* became increasingly a dead letter over the subsequent decades, the state itself, the metropolitan country, taking the lead in the excessive severity preached and practised. This applied particularly to the issue of the slave striking a white person. As the minister of colonies wrote to a colonial governor in 1726, if one tolerated this, "one would soon see an end to the subordination of blacks to whites". A memoir of 1729 actually recommended that all mulattoes or free blacks who put their hand on a white person were to be re-enslaved.

The respect demanded by the *Code Noir* for the former white master by the former slave after manumission was now extended to respect by every free man of colour for every white person, representing, as it has been said, an incontestable aggravation of the status of the coloured freedman, a requirement eliciting henceforth, as special to their class, the crime of irreverence. This reflects what has frequently been elaborated on, the "veritable rage" with which authority, as occasion demanded, fell on its slave prey, leaving the impression in the texts and documents that what was involved here was terror more than being a tactic: terror in the colonies is a climate, an atmosphere, emerging from the arrival of the slaves and never thereafter to leave the whites. As the Swiss Jesuit Gibler comments, "with this we re-join the psychology of the Roman society at its apogee, marked by the same tensions" voiced by Seneca – so many slaves, so many enemies; Roman law required all the slaves in the household to be killed if one had killed the master.

The highly touted Spanish policy of humanitarianism and tolerance under the influence of Catholicism is singularly absent in this particular in the *Código Negro Carolino*, the 1785 code for Santo Domingo. The code required all blacks and persons of colour, slave and free, to "be humble and respectful to each white person as if each was his master or lord". The code as a matter of policy regarded as necessary the establishment of "the most comprehensive subordination" on the part of the slave "toward the white population", as this was to be "the fundamental basis of the internal policy of the colony". The slave codes were at pains to enforce the legal subordination of the slaves. The *Code Noir* prohibited the carrying of weapons (article 15), slave assemblies or congregations at night (article 16), and flight or desertion; gave powers of arrest to whites in respect of assemblies; and prescribed the death penalty for the third attempt at desertion, as well as severe fines for freed men or whites who gave shelter to the runaways.

The general picture presented in the southern United States suggests a diet adequate in quantity; but the starchy, high-energy diet of cornmeal, pork and molasses produced specific hungers, dangerous deficiencies and a special form of malnutrition. It was a case of protein hunger; there was no lean meat, milk and eggs, because there were insufficient livestock. Vitamins and minerals were short, resulting in beriberi, pellagra and scurvy. Of a sample of over 8,500 slaves over fifteen in the three states of Georgia, Mississippi and Louisiana, one in eleven was either physically impaired or chronically ill. It was largely an economic problem – planters trying to save money and reduce plantation expenses – while the land given

European Christianity and African Slavery | 149

to the slaves for growing their own foods was usually of the poorest quality, so as not to encroach on the cotton kingdom. From this point of view, the French in the Caribbean were emphatic that, as part of the campaign to reduce costs, the slaves were not to be encouraged to develop a taste for the high-cost imported French foodstuffs.

Baptism made slaves no more free than it made penguins. A pious lady, asked if her black maid was to be baptized, replied, "You might as well baptize my black bitch." Britain's Bishop Berkeley was a little less coarse: blacks were "creatures of another species who had no right to be included or admitted to the sacraments". The bishop seemed not to have known his St Paul, who sent back Onesimus to his master to serve as both slave and as "more than a servant, a brother beloved", indicating that Christian conversion had changed a bondsman's spiritual condition but not his legal obligation. But the southern states soon learned from Baptist and Presbyterian revivals that authentic Christianity made blacks better slaves.

The Apprenticeship Decree of 1840 extended to the age of twenty-five the period during which the *manumiso* must be apprenticed to a "patron" and official surveillance continued. The apprentice was guaranteed a salary of twelve to twenty-four pesos a year, had no freedom to choose his residence, could not marry before twenty-five, when he became a *peon*, legally free, but required to register with the local judge and to carry a booklet without which he could not be given a job.

Even in 1810 slaves represented no more than 5 per cent of the population of Venezuela, and the tendency was pronounced for them to be used more in domestic service than in agriculture. By 1854 slavery was in every sense a social and economic liability rather than an economic asset. Yet the abolition was resisted to the very end, and abolition without compensation was denounced – the note is strikingly modern – as communism. Gwendolyn Hall ends her analysis of the Spanish slave code: "The *Código Negro Español* did indeed claim in its preamble that it was a codification of existing slave law in force in the Spanish colonies. The claim was false. It was copied largely from the French *Code Noir* of 1685, and from the *Ordinances de Louis XIV*. A search of Spanish slave law predating the 1789 code reveals a conspicuous absence of concrete protective measures." How did the vaunted Spanish slave codes show up in practice on the Cuban sugar plantation? Fraginals replies: the books kept on the plantations, and especially the so-called balance sheets of the sugar harvest, reveal the following:

1. There were no days of rest as such on the plantations, although legal precepts established Sundays and religious festivals as rest days.

150 | THE BLACKEST THING IN SLAVERY WAS NOT THE BLACK MAN

2. There were no hours of rest or free time as such. Free time was eliminated, all biologically available hours being employed in production.

3. When, for reasons beyond their control, the slave owners had no productive work for the slaves to do, they devised unproductive work for them, such as moving objects from one place to another and then returning them to their place of origin. A slave without work was an element of dissolution for the whole system, a factor of possible rebellion.

4. The work day during harvest time was sixteen to eighteen hours during the period of maximal barbarity of the slave system. For the rest of the year, it was fourteen to sixteen hours. In 1842, the legal limits set to "soften" the life of the slave were fifteen hours in harvest time and twelve hours for the rest of the year. A planters' commission had this law repealed, arguing that sixteen was the acceptable minimum.

Finally, suicide. In the decade 1840–1849, 83 per cent of suicides in Cuba were committed by black slaves. "There was, on average, one suicide per plantation every two years. Collective suicide was common during the most barbaric period; there is on record the extreme case of forty-three black slaves committing suicide after an unsuccessful uprising."

The paeans to the Spanish slave regime rested not only on Catholicism but also on the assertion that the race relations of Latin peoples were superior to those of Anglo-Saxons. Today one considers the Scandinavian people rather than Latins leaders in the field of healthier race relations. One of these Scandinavian countries, Denmark, had Caribbean possessions and developed a slave system of its own. Let us therefore look at the principal elements of the two slave codes of the Danish Virgin Islands: the code of 1733, the Gardelin code, so called after the then governor; and the code of 1755, Governor Lindemark's code, when the Danish Crown assumed formal ownership of the islands, following the 1741 proclamation of Governor Moth laying down special articles for Negroes.

1. Flight and desertion of slaves, the dominant feature of the 1733 code: death penalty for ringleaders after torture with red-hot pincers, at three separate public locations. Others in conspiracy to run away would lose a leg if not pardoned by the master. Penalties from death to leg amputation and to branding and whipping for absences over six months, three months, fourteen days, and for failure to report

desertions. The 1755 code prescribed harsher penalties; it removed corporal punishment for short absences and alternatives to the death sentence.

2. Deference to whites enforced, the alternative being regarded as prejudicial to the social order. Even menacing gestures or insulting words were punishable by the applications of glowing pincers followed by hanging; or, if the insulted white so desired, amputation of the slave's right hand. A slave meeting a white man was required deferentially to step aside for the white to pass, on pain of corporal punishment (1733 code).

3. Sumptuary legislation. The slave was not to be seen in clothing of any "consequence" without a certificate from his master (1733 code).

4. Freedom of movement. No plantation black was to be found in the town after the beating of the evening drum; the penalty for violation of the curfew was a thorough beating (1733 code).

One student of the slave regime of the Danish Virgin Islands has concluded: "The slave as property, consigned to servitude by the Almighty, and petrified in dumb superstition by his ignorance, had only obligations but no rights, not even in respect of those essentials of food, clothing and shelter that made him a more efficient unit of production." A commission appointed by the Crown in 1791 to seek to ameliorate the slave system "was not prepared to make any statutory inroads into the master's discretion in matters relating to food, clothing, housing, pre and post-natal care, or care of children and the sick. These were areas comprehended by the sacred right of property, which the commission had no intention of violating". As late as 1805, the secretary of the abolition commission (on the slave trade) was "reiterating its position that a comprehensive *code noir* was not an urgent priority; that its immediate concern was a police code which would reflect what was customary among better planters".

The *Code Noir* enjoined on the slave owners to govern the slaves like good fathers of families (article 54). We have examined the slave codes of the European countries, Anglo-Saxon, Latin and Nordic; Catholic, Puritan, Protestant and Lutheran. We can now ask, with Gwendolyn Hall, "Was all this savagery really necessary?" Was it necessary to chain a man of sixty for twenty-five years to a tree with a chain twenty-five feet long? Was it necessary to keep a Senegal black of eighty-seven, with twenty-two children, in slavery? She herself replies: "Given the insecurity of the system, the rebelliousness of the slaves, the relative ineffectiveness of both legal security measures and methods of socialization such as religious conversion and

152 | THE BLACKEST THING IN SLAVERY WAS NOT THE BLACK MAN

indoctrination, it appears that paralysing the hand that might strike down the master through the most naked form of terror was the cement that held the system together."

As Pauleus Sannon has concluded of St Domingue, in his history of Toussaint L'Ouverture: "a collection of beasts of burden exploited by beasts of prey".

The Slave Personality

A Brazilian scholar, Emilia Viotti da Costa, in a paper on "Slave Images and Realities" presented to an international conference in 1977, on Slavery in New World Plantation Societies, wrote as follows:

> Creating a black community represented resistance to slavery because slavery implied not only the subordination and exploitation of one social group by another, but also the confrontation of two ethnic groups. The slave could resist in different ways: as a slave to his master, as a black man to the white man, and as an African to the European. In this context cultural resistance could be interpreted as a form of social protest. The existence of two communities, one white and the other black, allowed the slave to move from one world to the other. Within the net of ambiguous interrelationships created by the system the slave had a chance to play different roles. . . . The need to function in two different and antagonistic worlds created for the slave the possibility of using several masks. He had one for his master, another for his companions, a third for his family and probably another for himself. His personality was a synthesis of often conflicting selves.

Or, in the words of the Jamaican slave song, "Got one mind for the boss to see, got another mind for what I know is me." It was varied slightly in South Carolina, "One life they show their masters and another life they don't show."

One mask, the mind for the boss to see, is the conventional viewpoint expressed by two different and contradictory personalities. The first, Booker T. Washington, associated with countless others in his analysis of the emancipated blacks as a "simple people . . . freed from slavery and with no past". The second, Ulrich B. Phillips, the traditional historian of the Slave South, dismissed the slaves as people "with hazy pasts and reckless future . . . they lived in each moment as it flew". He saw slavery as a "safeguard of civilization and orderly government", and the plantation as "a school constantly training and controlling people who were in a backward state of civilization . . . the best school yet invented for the mass training of that sort of inert and backward people which the bulk of the American Negroes represented". He contemptuously dismissed the blacks in the American Revolution as "a passive element whose fate was affected only so far as the master race determined". Morison, for his part, had reason to believe that the slave (whom he nicknamed Sambo) suffered less than any other class in the South from slavery, while Turner justified slavery as "the mode of dealing with the Negro".

These opinions reflect the conventional view that slaves could learn only from their masters, so that slave culture, a source of slave belief and behaviour, was at best "imitative". As expressed by Franklin Frazier, the distinguished black sociologist, "force of circumstance caused the slaves to take over, however imperfectly, the folkways of the American environment", finding "within the patterns of the white man's culture a purpose in life". As expressed by Gunnar Myrdal, the Swedish analyst of the American dilemma of race relations, "American Negro culture is not something independent of general American culture. It is a distorted development, or a pathological condition, of the general American culture."

Like master, like man. W.E.B. Du Bois is emphatic that the lack of a white work ethic among blacks is due to their tendency to follow – follow the example of their former masters. Joaquim Nabuco, the outstanding Brazilian abolitionist, stressed that there were "two contrary types, and at bottom the same – the slave and the master". Eugene Genovese, the American scholar, reminds us that for reasons common to the slave condition, all slave classes displayed a lack of industrial initiative and produced the "lazy Nigger", who, under Russian serfdom and elsewhere, was white. Turning now to the slave's other mind which he knew to be his, Roger Bastide has presented the case for African slaves in the New World: "To make life possible, they hammered out a new cultural pattern of their own, shaping it in response to the demands of their new environment." First, there was the question of language. Leaving out of account the increasing evidence that oral communication between slaves of different African "nations" was not as difficult as has traditionally been represented, the African slaves developed their own New World languages. There was Srinam English, Negro English, in Suriname: Taki-taki has been assessed as demonstrating the "existence of a slave consciousness that refused to be limited by the whites' conception and manipulation of it". As against the French view that only the white of the French language was able to create the Creole of Haiti, Suzanne Sylvain-Comhaire has countered with the predominant African influence in its formation. The contemporary Haitian version is "derived from French vocabulary but built on African syntactic ordering, which made communication easier between slaves of different ethnic origins". To quote Sterling Stuckey: "Slaves were able to fashion a lifestyle and set of values – an ethos – which prevented them from being imprisoned altogether by the definition which the larger society sought to impose." The ethos was an amalgam of Africanisms and New World elements which helped slaves, in Guy Johnson's words, "feel their way along the course of American slavery, helping them to endure."

The first major field for this syncretism was religion. In Brazil the first inclination was, on the part of both the Crown and many planters, to permit the Africans to enjoy their music and dancing and dramatic skills on such special occasions as religious feast days and processions. They saw the African rituals as performing a social function analogous to Catholicism, an instrument of social control. So it was with the John Canoe dance in Jamaica, closely associated with survivals of African religion and magic. In Suriname, however, the *watramama* dance, among others, was proscribed by penal regulations in 1874 as idolatry. The Catholic clergy in Brazil protested vigorously, seeing the African rituals, the *batuques* and *calundus*, as important carriers of African traditions. As da Costa writes:

> Reinterpreting Christianity in their own terms, blacks found ways of converting their African gods into Catholic saints. Through this syncretic process they could pray to our Lord of Good and Saint Anthony or Saint George, while worshipping Oshala, Xango or Ogum, and they could make offering to Yemanja while praying to Our Lady of the Rosary. The African gods' pantheon was transported to the New World and could survive, though not intact, in the bosom of Christianity. Slaves in Brazil found in their *batuques* and *calundus* as well as in Catholic rituals the means of creating an identity independent of their masters.

The only African institution to withstand the triumph of Catholics was the cult of the dead. Black and white Catholicism were two very different things. The blacks organized special fraternities of their own, under the patronage of black saints – for example, St Benedict the Moor. There were special fraternities for Yoruba and for Congo, the same division into "nations" developing within the ecclesiastical organization facilitating the perpetuation of African languages and African religious beliefs. Rivalry between the "nations" dominated the sodalities. Mozambique fought with Congo over the location of the statue of Our Lady of the Rosary, which once appeared in the ocean. Jamaican Baptists subordinated Christ to John the Baptist. But the syncretism – reconciliation of Catholic and African – was a two-way street; the other side was the Africanization of the Europeans, white Spanish women in Bahía submitting to the authority of black priests; the de-Europeanization of the whites – as Ramos puts it, "In Bahia all classes, even the upper class, have a tendency to become Negro." All of this is well brought out in the story of Chico Rei, an African king taken prisoner, enslaved and saving enough money to buy the freedom of his whole family and then the entire tribe, as well as slaves from other tribes. He established a "veritable state within a state", with king and Catholic brotherhood, that built the Church of the Rosary, one of the most beautiful churches in Curo Preto.

The third example of religious syncretism was Haiti and its voodoo, banned in St Domingue from 1704, thus described by a Haitian writer: "A religion peculiar to the slaves, derived from their African background and constituted through the creolization of ancestral beliefs and rites, and joined in adaptive syncretism with the religion of their masters; voodoo was rooted in the difference between the gods of the white and the gods of the black." Thus it was that the Haitian *Vodun* was drastically changed from its African manifestation. Prohibited by the first three Haitian rulers – L'Ouverture, Dessalines and Christophe – the break of the Haitian connection with Africa with independence, except for the solitary case of Christophe's recruitment of a palace guard of four thousand from Dahomey, meant that, to quote Bastide, "Vodun was thus free to develop in such a way that it is not, strictly speaking, an African religion any longer, but rather the island's 'national' creed."[3] What it expressed is not so much the desire for a "return to Africa" as something quite different – the sum of all that is specifically and originally Haitian, at least as regards the island's agricultural population. The *loas* (spirits) exist side by side with creole spirits, progressively enriching the religious pantheon, so that it has ceased to be Dahomean and may now be regarded as national.

But it was the songs of the blacks that show up the absurdity of theories which conceive of slavery as a closed system which destroyed the vitality of the black slave and left him a dependent child. In their songs the slaves were able to create an independent art form and a distinctive voice, to quote Lawrence Levin, "the aesthetic realm was the one area in which slaves knew they were not inferior to whites". In the memorable phrase of W.E.B. Du Bois, in their songs "the soul of the black slave spoke to man".[4]

The slave songs were in the first place and basically a total rejection of all the facets of slave life. One of the most outstanding of such songs went:

No more peck o'corn for me
No more driver's lash for me
No more pint o'salt for me
No more hundred lash for me
No more mistress call for me.

An explicit call to secret meetings: "Steal away, steal away, steal away to Jesus." Nothing more likely. "Sometimes I feel like a motherless chile, a long ways from home" went to the heart of every slave mother separated from her children.

For the non-slaveholder, the poor white, the blacks felt unmitigated scorn. They were "po' buckra", "white trash". They might refuse to do domestic service, to clean the planter's boots, to wait on his table and do menial work in his house; they called that "nigger's work". They might insist they were the companion, the equal, of the white planter. The blacks knew better. Governor Fénelon in Martinique begged the French authorities not to send over white immigrants from Acadia, or white ploughmen; they would be laughed at unmercifully by the black slaves. As Frederick Douglass put it, "It was considered as being bad enough to be a slave; but to be a poor man's slave was deemed a disgrace indeed!" The black took the view that "he ain't used to waiting on low rank people".

Southern planters in the United States, regarding their slaves as identified with the family, were surprised to encounter slaves with surnames. Slave law had denied them surnames; the slave was always *nullius filius*, nobody's son. "Why do you call Henry Mr Ferguson?" one white woman asked the black "Mammy". The reply was, "Do you think 'cause we are black that we can't have no names?" The slaves often chose surnames which differed from those who owned them, but hesitated to use them to the whites. Gutman states that "analysis of the surnames slaves retained shows that such decisions served to shape a social identity independent of slave ownership". With emancipation the whites realized that the old order, social and moral, had collapsed. One white man wrote:

> There will soon be no more old mammies and daddies, no more uncles and aunties. Instead of "Mamma Judy" and "Uncle Jacob" we shall have our "Mrs Ampey Tatoms" and our "Mr Lewis Williamses". The sweet ties that bound our old family servants to us will be broken and replaced with envy and notice that the negroes seldom or never take the names of the present owners in adopting their "entitles" as they call their own surnames, but always that of some former master, and they go back as far as possible; it was the name of the actual owner that distinguished them in slavery, and I suppose they wish to throw off that badge of servility.

Whatever the slave owner might do to renege on his legal obligations to provide for his slaves' welfare or to make extra profit of him, the slave's personality and identity were seen most frequently in his looking after his own welfare. The Haitian historian Fouchard emphasizes that it was the slave who provided his own bed for his slave cabin and such furniture as it

European Christianity and African Slavery | 157

contained – chairs, rugs, blankets, calabash, candlesticks and pottery. Slaves preferred to be given a garden to grow their own food and feed themselves, notwithstanding the prohibitions of the law. The despised slave food is today among the ethnic delicacies – salt fish is now soul food. The slave continued to roast his corn and eat it on the cob, no matter how much the Europeans sneered at it as cattle food. The slave clothed himself, made his own hats, trousers and shoes. It was not the master, insists Fouchard, who saw to it that the slaves bathed – three times a day for the women, adhering to their African hygiene. It was the slave, insists Fouchard, who developed his vegetable toothbrush when the toothbrush was unknown in France, where even in 1972 the tradition was one in four using toothbrushes, one in seven homes where the same toothbrush was used by five people.[5]

The slave personality also had its political aspect. Du Tertre might pontificate that other causes than the desire of liberty motivated flight and desertion. Debbasch might assert that the principal cause was that the maroon was a sick man. Some professor once said that it was only in the middle of the eighteenth century that the philosophers had adumbrated the natural right to liberty and thus the slaves could not have been motivated by a desire for freedom. The slave answered in song:

> He delivered Daniel from de lion's den,
> Jonah from de belly of de whale,
> And de Hebrew children from de fiery furnace,
> And why not every man?

Try as they would, they could not deny the slave's humanity. His resistance was not only cultural and religious, it was also political. A Jamaican slave song went as follows: "Me no horse, me no mare, me no mule, / No use me ill, obisha (overseer)."

But the rivalry among the "nations" was reinforced by the jealousy between the classes – witness Turner and the field slaves as well as his relations with the house slaves. The Brazil slave *mot* of the nineteenth century made this clear: "Field worker becomes butler, does not look out for his former peers."

Spanish and Portuguese America kept up the tradition of the European literary contests of the troubadours. This became a contest between white and black improvisers. A black in Brazil sang on his white competitor: "It was a white man, Judas / Who betrayed our Lord."

A black reply to mockery directed at his colour:

> White paper is worthless in itself
> But write on it

With black ink
And it is worth millions.

Ambiguous? Black on white? In Argentina, a black competing with Martín Fierro sang: "I too have something white about me / The whiteness of my teeth."

"Whenever you see a black face, you see a thief," said the overseer to Marly, in a Jamaican novel of the early nineteenth century. The slave gave it back with compound interest: "What I take from my master being for my use, who am his slave, or property, he loses nothing in the transfer." Marx should have gloried in this attack on the misappropriation of surplus value. But the slave went further: accused of an imitative culture, he understood it was only a limited imitation. A black proverb runs like this: "When black man tief he tief ha'f a bit, when buckrah massa tief he tief whole plantation." In the Brazilian version: "When the black man steals he goes to jail, but when his master steals he becomes a baron."

In every Sambo there might be a Spartacus. One of the great analysts of the US slave system on the eve of the Civil War, Frederick Olmsted, wrote as follows: "I begin to suspect that the great trouble and anxiety of Southern gentlemen is: How, without quite destroying the capabilities of the negro for any work at all, to prevent him from learning to take care of himself."

Slavery through the Eyes of the Slave

However much in recent years the view has gained ground that the slave had a personality of his own, it is the slave owner's, the slave trader's, the imperialist country's view of slavery which have been dominant. By the nature of things the slave's own account of his own experiences would be limited in quantity if only by considerations of literacy, the hostility of those to whom his account might have been available, the difficulties of preservation of his material. But the material exists, however limited, in letters by slaves, in speeches by slaves and ex-slaves, in interviews by journalists and officials, in reports of direct dialogue with official commissions, as for example, the Freedmen's Bureau in the United States. The little that is available affords a profound insight into the mind of the slave, his private world, his struggle for survival, his family life, his confrontation with authority. We can today attempt a picture of slavery through the eyes of the slave, drawn from his own first-hand accounts.

Take slavery itself, as an institution, as a system. The views of this slave or that slave or the other slave, pieced together, emerge like this, in terms of their own expressions, language, presentation, each, so to speak, saying, in the words of Langston Hughes, "I speak in the name of the black millions."[6]

> There is no sin which man can commit, that those slaveholders are not guilty of.
>
> What I want to make you understand is, that A SLAVE CAN'T BE A MAN!
>
> (Description of one plantation): "It was well stocked with cattle, and some fifty head of niggers."
>
> Slavery is the father of lies . . . there never was anything to beat slavery for lying.
>
> I am led to the conclusion that the slave who can take care of himself and master can certainly take care of himself alone.

Code Noir and slave codes were one thing; the conditions of existence for the slave were something else. The slaves reporting:

> Man and wife draw half a bushel (corn), and two or three herring. What, if you hold em up in tumb and finger, de wind would blow 'em away, so salt eaten. Masters often give servant ninepence to get food for dog; yes, he would pay dog's board, but leave the slave to take care of himself.
>
> You had to get your victuals standing at your home.
>
> We wuz not 'lowed tuh have any pockets in our breeches 'cause dey thought we might steal sumpin'.

And the slave's family?

> (Planter to son). "Do you talk to me about a nigger wife?"
>
> This custom of the husband going to the wife's home on Saturday night was one of the peculiarities of the slave system.
>
> Why, they mind no more selling children away from slave, than they do calves from a cow.
>
> The suffering of children in slavery will never the half of it be told; especially if the mistress suspects that the child is a little too nearly like master.
>
> You bring up a tier of children by your wife, and another tier of children by your slave women. By and by your children grow up, and those you had by your wife have children by those you had by your slave women, and then you take these same children and sell them.
>
> The slaves used to debate together sometimes, what could be the reason that the yellow folks couldn't be trusted like the dark ones could . . . we concluded it was because they was sons of their masters, and took after their fathers.

But nothing could quench their thirst for freedom. They would run away, forging the slave pass when necessary, hiding in the swamps: "I felt safer among the alligators than among the white men." "Run Nigger Run" was the song they made up about evading the white patrols for runaways. They

160 | THE BLACKEST THING IN SLAVERY WAS NOT THE BLACK MAN

knew all the fraud involved in the so-called arrangements for purchasing their freedom, involving enormous overwork, only to be cheated at the end and be sold to another master as they paid off the purchase price to the former. But the spirit of freedom could not be tamed. One slave who had purchased his freedom wrote to his former master proposing the purchase of his family: "You must not consider that it is a slave talking to 'massa' now, but one as free as yourself."

The slaves had a great contempt for the Founding Fathers, for Washington with his parties, card-playing and wine-drinking, and slave owner to boot; for Jefferson with his family of four by Sally Hemings and the "uncertainty to us slaves" resulting from his death in 1826, when he freed only seven of his slaves; all the rest were sold from the auctioneer's block, by order of Jefferson, who had once been overheard by his slaves in argument with Lafayette, who thought Jefferson should free them. The slaves did not think much of proposals being canvassed by the Freedmen's Inquiry Commission in 1863: "Suppose the United States Government should give the colored people of South Carolina, Georgia and Florida a vote of their own, would they rather be by themselves and have their own judges, magistrates and officers of the government, or have white men to live with them and mix up with them?" The slaves had some interest in Liberia, which one of them described as "a fine country, fine delicious fruits from her enough to attract the noblest minds". But as one put it, explaining that Liberia fulfilled the scriptural description of the Promised Land: "The good Lord never left nothin' undone in Africa, for He knows how afraid the negro is of work. So God just made everything right to his hand so he could get it without the least bit of trouble."[7]

This remarkable volume of *Slave Testimony: Two Centuries of Letters, Speeches, Interviews, and Autobiographies*, a monument to the dedication and diligence of John Blassingame, is very revealing of the slave personality: "one life they show their masters and another life they don't show," 75.

6.

The Calvary of Free Blacks

A race has been freed, but a society has not been formed.
                    Governor Lord Harris (1846–1853).

The British planters in the Caribbean made a bitter and determined last-ditch stand to prevent the inevitable – the abolition of black slavery and the sugar monopoly. One of Jamaica's leading planters, Sir Rose Price, resident in England as lord of the manor of Trengwainton House in Penzance, with its "Chinese wall", wrote a pamphlet which he injected into the 1832 elections in Britain in connection with the first Reform Bill. Price's pamphlet, published at his own expense, was entitled, "Pledges and Colonial Slavery, to Candidates for Seats in Parliament, rightly considered". Price's theme was that, while slavery was odious, it was preferable to the life of a free labourer in England, and that English slavery was infinitely superior to the dreadful slavery of foreigners.[1]

Considering the "necessities" of life, which took nearly one-tenth of the English labourer's weekly wage of twenty-six shillings, Price compared the black's fare:

In the room of meat; – the negro has salt and herrings.

For Bread; – He has yams.

For Butter; – He has honey and treacle.

For Potatoes; – The plantain *and substantial cocoa root* . . . and . . . the large sweet potatoe.

For *a little Sugar;* – He has ten times more than the English labourer.

For Tea; – He has abundance of Coffee.

For Beer; – He has grog, or punch . . .

For Coals; – He has as much wood as he pleases.

For Candles; – He has the castor oil in abundance . . .

For Rent; – *He has his own house, which is as much his own as any building erected on a leasehold estate in England, which goes to whom he pleases at his death, with his other property*, which I firmly believe, was never deviated from, *when no law existed to secure it to him.*

162 | THE BLACKEST THING IN SLAVERY WAS NOT THE BLACK MAN

Price continued:

> More I need not say to prove that the Negro counts not to toil *for his victuals*, the greatest object of a poor white man, many of whom both in England and Ireland, have been starved to death. . . . *It is a fact, which cannot be contradicted, that one months easy labour in the year, will provide a negro and his family, in the island of Jamaica, all necessaries of life in abundance. The important question, therefore, is how is he to occupy his time the remaining month of the year, when he is no longer compelled to labour? and what inducement has he to labour as a free-man?*

Price answered his own questions – unconditional freedom was "*utterly impossible, unless it is intended to abandon the West Indies to the negroes*, to live in idleness and vice!" The Negro should be

> coerced to labour, *by direct means*, otherwise he will cultivate no land, except for the purpose of procuring such necessaries and comforts for himself and family *as he may desire*. . . . As coercive labour *is not a state of freedom*, it would appear he is destined by Providence to labour in a state of slavery, *of some sort or other*, till the curse of Adam is removed from the face of the earth, and from the brow of man at Gods appointed time. The freedom of black men is attended with difficulties (by the laws of nature and God himself) *which never impeded the freedom of white men*. Nature presents every reason for the white man's freedom as *a fellow labourer on earth*; and every reason, for the black man's bondage, *as such, to cause the earth to produce its abundance.*

Another member of the family, Thomas Price, claimed that blacks preferred squatting to working for wages. "As a general rule the negro is not satisfied with his condition unless he has a horse, a blue tail coat and a certain amount of land." He added that they came down from the mountains to work for a couple of days and then returned with a bottle of Bass ale. But their enemies were saying they drank only champagne, and two days' work would hardly provide them with a horse and blue tailcoat. Lord Bentinck, member of a select committee of the House of Commons, asked Price whether the lack of continuous labour of which the planters complained was not the fault of the planters themselves?

> A: It is very possible that the planters may not have given them continuous work.
> Q: What you want is this, that at any moment when it suits your convenience you may be able to put your hand on the labourer?
> A: Undoubtedly, you could not have better expressed my meaning.

In December 1832, on the eve of emancipation in the British colonies, Lord Howick, under-secretary of state for the colonies, prepared a long

The Calvary of Free Blacks | 163

memorandum on the problem anticipated with the changeover to free labour. The problem and proposed solution were stated as follows:

> It is impossible therefore to suppose that the Slaves (who, though as I believe not more given to idleness than other men are certainly not less so) would if freed from control be induced even by high wages to continue to submit to a drudgery which they detest, while without doing so they could obtain land sufficient for their support. . . . I think that it would be greatly for the real happiness of the Negroes themselves, if the facility of acquiring land could be so far restrained as to prevent them, on the abolition of slavery, from abandoning their habits of regular industry. Accordingly, it is to the imposition of a considerable tax upon Land that I chiefly look for the means of enabling the planter to continue his business when emancipation shall have taken place.

Thus the sugar plantation was to continue minus the black slave. To enable the planter to continue his business after emancipation, steps must be taken to make it difficult for the former slaves to own land, which in official eyes, was tantamount to abandoning their habits of regular industry and, as stated precisely in British Honduras in 1839, tending "to discourage labour for wages". In the words of Taylor, of the Colonial Office bureaucracy, the free black must acquire habits of "self-command and voluntary industry", to be "saved from a life of savage sloth and the planter from ruin".

The policy eventually adopted by the British Government was to make emancipation gradual. For seven years after emancipation the slaves – excepting children under six, who were to be free without restrictions – were to become apprentices obligated to work for their masters for three-quarters of their time in a day fixed at ten working hours, between forty and a half and forty-five unrecompensed hours per week. This arrangement was generally regarded by the planter class as part of the financial compensation, whereby they were guaranteed forty and a half hours of work each week for some years. The apprentices were still subject to corporal punishment, but this could only be administered by special district magistrates. The master was responsible for supplying to the apprentices food, clothing, lodging, medicine, or, in lieu of food, adequate provision grounds and leisure time in which to cultivate them. The apprenticeship scheme, never bothered with in Barbados and Antigua, with their superabundance of labour, was ultimately abolished in 1838, two years ahead of schedule. Antigua, according to its governor, with tongue in cheek, preferred "the confidence generally reposed in the superior intelligence and good disposition of the labouring population". In Suriname the same principle was followed – a period of ten years under contract as hired labourers under the special supervision of the state. But unlike the British

164 | THE BLACKEST THING IN SLAVERY WAS NOT THE BLACK MAN

colonies, corporal punishment was strictly prohibited, and the ex-slave was free to conclude a contract with an employer of his own choice. The drift to the capital was encouraged thereby, the ex-slave preferring to live closer to the urban areas. The "released persons" in Paramaribo increased from 5,629 in 1864 to 6,921 in 1872.

In accordance with the theories then in vogue in England with Gibbon Wakefield and his theories of colonization, the British Government stepped in to ensure that, at the end of slavery and apprenticeship, it would be well-nigh impossible for the freedmen to become landowners. In Trinidad, for example (where, as we have seen, there were only twenty thousand slaves at emancipation), Crown land was disposed of after the end of apprenticeship only in minimum quantities of 340 acres (later raised to 680), at a minimum upset price of £1 per acre (raised in 1847 to £2). The land was for new capitalists and not for ex-slaves. The government, by locking up the Crown lands to all but the rich, had made it impossible for a landed class, whatever its colour, to grow up to fill the gap between the plantation and the landless proletariat. The British Government fully agreed with the policy of envisaging the sale of public land in terms of sugar only; nothing should be done to accelerate the dispersal of agricultural labourers so greatly needed by the planters. So between 1847 and 1865 only 3,423 acres of Crown land were sold in Trinidad, in 779 transactions; of these, only 453 acres were bought by sugar planters. As a Trinidad historian, Fraser, has written, it was not the interest of the large sugar planters to encourage the growth of a free peasant class, but it was emphatically in the interest of the colony to do so.[2]

In British Guiana, with much virgin land available for those who wished to opt out of the plantation economy, there was a bitter war between peasant and planter, in which the latter had the fullest support of the machinery of government, both local and imperial. The first act of the planters after emancipation was the deliberate destruction of the fruit trees and provision grounds, in an effort to make the black man dependent on plantation labour. In 1836 the British Government directed that Crown land was only to be alienated in minimum parcels of a hundred acres, and at a price that would discourage peasant settlement. The freed blacks, however, got together and began to buy abandoned plantations and set up their own villages. The following table of purchases of land between 1838 and 1844 tells its own story:

Plantation North Brook	810,000 (84 workers)
Plantation Friendship	380,000 (500 acres, 168 workers)
Plantation New Orange Nassau	850,000 (500 acres, 128 workers)
Plantation Beterverwagteng	822,000 (300 acres, 88 workers)

The average price of these land investments was over £112 per acre. It at once meant that the workers exhausted all their capital in land, and had no funds to maintain the estates in sound operating condition – either to invest in the new sugar technology or to maintain the costly system of irrigation, drainage and sea defence works which production in British Guiana demanded. Worse still, the communal villages broke down and fragmentation began. But the power of the village movement and the rise of the new peasantry can be seen in the increase of the village population from 15,906 in November 1842 to 49,402 in June 1854. The government thought it was high time to step in to enable the sugar planter to continue his business and to prevent the further spread of communal villages. The principal steps in this policy were as follows:

The 1852 ordinance prohibited the joint purchase of land by more than twenty people;

The 1856 ordinance specified that if more than ten people purchased an estate, the land so held would be partitioned and the individual shares would be subject to compulsory monthly rates to be applied against the repair of roads and bridges and the maintenance of drainage and other vital services;

The 1861 ordinance raised the upset price of Crown lands from $5 to $10 an acre and fixed the minimum parcel at a hundred acres;

Official control of villages by 1862 and 1863 ordinances assessing village rates and making them recoverable at law and 1866 ordinance bringing villages under neutral control of a board of villages with power to create villages and borrow on their behalf.

With all Antigua's big talk about rejecting the apprenticeship proposals, the war of planter versus peasant was as bitter as elsewhere. Emancipation had removed the human degradation of slave status – the worker was no longer driven to work, he could appeal to a magistrate if wronged, his family was safe under his roof; but the roof was not his, nor the land, nor the freedom to avoid the daily routine of plantation labour. He either had to leave Antigua or find another place to live. But Antigua had, from 1700, an act relating to ten-acre lands by which owners of such undeveloped land on which taxes had not been paid were subject to forfeiture unless the arrears were paid. These lands were granted to disbanded soldiers in particular. The aim had been to develop a class of small white farmers. By 1835 most of the ten-acre lands had by right reverted to the Crown; but when the governor proposed settlement of the apprentices, the planters disagreed, all except the editor of the *Antigua Free Press*, who saw that such a move "would create a new

166 | THE BLACKEST THING IN SLAVERY WAS NOT THE BLACK MAN

and necessary order of men among us". By 1842, against the wish of the plantocracy, twenty-seven independent villages had been established, with 1,037 houses and 3,600 inhabitants; while the lieutenant governor was in December 1845 still exhorting, at the direction of the Colonial Office, the workers "for the sake of God, Country, Queen and Freedom to pay respect and continue to cut the canes". Comparing in 1854 the former situation with six thousand workers on properties with no return and nine thousand independent cultivators, the *Antiguan Weekly Times* concluded, "Antigua might indeed be poorer, but most Antiguans might be better off than before."

The lieutenant governor of St Kitts warned the ex-slaves in 1834 that "if any master chooses to say he will not have apprentices, you must not think that will release you from labour, there are other laws that will compel you to work". The principal was the military presence at the Brimstone Hill fortress, with some thousand armed slaves. The ex-slaves, however, vowed to resist apprenticeship and not to give up their houses or provision grounds: "They would give their souls to hell and their bodies to the sharks rather than be bound to work as apprentices."

In British Honduras, where mahogany and logwood replaced sugar, the battle to prevent the emergence of an independent peasantry was as acute as elsewhere, the same combination of imperial government and local bigshot conspiring to keep the small man, white, black, coloured or Amerindian away from mahogany operations. The earlier grants had all been free: in 1817 all unclaimed lands were vested in the Crown. But in 1838, the Colonial Office ordered a price of £1 per acre; at the very time the former apprentices were eligible for grants of Crown land, such grants were declared to be no longer gratuitous, in a colony where the old aristocratic settlers had at least eight to ten mahogany works and, with what the superintendent dubbed "rapacity", owned most of the land and most of the people; in 1835, 3 per cent of the free heads of families owned 40 per cent of the apprenticed labourers, while 81 per cent owned 7 per cent of the apprenticed labourers.

Jamaica after emancipation developed similar policies of seeking to force the freed slaves to continue to work on the lowland sugar plantations, in this case by either ejecting them from their provision grounds, which they had occupied as slaves, or by charging high rents for these grounds. The normal arrangement was one day's wage as weekly rent for the cottage and one day's wage as weekly rent for the use of the provision grounds. Another typical arrangement was to charge rent equal to one day's pay for each inhabitant of the cottage each week. These houses had been built and the ground planted by the former slaves in their spare time. The subtle policy

The Calvary of Free Blacks | 167

was aided by the importance attached by the blacks to their ancestral burial places. But the ex-apprentices, using money saved from the sale of their provisions and their paid labour, as apprentices, proceeded to buy up the land, especially the so-called back lands in the mountainous interior. Their view was that if they paid rent, they were free men and should be allowed to work for whom they chose. One planter observed in 1836: "If the lands in the interior get into the possession of the Negro, goodbye to lowland cultivation, and to any cultivation. You are aware, I dare say, that very many of the apprentices are purchasing their apprenticeship and buying five ten, fifteen, fifty and even a hundred acres." To stop this, the planters tried, without success, to introduce Europeans to the cooler interior mountain districts. The progress of the peasantry can be seen in the increase in freehold settlements under ten acres from 883 acres in 1840 to 20,724 in 1845; in settlements from ten to nineteen acres, an increase from 938 acres to 2,112.

Land hunger was the principal cause of the "Rebellion". A number of peasants sent a petition to the queen early in 1865 complaining of their poverty (due to drought and unemployment) and asking to be allowed to have some of "Her Land" to cultivate on a cooperative basis. The "Queen's letter" in reply on 14 June 1865 reads as follows:

> The prosperity of the labouring Classes, as well as of all other classes, depends, in Jamaica, and in other countries, upon their working for wages, not uncertainly, or capriciously, but steadily and continuously, at the times when their labour is wanted, and for so long as it is wanted; and that if they would use this industry, and thereby render the plantations productive, they would enable the planters to pay them higher wages for the same hours of work than are received by the best field labourers in this country; and, as the cost of the necessaries of life is much less in Jamaica than it is here, they would be enabled, by adding prudence to industry, to lay by an ample provision for seasons of drought and dearth; and they may be assured, that it is from their own industry and prudence, in availing themselves of the means of prospering that are before them, and not from any such schemes as have been suggested to them, that they must look for an improvement in their conditions.

And that: "Her Majesty will regard with interest and satisfaction their advancement through their own merits and efforts."

Thus, the very people who had been brought from Africa as slaves to produce sugar and render the plantations productive were now being told, as free men, that they must continue to produce sugar and nothing but sugar and render the plantations productive as the only source of their

168 | THE BLACKEST THING IN SLAVERY WAS NOT THE BLACK MAN

improvement and the only proof of their merits and efforts. The Caribbean colonies, freed from sugar that was slave-grown, remained under the domination of what were denominated by the Colonial Office "saccharine oligarchs", by a Trinidad newspaper the "saccharine dragon", by British Guiana merchants "saccharine despotism", and by a contemporary Cuban historian "saccharocracy".

For some inexplicable reason the whites and their governments, metropolitan and colonial, thought that agriculture and production meant, and could only mean, sugar. So did Trollope lament the Jamaica planter bemoaning the decline of sugar. So did Carlyle speak of the greater "nobility" of certain crops, and pontificate that "the gods" looked to Jamaica for "things far nobler than pumpkins" – such as spices, he claimed, ignoring the pimento of the Jamaica small settler. In 1859, planters of Hanover parish, claiming that the prosperity of colonial sugar depended on the plantations, pointed with alarm to the amazing growth of small freeholds. The planters continued to mumble demands for "continuous labour", but most of the time did not have full-time work to offer all the year round. As admitted in St Kitts, "Yes, there are labourers, but there is not labour enough." It was this peasant whom Carlyle denounced as Quashee and lambasted for his subsistence economy. It was precisely not a subsistence economy. In Portland, in 1858, there was one freehold property for every five inhabitants; by 1855 there were fifty thousand small proprietors, growing fruit, yams, plantains, breadfrui and sugar for local consumption; ginger, pimento and coffee for export.

Note well – sugar for local consumption. A Jamaica plantation overseer, Beaumont, testified in 1836 before the House of Commons Committee on apprenticeship that he knew of at least twenty-eight sugar plantations practically managed by black men: "I have known estates managed for weeks together entirely by the blacks, and very well managed." But this, of course, was at the sacrifice of the interests of the white power structure. The planters naturally resisted, and turned to the young Scotsmen who were already familiar in the West Indies. For example, Robert Burns just narrowly missed in 1786 going out to Jamaica to take a job as a bookkeeper on a plantation at £30 a year, and many Scotsmen settled in the islands acquired by Britain in 1763. This was just plain vulgar white racism, based on the articulate, major premise that, as Noel Deerr phrases it, in speaking of Java and Hawaii, sugar cultivation required "the directing and driving force of a Nordic element" and coloured labour. It was totally repudiated by the French commission on emancipation, under the directing and driving force of that great radical politician Victor Schoelcher. Opposing

The Calvary of Free Blacks | 169

the frequent demand for the organization of labour as a "second form of slavery", Schoelcher justified the commission's rejection of any form of apprenticeship or compulsory labour for the emancipated slaves as follows:

> I prefer the most confirmed laziness to forced labour even without the whip. From the moment the slaves became free, it was necessary to concede to them the conditions of every free man. It would have been curious philanthropy indeed which, abolishing slave labour as infamous; would have imposed on the freedmen free labour under penalty of forced work. . . . In making men free the Republic could not impose on them laws other than those of common law, it would have been unworthy of it to give them independence with one hand to take it away with the other. Their liberty had to be a reality. In the colonies, as in France, the day of fictions is over. . . . To condemn a man, however black his skin, under whatever pretext, to work more than he wishes, so long as he works enough not to be a charge on anyone or trouble society, that, in our eyes, is a crime against individual liberty, that is to say a mortal offence to humanity.[3]

The problem never arose in Puerto Rico, where, as we have seen, abolition in 1873 found the island with less than thirty thousand slaves in a total population of over 650,000, both white and mulatto. Why the Spanish Government insisted on a three-year period of apprenticeship during which the ex-slaves were required to have a "patron" to clothe and feed them, to reside on the patron's estate and were denied freedom to move from one town to another without the patron's consent – all against the wishes of the majority of Puerto Ricans – remains obscure. There was no problem, as elsewhere, of accommodating the freedmen in the economy without disruption. It was not a plantation economy dedicated to monoculture, that is to say, sugar. In 1899, on the American takeover, the island had 38,170 farms less than a hundred acres in size, embracing 483,395 acres; of these 22,327 farms were less than four acres in size. This compared with 851 farms comprising 1,271,179 acres; representing 2 per cent of the total number of farms, they accounted for 72 per cent of the land devoted to agriculture. Coffee represented 41 per cent of total agricultural production, sugar 15 per cent and food crops 32 per cent. Most important of all, however, 91 per cent of the arable land in Puerto Rico was owner-occupied, as compared with 43 per cent in Cuba, with its pronounced absentee ownership.

In 1859–1860, William G. Sewell, on behalf of the *New York Times*, visited the British West Indian colonies, at the very period when the slavery issue was dominant in the United States, though he hastened to disclaim any intention "to draw from the results of British Emancipation any inference or to point any conclusion favorable or unfavorable to slave labour in the United States". These are some of his first-hand observations on the different colonies:[4]

Barbados: The planting interest of these islands may be characterized as one of unqualified selfishness. . . . It is a fact which speaks volumes, that within the last fifteen years, in spite of the extraordinary price of land and the low rate of wages, the small proprietors of Barbados holding less than five acres have increased from 1,100 to 3,537. . . . This is certainly evidence of industrious habits, and a remarkable contradiction to the prevailing idea that the negro will only work under compulsion. The idea was formed and fostered from the habits of the negro as a slave, his habits as a freeman, developed under a wholesome stimulus and settled by time, are in striking contrast to his habits as a slave. . . . There is very little doubt, and it cannot be intelligently questioned, that Barbados, under the regime, of slavery, never approached her present prosperous condition. . . . I can come to no other conclusion than that the island offers a striking example of the superior economy of the free system.

St Vincent: The returns for 1857 show that no less than 8,209 persons were then living in their own houses built by themselves since emancipation – illustrating, in the most satisfactory manner, the material progress made by the Creole labourers of St Vincent during the last twenty years. More remarkable still is the fact that, within the last twelve years, from ten to twelve thousand acres have been brought under cultivation by small proprietors, owning from one to five acres, and growing arrow-root, provisions, and minor articles for export. The statistical returns further state that there are no paupers in the island – quite sufficient, in my opinion, to disprove the erroneous idea that, unless compelled to work, the negro will lie all day in the sun and live on a piece of sugar-cane. I have seen nothing in the British West Indies that lends any countenance to such a supposition.

Trinidad: Today the number of Trinidadian Creoles attached to sugar and cacao estates is not more than five thousand; and this falling off in the native and natural labouring force has been attributed here, as in other islands – and, I must add, without very much reflection – to the effect of abolition, to the indolence of the negro, and his refusal to work except under compulsion. I am unable to arrive at any such conclusion. I have taken some pains to trace the Creole labourers of Trinidad from the time of emancipation – after they left the estates and dispersed – to the present day, and the great majority of them can, I think, be followed step by step, not downward in the path of idleness and poverty; but upward in the scale of civilization to positions of greater independence. The result which the planters apprehended – namely, that the emancipated labourers would prefer cultivating their own land when land could be bought at a nominal cost – might have been apprehended with equal propriety in any other country in the world where an abundance of rich territory offered the most tempting invitation to settlers.

Antigua: Judged by a commercial or a moral standard, Antigua as a free colony is considerably in advance of Antigua as a slave colony. . . . In 1846 there were in the island sixty-seven villages, containing 3,187 houses and 9,033 inhabitants. All these villages were founded and all those houses built since emancipation. In 1858, after another lapse of twelve years, two thousand additional houses had been built, and the number of village residents had risen to 15,644. . . . The progress made by the people of Antigua since emancipation would certainly justify an extension of their very limited franchise. . . . While agricultural labor in all the British West Indies is the great desideratum, and the cry for immigration is echoed and re-echoed, it is amazing to see how the labor which the planter has within his reach is wasted and frittered away; how the particular population upon which the prosperity of the colonies so utterly depends is neglected; how, by mismanagement and unpardonable blunders of policy, the life of the field laborer has been made so distasteful to the peasant that the possession of half an acre, or the most meagre subsistence and independence, seem to him, in comparison with estate service, the very acme of luxurious enjoyment. Can it be credited that through want of proper medical care the agricultural population of Antigua has been allowed, for twenty years past, to decrease at the rate of a half per cent per annum?

Jamaica: . . . I come to the West Indies imbued with the American idea that African freedom had been a curse to every branch of agricultural and commercial industry. I shall leave these islands overwhelmed with a very opposite conviction; and if I can convey to others anything like a truthful picture of Jamaica life, and of the civil and social condition of the people who are so erroneously supposed, by their indolence and improvidence, to have plunged themselves and their country in hopeless ruin, my task . . . cannot be a profitless one. I hope to be able to show to others as plainly as the conviction has come home to myself, that disaster and misfortune have followed – not emancipation – but the failure to observe those great principles of liberty and justice upon which the foundations of emancipation were solidly laid. The very highest influence has ever been exerted, and is still exerted, to support the old plantocratic dynasty and its feudalisms – things that were meant to die, and ought to have died, as soon as the props of slavery, protection, and other monopolies were removed.

General Observations: I have endeavoured to point out the two paths that lay open to the West Indian Creole after the abolition of slavery. The one was to remain estate serf and make sugar for the planter; the other was to rent or purchase land, and work for estates, if he pleased, but be socially independent of a master's control. I endeavoured to follow these two classes of people in the paths they pursued – the majority, who have become independent, and the minority, who have remained estate laborers – and I have shown that the condition of the former is infinitely above the condition of the latter. Is this anywhere denied? Can anyone say that it was not the lawful right of these people thus to seek, and having found, to cherish their independence? Can anyone say that, by doing so, they wronged themselves, the planters, or the government under which they lived? Can anyone say that they are to blame if by their successful attempts to elevate themselves above the necessitous and precarious career of labour for daily hire, the agricultural field force was weakened, and the production of sugar diminished. . . . Is it any argument against the industry of the laboring classes of America that a large proportion annually become proprietors, and withdraw from service for daily hire? Yet this is precisely what the West Indian Creole has done; this is the charge on which he has been arraigned – this is the crime for which he has been condemned . . . divested of such foreign incumbrances as "defects of African character", and other similar stuff and nonsense, it is simply a land question, with which race and color have nothing to do.

This was a white American speaking, through the prestigious *New York Times*. Did Abraham Lincoln listen to this observer of the results of the abolition of slavery, just one year before the Civil War began on 12 April 1861? Did the British Government listen to this white American observer on Jamaica just five years before the Jamaica Rebellion for land for landless peasants? From their reaction and action, they preferred the estimate of Trollope, the distinguished British novelist, who was in Jamaica in January 1859, perhaps just one year before Sewell. This is what Trollope had to say about Jamaica in his lament of the decline of the plantocracy:

> The first desire of a man in a state of civilization is for property. . . . Without a desire for property, man could make no progress. But the negro has no such desire; no desire strong enough to induce him to labour for that which he wants. In order that he may eat to-day and be clothed tomorrow, he will work, a little; as for anything beyond that, he is content to lie in the sun. . . . These people are a servile race, fitted by nature for the hardest, physical work, and apparently at present fitted for little else. . . . The negro's idea of emancipation was and is emancipation not from slavery but from work. To lie in the sun and eat breadfruit and yams is his idea of being free. . . . Work to them is an exceptional circumstance, as to us may be a spell of fifteen or sixteen hours in the same day.[5]

No one, reading Trollope, would believe that Sewell had reported the emergence of fifty thousand small proprietors, owning on an average three acres each, who, between 1834 and 1859, had exported 86 per cent more logwood, 10 per cent more rustic, eighteen times as much mahogany, and developed a new export trade in coconuts, beeswax, honey and arrowroot. The export of sugar in 1858 was almost as much as in 1841, rum had gone up 60 per cent and pimento had almost tripled, while coffee had declined by 20 per cent and ginger by 60 per cent. The growth of local food production

The Calvary of Free Blacks | 173

was demonstrated by the decline of imports of flour by 25 per cent, of meal by 40 per cent, of corn by 80 per cent and of pork by 40 per cent. The British Government chose to forget the asperity with which its principal officer in the Colonial Office, permanent under-secretary James Stephen – the "Mr Mother Country" of Wakefield's unfriendly gibes – had warned before emancipation of planter ascendancy:

> The deprivation of a mansion or an equipage painful though it may be is hardly to be set against the protracted exclusion from those common advantages of human life under which from the admitted facts of the case the slaves are proved to be labouring. . . . The ultimate end of human society – the security of life, property and reputation – must be preferred to its subordinate ends – the enjoyment of particular franchises.

But Trollope was in the tradition of Thomas Carlyle, the distinguished British essayist who, one year after Mill's *Principles of Political Economy*, Marx's *Communist Manifesto*, and the French abolition of slavery, published in 1849 his infamous essay "Occasional Discourse on the Negro Question", to prove that emancipation had been a blunder and had merely given rise to the "idle Black gentleman . . . rum-bottle in his hand, no breeches on his body, pumpkin at discretion, and the fruitfulest region of the earth going back to jungle around him". That the emancipated blacks refused to work on the sugar plantations but preferred rather to set up as peasant proprietors was precisely what Carlyle was opposed to. "Not a pumpkin, Quashee, not a square yard of soil, till you agree to do the state so many days of service." Slavery, therefore, was abolished, or was being abolished, principally on economic grounds, but except in the French West Indies, the former slave was tied down to the plantation and his master by contract, varying from three years in Puerto Rico to ten years in Suriname, the system lasting as long as thirty years in St Croix. But the more reactionary elements demanded perpetual serfdom, requiring the ex-slave to contribute so many days of labour per year.

The sugar planters of the British West Indies took the lead in proposing radically new measures, going beyond mere legal efforts to prevent, discourage or frustrate the emergence of a black peasantry. They had been through abolition and the termination of apprenticeship, and in 1846 were faced with the worst blow of all, the notice of equalization of the sugar duties in 1852, thus ending their monopoly of the British market. If they were to continue to produce sugar, they must do something drastic. Total British West Indian sugar production, in the years selected, was as follows – the position of Trinidad and British Guiana is compared with older colonies:

Year	1829	1832	1839	1847	1853
British West Indies	209,109	201,926	149,032	170,160	161,370
Trinidad and British Guiana	72,629	70,575	47,113	60,983	72,503
BWI % decline		-4	-25	15	-9
Trinidad and British Guiana % change		-3	-33	25	20
Trinidad and British Guiana as % of BWI	34	35	31	35	45
BWI as % of World Cane			19	6	12

Thus the sugar industry was on the verge of extinction in the smallest islands, had declined catastrophically in Jamaica, was barely holding its own in British Guiana and had increased in Barbados, Antigua and Trinidad, while it was becoming more and more insignificant in relation to world cane production and was obviously not equipped to face the superior science and technology of beet sugar. Trinidad and British Guiana combined contrived to produce more than the beet industry in the world in 1839; by 1847 their production had dropped to 60 per cent of world beet; and by 1853 there was a further decline to less than 40 per cent.

The British West Indian sugar plantocracy demanded a new supply of labour. The first expedient was the transfer of redundant and surplus labour to the smaller Caribbean islands. The superior opportunities of British Guiana and Trinidad produced a curious sideline to the British abolition of the slave trade in an attempt to transfer slaves and domestic servants from the older to the newer Caribbean colonies. Between the years 1808 and 1812, more than 7,500 slaves were imported into Guiana under licence alone, and between 1821 and 1825 a further 1,750 were imported. Between 1813 and 1821 Trinidad received over 3,300 new recruits, of whom nearly 1,100 hailed from Dominica and nearly 1,200 from Grenada.

It was the superior value of slaves and the greater fertility of the soil of Trinidad and Guiana which formed the background to this intercolonial slave trade. The cost of a slave in Barbados or Antigua was only £35 or £40; in Guiana and Trinidad it was from £80 to £90. The relative fertility of Demerara and Barbados, as judged by exports, was in the proportion of four to one. In Demerara it took two hundred days' labour to produce five thousand pounds of sugar, in Barbados four hundred. In the former the sugar was produced without any outlay of capital for manure, in the latter it required 25 per cent of the labour of the plantation. The canes in Trinidad produced saccharine matter in the proportion of 2.5:1 as compared with the

The Calvary of Free Blacks | 175

older islands; the average output of sugar was three hogsheads per slave, as compared with one in the older islands.

The arguments used by the planters in both the new and the old colonies were so specious that this alone should have aroused suspicion. The Greeks were bearing gifts, yet no one seemed to distrust them. The Consolidated Slave Act had insisted that removal should be in the interest of the slave, a direct encouragement to the planter to mumble humanitarianism for his purpose. Mr Boll was anxious – on grounds of humanity of course – to remove his three hundred slaves from Barbados to Trinidad; the rich soil of Trinidad did not need the labour of manuring, and he was eager "by such location to ease these Barbados labourers of the most grievous part of the toil which is employed on sugar plantations". The older colonies, it was argued, were overpopulated and could not feed their Negro population. On barren Antigua the law compelled a greater population to remain than it was capable of supporting, while their better interests called them elsewhere. Thus wrote Mr Charles Shand, "official conservator of the British Colonial interest", emphasizing "not only the sound policy but also the humanity of permitting the free emigration" of Negroes to colonies which were far better able to compete with Brazil than the older colonies. The poor black wretches, pleaded the governor of Trinidad, with a laudable philanthropy matched only by that of the planters in his government, had only six pints of cornmeal per week in the older islands, like Tortola and the lesser islands in its vicinity, the most miserable of all the colonies. In Trinidad, on the other hand, no one starved; a Negro had not only his pig, but half a dozen goats or dogs as well; while the richness and extent of the soil permitted the planters to give the slaves more ground for the cultivation of their own produce. A black could earn in Trinidad in one hour as much as in Tortola in one day. At the same time, so the governor argued, the richness of the soil diminished the labour of the slaves – a most dishonest or stupid argument which elicited from the Colonial Office the comment: "This is not only a *non sequitur*, but I should think a *nusquam sequitur*. Where the soil is rich less labour is required to raise a given amount of produce, but more produce will be raised, not less labour employed."

These arguments did not exhaust the armoury of planter casuistry. At a time when Trinidad cocoa was already beginning to feel the chill blast of Brazilian competition, Governor Woodford was expatiating on the advantages of transferring Negroes from the arduous operations of sugar cultivation in the older islands, to "the labour of this beautiful cultivation (which) is light, easy and comfortable, the Negro being sheltered during the heat of the day under a double shade as cool as it is refreshing, enjoying as much comfort and ease as a labourer in any climate can have a claim to". Not all the planters agreed with him. To some it seemed that to remove a slave from a sugar estate in one colony to a sugar estate in another would not, *ceteris paribus*, make his condition worse. But other things were not equal; there was a vast difference between sugar cultivation in Barbados and the breaking-up of new land for sugar cultivation in Trinidad.

One final plea remains to be considered. Trinidad and Guiana were Crown colonies. The Crown, that is, Parliament in England, made such regulations in the interest of the slaves as it thought fit. Spanish laws were retained, and the Spanish slave code was notoriously milder than the English. A Protector of Slaves was appointed, and the Orders in Council sent out by the mother country did really tend to mitigate some of the worse sufferings as they appeared in the self-governing colonies. Compulsory manumission, too, the purchase by the slave of his freedom, was easier in the Crown colonies. To forbid, therefore, the transfer of slaves to the Crown colonies, planters urged, was to admit that the laws in force were too bad for new slaves whom the planters wished to take there, in which case they were too bad for the slaves already in the Crown colonies. If compulsory manumission was impracticable in the old colonies, it was inconsistent to oppose the removal of slaves from a colony where the Orders in Council were not in force to a colony where they were in full operation. "If the order in council cannot go to the slaves," declared Attorney General Fuller of Trinidad, referring to the refusal of the self-governing colonies to pattern their legislation and reform their system on the Trinidad model, "the slave might be permitted to come to the order in council in Trinidad."

What dominated was the value of slave labour in the various colonies. In Jamaica and Barbados, with adequate supplies of labour, the compensation rate per slave was £19 5s in Jamaica and nearly £20 16s in Barbados. In Trinidad it was over £50 and in British Guiana almost £52; in British Honduras, with its limited slave labour force and its need for workers for the operations of mahogany and logwood, the compensation per slave, the highest for any British colony, was over £53 5s. The smaller Caribbean colonies made as much effort to prevent migration of their workers after apprenticeship as British Guiana and Trinidad made to attract them. "Emigration is our greatest evil," complained the planters of Montserrat. The Sloop Experiment was made to give two guarantees of £1,000 not to remove any workers without official permission. Between 1839 and 1846 the Caribbean migration to Trinidad was as follows: from Antigua, 203; from Montserrat, 2,218; from Nevis, 2,609; and from St Kitts, 963. Between 1839 and 1849 emigration was as follows: to Trinidad, 10,278; to

British Guiana, 7,582; and to Jamaica, 790.[6] Bounties were offered by the governments of Trinidad and British Guiana to immigrants as follows per head: Grenada and Tobago, $6; St Vincent, $8; Barbados, St Lucia, $10; Dominica, $12; St Kitts, Nevis, Montserrat and Antigua, $14; Tortola, $16; United States, $25; Canada and Bahamas, $30.

The second expedient was immigration from America, whether white or black. One curious angle to this post-emancipation situation relates to the former slave owners of the United States rather than the former slaves. British Honduras worked mightily to attract southern slave owners after the Civil War, going so far as to attempt to sell half a million acres at twenty cents an acre when the former Honduran slave was then required to pay $5 an acre. It was openly stated that the aim was to attract not whites with capital, but poor whites – anybody, in fact, to keep the blacks away from the land. The superintendent reported in 1867 that private offers were being made by white bigshots of a hundred acres free to every male adult from the southern states of America or of Anglo-Saxon origin. Similarly, in Brazil, after the civil war, many southern planters emigrated in a vast exodus, so intense that it alarmed the US authorities. Perhaps two to three thousand went, the Brazilian Government paying one-third of the cost of passages and distributing lands on a scale perhaps equalled only by the United States itself. One grant, for rice and sugar, was for half a million square metres. The only result of this migration was the Brazilian town of Vila Rica, as the southerners could not adapt themselves to the colour scheme and classification of Brazil.

The principal sugar planter of Trinidad of the day William Burnley pinned his hopes on North American free blacks and free people of colour. Some black loyalists of the war of 1812 with Britain had been sent to Trinidad and settled in companies in villages in South Trinidad; by 1842, 923 had been settled. To Burnley, squatting was an obsession; he was determined to stop sale of lands in small plots. He was satisfied that Trinidad could be cultivated to the mountaintops, and that with capital from the United Kingdom and an industrious and docile labour force, based on a thousand immigrants a year, Trinidad could drive Cuban sugar from the market and provide all Britain's needs. Becoming virtually an official agent in the United States, he excited false hopes and antagonized Trinidad public opinion, hinting at jobs in the public service and homestead grants of two acres of Crown land. In 1847, some 1,300 coloured emigrants came from the eastern seaboard, to red-carpet treatment and a public dinner in their honour. But the coloured Americans were not prepared to wield a hoe. They preferred British Guiana to Trinidad, where their skills as craftsmen and mechanics could better be utilized. By 1848 there were only 148 Americans still working on sugar plantations.

A third source of immigrants was Europe; the United Kingdom alone in the decade of the 1840s sent just under 1.7 million people to North America and elsewhere. The West Indian planters tried everywhere. Prussians came from Le Havre in 1840 to Trinidad; one in ten died in four months. Heavy mortality was experienced among Madeirans in Trinidad and British Guiana. Scotsmen went to Trinidad in numbers, running from the enclosures which turned their lands over to sheep; the Scotch overseer living on his saltfish and plantains was a stock figure in mid-nineteenth-century Trinidad – "ungodly Scotchmen", with their Presbyterianism. Trinidad competed with Venezuela for the services of German-Americans from Pennsylvania. No project was too outlandish to use in recruiting drives: someone announced a company in London to build a railway from Port of Spain in Trinidad to Port Royal in Jamaica. Between 1834 and 1849, 4,500 Europeans emigrated to Jamaica, principally from Britain (2,763) and Germany (1,067); 20,530 arrived from Madeira. After emancipation Brazil turned to Europe; between 1890 and 1929 the state of São Paolo received 2.3 million Europeans, principally Italians and Germans.

The West Indies were thus back at square one – they turned to Africa, seeking now not slaves but workers on contract. The principal source of African recruitment was the British naval squadron intercepting slave ships to Brazil and Cuba and taking the slaves to mixed commission courts. The slaves, when freed, were sent to Sierra Leone or to the West Indies. The following figures are instructive for the Liberated African Emigration Scheme; to September 1847 – 36,079, of whom British Guiana 17,169, Trinidad 15,011 and Jamaica 3,899. Between 1847 and 1848, from Sierra Leone 2,319, of whom British Guiana 936, Trinidad 211 and Jamaica 1,204. From St Helena 1,772, mostly to Trinidad. The immigrants were apportioned on the basis of one shipload for every 100,000 cwt of average export of sugar. This worked out at the following ratio: Jamaica, seven; British Guiana, six; Trinidad, four; Grenada, St Lucia and St Vincent, one each; St Kitts and Tobago combined, one. Small wonder that the United States refused to cooperate in British efforts to put down the slave trade on the coast of Africa, which it described as designed "to repair the consequences of the forced emancipation of their slaves".

"The monster is dead. The Negro is free." This was the theme of a mammoth demonstration in Jamaica on 1 August 1833, the date of emancipation. The exultation was premature – only the British Caribbean was involved. The monster of slavery was not dead. Spanish humanitarianism, led by Las

Casas, had sought to emancipate the Amerindian by enslaving the African. Nineteenth-century European humanitarianism sought to emancipate the African by enslaving the Asian. African "nigger" had been substituted for Amerindian attached to the *encomienda*. Now African "nigger" was to be replaced by Asian "coolie". Europe, pouring its millions into the New World and especially the United States, turned to the teeming millions of Asia as the new "mudsill" of society structured on white supremacy. India, China, Japan and the Philippines, in that order, were the new reservoirs of labour: India for the Caribbean economies in general; China, of great importance, for the Caribbean, with particular reference to Cuba, the western United States, Canada and Latin America (principally Mexico and Peru); and Japan for the United States, Canada, Peru and Brazil.

The saga of the abolition of slavery was not without its human element – at least in the British Caribbean. The British seemed to have difficulty in keeping count of all these islands. At any rate, they completely forgot one – Barbuda. Charles II once issued a large grant, at someone's request, to an island called Busse Island. Search as they would, no one has been able to find Busse Island to this day; perhaps it was a part of the lost Atlantis. But Barbuda did exist and still exists; it had been granted to the Codrington family in 1685 for fifty years, with the grant renewed in 1705 for ninety-nine years from that date, Codrington being required to pay to Her Majesty yearly and every year one fat sheep if demanded. Codrington developed Barbuda as a slave-breeding farm for his estate on next-door Antigua. Why could not more cotton be produced in Barbuda, he asked angrily in 1781. His manager was always full of predictions of an anticipated revenue that never seemed to materialize: "Paradise could not be more productive than he made Barbuda to be." In 1805, the grant was renewed for a further fifty years.

But when emancipation came in 1833 the draftsmen of the Abolition Act omitted to mention Barbuda, so completely had its existence been forgotten. What to do? Attach it to Antigua? The Antigua legislature declined the honour. The confusion between views of Barbuda as a private property and as a British colony, and of Barbudans as servants of the Codringtons and colonial citizens of Britain escalated into an international incident in 1847, when a French ship went aground at Barbuda. According to the original charter, the Codringtons had rights to flotsam and jetsam and wrecks, and it was more than a suspicion that vessels used to be lured to the dangerous coasts. What to do? Repossess Barbuda for the Crown? Grant a new lease? Give Barbuda a constitution of its own? Legislate to make Barbuda a part of Antigua? All these options involved action of some sort by Parliament, and no government in Britain would risk the possibility of defeat in Parliament over the fate of Barbuda. To renew the lease for fifty years, as was done in 1854, provided no security. What if a murder was perpetrated in Barbuda? Matters came to a head in 1858 with a riot in Antigua: a Barbudan house was burned down, the crowd destroyed the houses of all Barbudans, the police opened fire, eight people were killed and fourteen wounded, and martial law was declared.

And so the sore festered until 1898, when the Antigua legislature agreed that Barbuda would be a part of the colony. In the course of the long-drawn-out affair, one governor of Antigua saw light at the end of the tunnel. In 1891 he proposed the severance of Barbuda from Antigua and Anguilla from St Kitts, the two joined as a separate colony in his commission, legislated for by the general legislative council of the Leeward Islands and administered by the governor in federal executive council, with a development programme to encourage livestock for export throughout the Caribbean. In the light of later developments with the federal system and the secession of Anguilla, this may not have been a long-lasting solution. But the Colonial Office reply to the proposal most certainly was not a solution. The reply was that the scheme was approved if the governor could find the money needed, £20,000, to buy breeding stock and provide a ship. Was that the end? No way. Barbuda is today seeking to secede from Antigua.

7.

Asiatic Labour

Miscellaneous scraps of humanity.
Lord Hardinge, Viceroy of India, 15 October 1915.

The White Colonies

The issues involved in Asian conscription arose first in Australia with respect to Indian immigrants; the admission of Indians became an issue also in Canada some years later. The question of admission of Chinese and later Japanese then arose first in Australia and New Zealand, and then in Canada. The question of Asian labour in a country dominated by whites arose also in South Africa with the Indians and the Chinese. The United States faced the question of Asian immigration from China, Japan, the Philippines, India – on its west coast in particular. The basic issue in the colonial areas was the right of self-governing white colonies to determine and control their immigration policy.

To turn first to Australia and the issue of Indian immigration: the Australian colonies were then half convict, half free. At the end of 1845 there were twenty-five thousand English convicts in Van Diemen's Land, of whom 17,637 had been sent from 1841 to 1845; so outraged was colonial sentiment that the unofficial members of the legislative council threatened all to resign unless the British Government agreed to pay the total cost of the convict establishment, while some colonists petitioned the queen for the gradual and total abolition of the system. Despite this protest, Britain sent over 394 male and 318 female convicts in 1847. In 1846 a colonial correspondent of the *Times* called on Britain to "abandon at once and for ever the selfish and heinous sin of casting off on infant countries the scum and refuse of our own society". Western Australia was made a penal colony in May 1849; when transportation of convicts ceased in 1868, on the urgent representations of the other Australian colonies, nearly ten thousand convicts had been introduced. In 1850, 36,589 signatures were presented to the legislative council of New South Wales against the transportation of convicts, as compared with 525 in favour; 1,618 convicts had been sent out between June 1849 and April 1850. The British Government was

182 | THE BLACKEST THING IN SLAVERY WAS NOT THE BLACK MAN

adamant: the convict system would be maintained. Australia must be white, but convict. Lord Grey, secretary of state for the colonies, spoke as follows in Parliament in 1850:

> There are at this moment in the Australian Colonies not less than sixty-eight thousand persons upon whom the sentence of transportation has been passed, and who are now living in a state of perfect or qualified freedom, and in general earning their bread by honest industry, but who would have had no resource but to fall back into the commission of crime, if removal had not been made a portion of the punishment of transportation. This would have been not merely a great evil, but I think a great danger when I remember what we have heard of the army of *forcats* now in existence in France, and of the part which they have taken in all the late commotions in that country.

The British Government had powerful support in the country. In respect of similar opposition to the convict system in the Cape of Good Hope, the *Times* advised the white settlers that convicts were better than "dirty, lazy, and thievish Hottentots". The paper wrote on 29 March 1849:

> While ... we recognise the wisdom and public spirit of those who deprecate the perversion of any colony into a mere convict cesspool, we must remind them that England has rights as well as her dependencies, and that, possessing vast tracts of unused and unpeopled territory some thousands of miles off, she will not submit to the shame and cost of maintaining an annual burden of three thousand felons on her own soil.

The British Government was forced to back down. Australia would no longer be a convict settlement.

If convict labour was no longer available, what of other reservoirs? Was Australia to remain white as the United States, depending on European immigrants? Or were Asians to be admitted? The first to be presented for consideration were the Indians. The question of Indian labour was considered in New South Wales in 1839. The proposal was opposed because of the "paganism" and "colour" of the immigration suggested: "It would be an alien element, and a servile one as well." A committee headed by the Bishop of Australia reported in 1841: "Whatever defects may be chargeable upon the state of society here, it is at present so unmixed in its composition as to promise to supply materials for the fabrication of a social and political state corresponding with that of the country from which it derives its origin." A few Indian immigrants had been privately introduced, and formal requests had been made in 1841, and again in 1843, for the expenditure of public funds on their introduction. But the Colonial

Office was determined to keep Australia white. It was James Stephen, the personification of trusteeship, the active advocate of the emancipation of the African slaves, who gave the coup de grace to the proposal in language that must be embarrassing to all those in Britain and elsewhere who sing paeans to the humanitarian movement to which Stephen belonged. In a minute of 17 July 1841, Stephen wrote:

> To expedite the augmentation of wealth in New South Wales by introducing the black race there from India would in my mind, be one of the most unreasonable preferences of the present to the future, which it would be possible to make. There is not on the globe a social interest more momentous – if we look forward for five or six generations – than that of reserving the Continent of New Holland as a place where the English race shall be spread from sea to sea unmixed with any lower caste. As we now regret the folly of our ancestors in colonizing North America from Africa, so would our posterity have to censure us if we should colonize Australia from India.

Stephen's views prevailed. The secretary of state for the colonies, Lord Glenelg, emphasized that the use of "coolie" labour would bring rural work in the colony into disrepute; "It would consequently check the emigration of the British agricultural classes." Molesworth, one of the prominent colonial reformers, described indentured labour as "one of the innumerable descriptions of slavery to which, under various appellations designed to conceal its nature, colonists have had recourse when suffering under pressure of a want of labour".

Then came the discovery of gold and the emergence of sugar. The labour question became the dominant issue – whether Kanakas from the South Sea Islands, or Indians or Chinese or even Japanese. The labour question was the principal catalyst in the emergence of Australian nationhood, organized into a federation, with its White Australia policy. All non-whites were to be kept out – whether British subjects or not, whether Indians or emancipated West Indians or Chinese under British rule, all within the British Empire, or Chinese or Japanese outside the British Empire. Said one of the Labour papers, the *Sydney Bulletin* of 27 October 1900: "We must keep out the British nigger and the British Chinaman just as much as the non-British ones. They are just as black and just as yellow as the other sort." In the grandiloquent demagogy of Victoria's minister of education, an ex-Oxford don, "We are guarding the last part of the world in which the higher races, can live and increase freely, for the higher civilisation."

The White Australia policy had powerful repercussions, both domestic and international. On the domestic front, the colonies were divided, with some

184 | THE BLACKEST THING IN SLAVERY WAS NOT THE BLACK MAN

interests wanting Indian immigrants and some opting for black Kanaka labour. The government of India, British-controlled, always sympathetic to white Britishers anywhere, still had to make some pretence of safeguarding the interest of the Indian people. It did this by insisting upon two safeguards in respect of Indian immigrants: the recipient colonial government must be responsible for their welfare in general; it must appoint a Protector of Indians thoroughly acquainted with the language, social customs and character of the "coolies", the Protector being responsible to the government of India while being paid by the colonial government.

At international level, as far back as 1868 a shrewd French observer had predicted: "Some day a new Monroe Doctrine would prevent old Europe, in the name of the United States of Australia, from setting foot upon a single isle of the Pacific." In their attempts to prohibit Asian immigration, the advocates of the White Australia policy had chafed under their inability to negotiate directly with the governments of China and Japan. When the British pleaded their international commitments to China, a New South Wales spokesman retorted:

> If China has the right to declare at which of her ports alone Europeans might land, Great Britain had the same right, if she saw fit, to declare at what ports in Queensland or Australia Chinese might land. Great Britain might declare by proclamation, subject to these treaty rights, that Chinese should not be at liberty to come to Queensland or New South Wales or any of the gold-producing colonies, and then they would be protected at once, and the treaty would not be broken.

When Britain pleaded her commercial treaty with Japan, Australia declined to adhere, as was her right, to the treaty. Australia claimed that immigration was a question solely for the Australian colonies to decide, and they would decide it for themselves, "utterly irrespective of the views of Downing Street". When once the law permitting landing of immigrants on certain conditions was broken, this was the language of the colony's premier in Parliament:

> If in doing so we have infringed any law, I say that this House is bound in honour to indemnify us, because . . . we have obeyed the higher law of conserving society. Neither for Her Majesty's ships of war, nor for Her Majesty's representative on the spot, nor for the Secretary of State for the Colonies, do we intend to turn aside from our purpose, which is to terminate the landing of Chinese on our shores for ever.

Matters came to a head in 1897 when representatives of the British Empire, including Indian princes in all their dignity and splendour, assembled in

London to do honour to Queen Victoria on the occasion of her diamond jubilee. The British Government took the opportunity to examine and explain frankly the entire question of Indian emigration to the self-governing parts of the empire, with particular reference to the exclusion bills of several Australian colonies, which had not been accepted by the British Government. Spokesman for Britain was the secretary of state for the colonies, Joseph Chamberlain, an ardent imperialist and, protagonist of the then-popular doctrine of the cooperation of the three great Anglo-Saxon powers, Britain and her empire, Germany and America. Chamberlain, in a major speech to the Australian representatives spoke as follows on the exclusion bills:

> I have seen these Bills, and they differ in some respects one from the other, but there is no one of them, except perhaps the Bill which comes to us from Natal, to which we can look with satisfaction. I wish to say that Her Majesty's Government thoroughly appreciate the object nod the needs of the Colonies in dealing with this matter. We quite sympathise with the determination of the white inhabitants of these Colonies, who are in comparatively close proximity to millions and hundreds of millions of Asiatics, that there shall not be an influx of people alien in civilisation, alien in religion, alien in customs, whose influx, moreover, would most seriously interfere with the legitimate rights of the existing labour population. An immigration of that kind must, I quite understand, in the interests of the Colonies, be prevented at all hazards, and we shall not offer any objection to the proposals intended with that object.
>
> We ask you also to bear in mind the traditions of the Empire, which make no distinction in favour of or against race or colour – and to exclude by reason of their colour, or by reason of their race, all Her Majesty's Indian subjects and even all Asiatics, would be an act so offensive to those people that it would be most painful, I am quite certain, to Her Majesty to have to sanction it.

The Colonies in Asia, Africa and the Caribbean

The Indian migration of the nineteenth century was a vast exodus of impoverished peasantry overwhelmed by famine – seven famines in the first half of the nineteenth century (estimated 1.5 million dead), twenty-four famines in the second half of the century (estimated 28.5 million dead), with eighteen of these famines in the last twenty-five years of the century. This movement sent millions of Hindus (with some Moslems also) all over Southeast Asia – Burma, Ceylon, Malaya, Mauritius and Fiji – to many parts of Africa – South Africa, especially Natal, East Africa and Madagascar – and the Caribbean – British, French and Dutch. But for British opposition,

186 | THE BLACKEST THING IN SLAVERY WAS NOT THE BLACK MAN

they would have gone also to Cuba, Brazil and Peru. Peru's request was coldly received in Britain; the Cuban request in 1881 was met with the reply from the viceroy of India that Cuba "would be the last place which we should choose". After they were introduced into East Africa – Kenya, Uganda and Tanganyika – principally in connection with railway construction (at the peak, nineteen thousand Indians were indentured for the Uganda railway), a proposal was put forward in 1893 for the importation of Indian labour for coffee and cocoa plantations in the Niger delta in West Africa. The king of Hawaii in 1883 sought to import Indian women to make up for the imbalance of males in Hawaii. The Dutch wanted Indian "coolies" for – of all places – the Dutch East Indies in 1880. Madagascar called for *coolies hindous* for railway construction in 1902, as did the Sudan in the same year. Both German East Africa and German West Africa toyed with the idea, but were rebuffed by the British Government, as was Southern Rhodesia. Some Indians indentured for railway construction in Natal ended up, after their indenture, working on railways in Mozambique.

Growing sugar (Mauritius, Natal and Fiji), tea (Ceylon), rubber (Malaya) and constructing railways in Africa, these Indian emigrants resulted in substantial Indian minorities in a number of countries by the middle of the twentieth century. The Indian population in Asia in 1946 numbered approximately 2.5 million.

Country	Numbers
Ceylon	732,258
Burma	700,000
Malaya and Singapore	604,508
Fiji	133,941
Mauritius	285,111[1]

The conditions under which this emigration was permitted by the government of India, the colonial governments involved, and the British Government itself were deplorable, to say the least, and fully justified the appellation attached to it generally, "the new slavery". The British novelist Trollope, lyrical as ever where British rule in the West Indies was concerned, had this to say about Indian immigration in 1859 in reference to the West Indies: "These men could not be treated with more tenderness unless they were put separately each under his own glass case with a piece of velvet on which to die. In England we know of no such treatment for field labourers."[2]

Indian indentured immigration was responsible for serious political strains in the Commonwealth between Indians moving aggressively to self-government and independence on the one hand, and the areas of settlement in Asia and Africa which had their own political ambitions on the other hand. India suffered a resounding defeat in Southeast Asia, which had moved or was moving itself to independence. In Burma, where in 1946 there were over 750,000 Indians, less than 4 per cent, of the population, the Burmese, whose capital, Rangoon, was like an Indian city, objected to Indians marrying Burmese girls who might be abandoned when the Indians returned to India. "What use will Home Rule be to us if it is given by the English when the Burmese nation has become half-caste by gradual extinction?" There had been serious anti-Indian riots in 1930, 1938 and 1940, and Burma was adamant that it would no longer be associated with India in the Commonwealth. It separated from India in 1937. Gandhi asked Burma to postpone negotiations on immigration until both India and Burma were free; Burma ignored him.

Nehru, secretary of the All-Indian Congress Committee before independence, presented a paper in 1927 entitled, "A Foreign Policy for India". The paper said in respect of the Indian overseas:

> What is the position of the Indian in foreign countries today? He has gone either as a coolie or as a mercenary soldier on behalf of England . . . a hireling of the exploiter. . . . We thus see that there is no possible place for our country in the British group of nations, and it is idle to talk of India becoming a member of this group. . . . An Indian who goes to other countries must cooperate with the people of that country and aim himself for a position of friendship and service The Indians should cooperate with the Africans and help them, as far as possible, and not claim a special position for themselves.

By 1927 it was Burma and Ceylon calling the tune and there was probably no prospect of a reconciliation. But as for Nehru's view, unfamiliar to most of the Indians overseas, there might still have been time for reconciliation in East Africa. The Citizenship Act of 1948, the Pakistani Residents (Citizenship) Act of 1949 and the Ceylon (Parliamentary Elections) Amendment Act of 1949 settled all the issues from Ceylon's point of view, while Nehru, quite clearly not fully appreciating the gravity of the situation, was still refusing to haggle over bargaining points and still believed that the issues should be resolved by reference to principles; and so the questions outstanding were unresolved by the time of Ceylon's independence, and then they were decided unilaterally by Ceylon.

So we can now turn to the Indians in the Asian Crown colonies. There are two in the Pacific, Fiji and Mauritius – in 1948 Fiji had 125,000 Indians as against 121,000 Fijians; in Mauritius in 1944, there were 265,247

Indians, or over two-thirds of the entire population. Early Indian requests in 1926 for some sort of official Indian presence in Fiji were turned down on the ground that under the terms of the original deed of cession under which the Fijian chiefs accepted allegiance to Queen Victoria it was impossible; so there were three seats for Indians, three for the Fijians, with six for the British. Further, the appointment of an agent of the government of India was undesirable even in the interest of Indians themselves: "It is through their representatives in the legislature and not to the agent of another government that they should look to express their point of view." With independence Fijian nationalism came into its own. Based on the ownership of 98 per cent of the land which had been rendered inalienable, a movement emerged for the repatriation of all Indians.

Matters came to a head when, in 1968, Indians triumphed in the elections over the Fijians. This was reversed in another election in 1972. The seesaw led to two general elections in 1977. In the first, the Indians won. But the overwhelming Indian majority disintegrated into factionalism or communalism – individual rivalry over leadership, and rivalry over language and province of origin. As an Indian analyst has written, "Allegiance to one's subculture, whether grounded in religion, language or province of origin, is more powerful than allegiance to the wider Indian community." The result has been, according to one argument, that Indian disunity has contributed to Fiji's stability. Large-scale Indian emigration has followed, to the United States and Canada in particular.

In Mauritius, Governor Sir Bede Clifford (later to be posted to Trinidad and Tobago to expound the curious philosophy he had developed on the basis of his South African experience) stated bluntly that the whites constituted the indigenous population. The 1948 elections elected eleven Indians (but no Muslims), eight creoles; but, the Colonial Office pointed out, there was no real party alignment in the legislature – "Indian divides against Indian, coloured against coloured."

The ethnic balance appears rather different with independence. The Indian majority is decisive and complete. Little India, Mauritius is called. But the potential for division is there. In a legislature of seventy members, there are thirty-nine Hindus and ten Muslims, and an Indian prime minister presides over a cabinet of whom fourteen are Hindus and one Muslim. Of the sixteen main languages of India recognized by the Indian Constitution, seven are painfully entrenched in Mauritius – Hindi, Urdu, Tamil, Telugu, Marathi, Gujarati and Sanskrit. Hindi has pride of place, but as it has been said, one-quarter of every section of the Hindu community is doing something to foster the study of its particular language. All the

Asiatic Labour | 189

four major religions of the world are present: Hinduism (over half of the population) which all sects and divisions, Islam (one in six), Christianity (more than one in four, spread over different sects) and Buddhism (3 per cent of the population). It is a scene, as one observer notes, in which Christian church music, temple bells, the call of the muezzin and the gongs of the pagoda are heard.

The Caribbean

Trinidad pinned its hopes mainly on Asian immigrants. There one of the principal planters (British) sought to justify it in 1814 as a catalyst in the early extinction of "that baneful system of slavery":

> It may be considered as an axiom, that without a change in the materials of which the population of the island is composed, no beneficial alteration in its actual state can be effected . . . to effect a salutary change a new colony must be introduced, healthy and free, with habits and science ready formed, and sufficiently numerous to stand unsupported and distinct from our present population on its immediate arrival; subjected to a competition with such a vigorous race, the sickly, the expensive system of slavery could never maintain itself. Proprietors of estates would soon discover the advantages of substituting the hired labour of free men for the forced and reluctant service of purchased negroes. In this mode the present vicious system might gradually and without detriment to the West Indian proprietors be finally terminated.

As early as 1838 British Guiana began to experiment with Indian immigrants. The pioneer in this aim to "make us, as far as possible, independent of our negro population" was the sugar planter and former slave owner Gladstone, father of the future prime minister. Indian indentured immigration was nicknamed "the Gladstone slave trade". Gladstone considered that, in stocking his plantations in Guiana, one female to nine or ten males "for cooking and washing is enough".[3] Three hundred and ninety-six immigrants arrived in May 1838 on five-year contracts to work nine to ten hours per day at a daily wage of sixteen cents plus food allowances; the standard daily task in the colony was seven and a half hours and the basic wage thirty-two cents per day. The best commentary on the treatment of the immigrants was the report that two hundred of them had "cut through the bush due east in the hope of reaching Bengal"!

By 1843, 118 of the immigrants had died, a death rate of fifty-nine per thousand. Britain stopped the costly experiment and British Guiana turned to the other British colonies in the Caribbean, Sierra Leone and Madeira – eight thousand immigrants arrived in 1846: 4,300 from Madeira, over 2,700 from the West Indies and 1,100 from Africa. From 1846 to 1848, 24,848 labourers were introduced – 11,025 from India and 10,036 from Madeira. The case for the planters was considerably strengthened when in July 1842 a committee of the House of Commons on the West Indian colonies resolved, inter alia, "that one obvious and most desirable mode of endeavouring to compensate for this diminished supply of labour, is to promote the immigration of a fresh labouring population, to such an extent as to create competition for employment". The French sugar planters put it more precisely: on condition that no account is taken of the former slaves and their descendants.

The Colonial Office had a warning about the effect of Indian immigration. It came from a former permanent under-secretary, who in 1860 was lecturing at Oxford on colonization and colonies. From 1842 to 1872 Mauritius received 352,785 immigrants from India. Its sugar production had more than tripled – from 34,340 tons in 1842 to 122,288 in 1872. Merivale's warning – curious because of the fact that he must have had some share in the permission and assistance granted to the West Indies to recruit labour from the same source – reads as follows:

> In everything but the compulsion and the cruelty, the immigration trade is but a repetition of the slave trade, and the economy of Mauritius resembles that of Cuba. Such a colony is but a great workshop, rather than a miniature state. And, whenever a serious check in its prosperity occurs, in the ordinary cause of commercial vicissitude, it may be that this wealthy community will see cause to envy the far less brilliant but more solid fortunes of such regions as Barbados.

The French Government had resisted all British efforts to abolish the slave trade and to agree to a reciprocal right of search of suspected slave ships by the warships of the two countries. Eventually agreement was reached in a convention of 1861 whereby France agreed to abandon its African emigration in return for British permission for France to recruit Indians in India and transport them to the French colonies. At the end of 1869 there were 9,590 Indians as against 6,462 Africans in Martinique; at the beginning of 1877 the numbers were 11,713 Indians and 6,487 Africans.

Small wonder that the immigration was generally described as "the new slavery". The mortality rate was reminiscent of the Middle Passage. The death toll in Trinidad in the 1850s was alarmingly high – over 5 per cent on one ship, 9 per cent on another, 8 per cent on a third, over 10 per cent on the fourth, 19 per cent on a fifth, 12 per cent on the sixth, 21 per cent on the seventh and nearly 8 per cent on the eighth. These eight ships, between 1852 and 1858, carried 2,661 immigrants: 306 died, a mortality rate of 11.5 per cent.[4] This compared with a mortality rate of less than 2 per cent between 1848 and 1872 among 340,300 British emigrants to Australia, New Zealand and South Africa.

The new immigration differed in one fundamental respect from the old slavery. The planters had purchased their slaves themselves. The new immigration was subsidized by the entire community, that is to say, the emancipated slaves had to pay part of the cost of outside workers deliberately introduced to compete with them and keep down wages – a governor of British Guiana called it, in 1855, "a bonus paid by the community for the production of sugar".

The conventional arrangement was that the sugar planter paid two-thirds of the cost of immigration (including repatriation) and the community one-third, principally in the form of import duties on the essential food and drink requirements of the black population. The cost of immigration to British Guiana was over five times as large in 1862 as in 1851; the total expenditure for the years 1851–1862 was £1.63 million, during which period the immigrant population doubled. To meet this cost, an ordinance of 1855 doubled the duties on pickled beef, pork, fish, beer and soap and raised the excise duty on rum by 12.5 per cent. Where the cost of immigration accounted for 17.7 per cent of total government expenditure between 1855 and 1862, this increased to 19.7 per cent between 1863 and 1869. As a top Colonial Office official admitted in 1873: "The fact remains that one class – receives from taxation imposed upon other classes . . . assistance in carrying on its business. Political Economy must blush for a financial system like that of British Guiana."

Yet in 1874, the British Guiana and Jamaica planters asked that the general taxpayer's contribution should be increased from one-third to one-half. The governor of Jamaica exploded: "One is led almost to the conclusion that no system for the future will be satisfactory to them which does not provide at the public expense for the payment of the estates' weekly wages as well as the whole cost of the introduction of the immigrant to be employed." All at the cost of the emancipated blacks who were denied the land and denigrated as shiftless and lazy – the same people who, as the same governor replied to an audience in Britain which enquired what the blacks were doing, spent their time paying the greater part of the taxes.

The Indian immigrant was normally indentured to a plantation for five years. The terms and conditions of labour were specified in colonial ordinances. The essential features were: a six-day week of nine hours; a wage of twenty-five cents a day; fines or jail for absenteeism; larger fines and larger jail sentences for desertion. The ordinances specified the food rations the employer was to provide for the immigrant during the first twelve months, made provision for plantation hospitals and medical care, and laid down specifications for immigrant housing. The colonial saying was that on well-run plantations, "Every coolie was either at work, in hospital, or in gaol."[5] If this was free labour, it was, to paraphrase Carlyle, freedom plus a constable. As the whip was the discipline of slavery, the jail was the discipline of indenture.

The result was one of the most inefficient systems of labour ever developed. In five years in British Guiana, 31,900 cases related to breaches of immigration ordinances were brought before the magistrates, involving 18 per cent of the indentured population. The 1872 record showed 47 per cent resulted in conviction, 40 per cent withdrawn, 12 per cent acquitted. In Trinidad, from 1909 to 1912, there were 7,899 prosecutions of Indian immigrants: 2,668 for desertion; 1,466 for absence from work without lawful excuse; 1,125 for refusing to begin or finish work; 983 for vagrancy; 603 for neglecting to obey a lawful order; 412 for habitual idleness; 355 for using threatening words to those in authority; 346 for breach of hospital regulations; 271 for refusal to obey a lawful order; 255 for absence from the plantation without leave; 71 for damaging the employer's property; and 52 for persuading immigrants to strike. In respect of 6,777 of these prosecutions, 2,009 immigrants were fined; 1,532 imprisoned; 1,027 convicted and reprimanded or discharged; 1,441 discharged for want of prosecution or lack of evidence. Thus, one in every four immigrants in these three years was fined, and one in every five sent to jail.

In French Guiana in 1875, the man-days lost in hospital were about equal to the man-days worked; each immigrant worked on an average twelve days per month; for every day worked, one was spent in the hospital. In 1895 in Trinidad, for 10,720 immigrants there were 23,688 admissions to hospital. Every immigrant was hospitalized at least twice a year. The loss was estimated at 165,816 man-days. On the records of approximately two thousand indentured immigrants in the period 1892–1895, two out of every three days were worked; the other was lost to the plantation. Eleven per cent of the time was lost through sickness. The immigrant mortality was frightening, reminiscent of the seasoning of the black slaves. Of 11,437 immigrants distributed to plantations in British Guiana from 1845 to 1849, 2,218 died and 2,159 were "unaccounted for" – in other words, they had died. The death rate per thousand reached, in 1861–1863, the astronomical figure of 64.8 per thousand; a decade later it was 34.7. On the largest Trinidad plantation, one out of every six working days was lost through desertion and absence without leave. In British Guiana, of

105,205 immigrants introduced between 1874 and 1898, one out of every eight deserted. After 1864 the law in British Guiana stipulated that an indenture could be extended by twice the length of the period of desertion. The law forbade the immigrant to leave the plantation without a pass from the manager.

The immigrants were exploited throughout. A commission of enquiry in 1876 in British Guiana found that the average number of hours worked in the sugar factory building was half as much more than the legally required unit; field gangs commonly worked from 4 a.m. until midnight, and one case was identified of twenty-three hours of continuous labour. For a parallel one would have to go to the comparable period of African slavery in Cuba. On one plantation wages actually paid were 40 per cent of the legal rate; as the 1870 commission testified, "The ability to contract on equal terms with his employer is not within the reach of the indentured immigrant." Under a British Guiana ordinance of 1868, all wages could be stopped for work badly done or incomplete. Adamson's conclusion about the system of indenture reads as follows: the immigrant was "bound in every important aspect of his existence, physically by the pass system, legally by contract, and economically by the limiting effect of indenture in his ability to bargain freely about wages". The West Indian black had a description for it – "slave coolie".[6] Was all this necessary? According to Adamson, as far as British Guiana is concerned, "the sugar economy could have operated without indenture from as early as 1870". The planters brought in more labour than they really needed – not having to pay its full cost – in order to reduce workers even below the legal wage of twenty-five cents a day.

Science and technology, rather than superior social organization, were the cause of the astonishing triumph of beet. Cane was superior to beet in sucrose content, the percentage being eighteen to ten, but cane involved more manpower than beet, while by improving varieties the sucrose content of the beet steadily increased – from 4 per cent in 1800 to 11 per cent in 1884, to 17 per cent in 1918. Beet became the great school of scientific agriculture – the deep plough, an improved agricultural rotation, higher yields through better varieties, the relationship of livestock rearing, the increase of rural employment, superior factory technology allowing for the centralization of factories. The average production per factory in Germany increased from 679 tons in 1866 to 4,587 tons in 1896. What Germany produced in eleven factories in that year, Barbados produced in 440 factories; what Germany produced in four factories required 140 factories in Jamaica. Four factories in Trinidad and three in British Guiana were needed to produce what one factory did in Germany.

194 | THE BLACKEST THING IN SLAVERY WAS NOT THE BLACK MAN

The British West Indies had been nurtured on dependence on the British market until the sugar duties were equalized in 1852. In the following year, Britain's imports were provided 17 per cent by British cane colonies, 69 per cent by foreign cane areas and 14 per cent by the beet industry. The proportions in 1896 were 10 per cent British cane, 15 per cent foreign cane and 75 per cent beet. The British West Indies turned to the United States. British Guiana, which exported less than 1 per cent of its total exports to the United States between 1838 and 1853, exported to that market 45 per cent between 1898 and 1900. For the same periods exports to the United Kingdom declined from 95 per cent in 1838 to 47 per cent in 1898. The percentage of British Guiana sugar sold in the US market increased from 15 per cent in 1884 to 75 per cent in 1897; by comparison, the British market absorbed 83 per cent in 1884 and 24 per cent in 1897. Trinidad's sugar exports to the United States increased from 51 per cent in the years 1881–1885 to 67 per cent in the years 1886–1890; the figures for the United Kingdom in the same periods were 46 per cent and 32 per cent respectively.

Then came catastrophe – a combination of two forces. The first was the American annexation of Puerto Rico in 1898 and its special status in Cuba, leading to large-scale increase in American capital investment in cane sugar. The second was the increase in American domestic production under protection. Cane sugar production in Louisiana increased from 49,460 short tons in 1840 to 347,701 tons in 1897. By the last decade of the nineteenth century various American states had begun to subsidize their beet sugar industry. From 1,300 tons in 1838, production increased to 40,300 tons in 1897; stimulated by subsidies and the tariff, it would increase progressively until in 1920 it topped the one million mark. The Republican Party's platform in the 1896 presidential election committed the party to "such protection as will lead to the production on American soil of all of the sugar which the American people use, and for which they pay other countries more than $100,000,000 annually". The president of the American Beet Sugar Association, in congressional hearings at the end of 1896, vigorously attacked cheap labour contracts, cheap Asiatic and Hawaiian labour and raw material and the twenty-four-to-forty-eight-cent labour in some cases, and coolie labour in other instances, with which California and Nebraska could not possibly compete.

Much of this was pure propaganda. Louisiana experimented with Chinese contract labour; a description of the Chinese read: "He can't plow, he can't run a cultivator, he can't steer a mule, but otherwise, his performances are admirable." Texas turned to convict labour: "successful convict farming on a large scale", as it was described, involving 2,300 in all, at a cost of $14 per month each to the state. The black sharecropper was gradually superseded by the wage labourer; the monthly wage in 1867 was $9 with rations and $14–$15 without rations. A survey in 1911 of Louisiana cane plantations with a labour force of more than five thousand showed that 52 per cent received a daily wage of less than ninety cents; average annual earnings of black workers rarely exceeded $2.40. A survey in 1937 of resident labour families showed that three out of four reported a gross cash income of from $250 to $500; but 7 per cent reported less than $250. By 1905, after an immigration convention, Louisiana turned to Puerto Rico and Italy and called for the "docile", "industrious", "submissive" Filipino.

In 1911, the British Beet Sugar Council, comparing beet and cane, exulted as follows over the former:

> Whenever you see a success of cane sugar production, you will notice it a blight on everything else. You will find the employees in the field and factory ignorant, degraded, poorly clothed and fed, and with no social advantages whatever. A beet sugar factory presents an entirely different picture. You will find every convenience of a prosperous civilised community and that it has attracted to itself a busy centre endowed with all modern improvements. . . . To the district come all the social and educational advantages that accrue to closer association of the population.

The reality was otherwise. European labour in beet sugar in the early twentieth century was paid twenty-five cents a day in Russia, thirty-six in Denmark, forty-five in Hungary and forty-seven in Germany. Not only was the Russian beet industry based largely on the labour of serfs, the nobles had virtually unlimited recourse to state funds for mortgages on their serfs. In 1859 seven million serfs were mortgaged, two out of every three in the country, and the money owed to the state was 425 million roubles; in some cases, the nobles had up to thirty-seven years to repay. With all of this, Russian refinery yields averaged three to four pounds of sugar per hundred pounds of beets in mid-century, as compared with a yield of five to six in Germany and France. American capital investments in cane sugar in Cuba and Puerto Rico would be based on cheap labour, including, in the case of Cuba, cheap black labour imported from Haiti and Jamaica. The American beet industry came to depend on Mexican contract labour, which was receiving, as late as 1935, an average annual income per family of $340.

The British West Indian sugar planters – except in Trinidad and British Guiana – failed because they did not keep up with the progress of science and technology. The steam engine on a Cuban central or the diffusion process in a beet sugar factory were up against the competition of the windmill in the older British colonies producing brown sugar. The steam plough came to Antigua only in 1863. The railway was rejected in favour of the familiar donkey cart, or black man's steed. The absence of central factories with modern equipment meant that Antigua required 13.37 tons of cane to make one ton of sugar, instead of ten tons. Barbados suffered a loss of 43 per cent in total production; only 75 per cent of the sucrose in the juice was extracted. In 1870 the process of diffusion was installed in only one factory in Trinidad, as compared with fifty-two beet factories in Austria and thirty-six in Germany. If Trinidad and British Guiana were more modern in outlook and methods than the older colonies, they paid a high price for this – an increase in absentee ownership. In 1870 in British Guiana, fifteen plantations were wholly or partly owned by resident proprietors, eighty-five by absentees and thirty-five by colonists who were merchants, attorneys or managers of other plantations. The percentage of absentee ownership increased from 77.7 per cent in 1872 to 83.5 per cent in 1884. By 1890, sixteen of the twenty resident planters then surviving were partners of absentees. By 1904 the four large absentee companies, led by Booker Bros McConnell and Co., controlled almost 75 per cent of the British Guiana sugar economy. Booker alone, with over one-quarter, was on the road to being able to boast that British Guiana had become Booker's Guiana. In Trinidad in 1896, absentees owned thirty-six of the fifty-six sugar plantations; the two largest absentees accounted for thirteen, nearly one-quarter of the whole.

Thus the British West Indian sugar industry was in all essential particulars a British industry, supported by the British Government, protected by a colonial government dominated by agents of the absentee British capitalists, dependent on immigration of Indian workers whose cost was to a large extent paid for by the black taxpayers. Britain took care of her own, always with the reservation that Britain's free trade policy was not affected. It was estimated that Britain, in the thirteen years before 1883, gained £28 million from cheap beet sugar produced under the European bounty system. The price of unrefined sugar fell by half between 1890 and 1800; British per-capita consumption increased from sixty-eight to eighty-three pounds.

The British Government did all it possibly could to hasten the impending bankruptcy. The chief weapon was the Encumbered Estates Act of 1854; ostensibly to help distressed planters, the act gave priority to English creditors, especially with its emphasis on the consignee's lien – debts to merchants took precedence over even earthquake loans. West Indian estates changed hands for a song; of thirty-two sold in Jamaica, at a time when

168 had been abandoned, the price ranged from £100 for a hundred acres to £4,500 for 2,388 acres. An Antigua estate of 161 acres, with encumbrances of £27,000, sold for £700. Judicial proceedings in England rather than the West Indies facilitated this; British excuses were the slowness of West Indian courts and the high charges of West Indian lawyers. Such sales facilitated concentration in fewer hands; in Jamaica twelve estates were sold to one person, nine to another, in Tobago seventeen to one person. A British Royal Commission in 1882 indicted the Encumbered Estates Court (to which the West India Committee in London had contributed £200) for its recognition of the priority of the consignee's lien: "There was no express law by which a person furnishing an advance for supplies had any lien on the corpus of the estate itself, and furthermore to assert that it had priority over other mortgages and claims on an estate was definitely not recognised by any law of the British West Indies."

The upshot of it all: Britain had never had it so good. If Germany and other countries in Europe taxed their population to give the British consumer sugar at a cheap price, why complain? asked the secretary of state for the colonies. In England in 1876: "The natural market of the West Indies was America, not Europe," "the great boon of cheap sugar" was the gift of "cosmopolitan benevolence", and, in the view of the Board of Trade, it "outweighed any disadvantage caused to a minor interest supplying but 178,376 tons of the total 931,168 tons consumed in the United Kingdom" in 1880. A select committee of 1879 had unctuously envisaged the abandonment of sugar cultivation in the West Indies, with half of the production disappearing in ten years. If, as the German beet interests explained in 1884, their object was not to give Britain cheap sugar but to ruin the West Indian sugar industry and thus obtain a monopoly and raise the price of sugar at will, unless they were referring to Cuba, then they were flogging a dead horse. Britain would not interfere to penalize the beet sugar industry for giving subsidized railway rates to sugar growers, for, after all, West Indian production was based on subsidized indentured labour, while Britain was not sure that Canada would not jump on the beet bandwagon.[7]

Ultimately we are all dead! So too was indentured immigration, but not before 1917, twenty years later. Was the immigration reduced? In the twenty years after 1897 (the last three years being years of war), the immigrants into British Guiana totalled 45,348 as against 85,937 in the twenty years before 1897 – a reduction by one-half. The figure for Trinidad is a reduction from 49,110 to 38,513, a reduction of about a quarter. For both colonies, therefore, where eight had come before 1897, five came after 1897. The annual average of importation was still 2,260 in British Guiana

198 | THE BLACKEST THING IN SLAVERY WAS NOT THE BLACK MAN

and 1,925 in Trinidad in the years 1897–1917. The planters were dominated by the obsession which one in Demerara thus expressed to Trollope: "Give me my heart's desire of coolies and we will supply the world with sugar."[8]

But what the West Indian governments would not do on grounds of economic policy they had to concede because of financial stringency. The cost of repatriation of the indentured immigrants became increasingly intolerable. One of every four immigrants to Trinidad and British Guiana returned to India, involving five free passages for four immigrants. In some years the number of departures exceeded the number of arrivals. Reindenture for another five-year term was not popular, amounting to six out of every hundred in British Guiana from 1874 to 1895. To induce the Indians to remain after indenture, the governments began to make grants of land: 844 grants totalling thirty-two thousand acres in British Guiana between 1891 and 1913. Land distribution in Trinidad, whether grant or sale, totalled fifty-four thousand acres from 1885 to 1895 and from 1902 to 1912. The stone which the builders rejected in 1841 where the black ex-slave was concerned; the same was made the head of the corner where the ex-indentured Indian immigrant was involved. Worst of all, from the planter's point of view, the Indian small farmer began to grow cane for sale to the central factory. In 1896, a total of 75,262 tons of cane was purchased from 3,712 small farmers in Trinidad.

While this was going on, and indentured labour continued to be imported with public subsidy to prop up a dying industry, the black workers were emigrating in large numbers – especially to build the Panama Canal, but also to work on the Costa Rican banana plantations and, of all things, the Cuban sugar plantation. The principal colonies involved were Jamaica, where the government would not make land available, and Barbados, where all the land was already taken up by plantations. It was against this background that Dr de Boissière, a local white of French extraction in Trinidad, asserted in 1890 that such labour as Trinidad still needed should have been sought not in India but in Barbados. He said: "History will pen a terrible indictment of neglect against the administration of the last thirty years for not having organised a system by which this natural and free Immigration, involving as it does scarcely any cost, would have been taken advantage of, and efforts made to retain it."

So there it was. By 1897, sixty years after the termination of apprenticeship, we at last are told that sugar ought not to have been given priority over food crops, the plantation ought not to have been pampered at the expense of the peasantry, semi-slave labour should not have been emphasized over free labour, immigration from India should not have been subsidized by the general taxpayer, such immigrants as were needed should not have come from Asia but from the West Indies.

There was still a final condemnation of the system of indentured immigration. It came from a Trinidad lawyer, one of her ablest sons, white, who became mayor of the capital city of Port of Spain. Alcazar testified as follows to the Royal Commission:

> It is recognised that by making him brutally callous to the rights of others and blunting his moral sense generally, slavery does at least as much harm to the slave-owner as to the slave himself. Now, however akin to slavery the coolie's indenture may seem, it has on him no marked degrading effect, because what above all demoralizes the slave is the hopelessness of his lot, while the coolie knows that at the end of his five years he must be set free. On his employer, however, the effect is much more similar to that of slavery, for if one-fifth of his bondsmen are set free every year, a fresh fifth at once take their place. Its effect on the employer, the system is not very different from slavery, with the gaol substituted for the whip. And one of the worst consequences of Indian immigration in Trinidad has been to keep its educated classes at the moral level of slave owners.[9]

How Did the British See Indians?

Who were these Asian immigrants? It was not possible for the early Europeans – whether Portuguese, Dutch, English or French – to dismiss them, as they had dismissed the Africans, as images of lower hemisphere, without arts or manufactures or civilization. The history of ancient India was not unknown. It was generally understood that the civilization that developed along the Indus belonged with its counterparts, on the Tigris-Euphrates in what is now known as Iraq and along the Nile, to the first great civilizations of the world. By 2300 BC two great cities had emerged as centres of the Indus civilization – Mohenjo-Daro and Harappa, with wide streets, evidence of civil planning; substantial houses, some with ballrooms; copper and bronze tools. We also know that the inhabitants of the Indus valley could write, and the raised citadels that dominated both cities suggest a highly centralized government, probably a theocracy. The use of uniform standards of weight and length, among other evidence, suggests, as one specialist has claimed, "the vastest political experiment before the advent of the Roman Empire".

How did the British see these Hindus? To the conquistador, Warren Hastings, "the Hindu appears as being nearly limited to mere animal freedoms and even in them indifferent". An Anti-Slavery Society pamphlet of 1841 condemned the "idolatrous and sensual services of the Hindu temples". The *Spectator* in 1866 spoke of that "strange pit full of jewels, rags, and filth, of gleaming thoughts, and morbid fears, and horrid instincts – the Hindoo mind". In the eyes of the Church Missionary Society, the Hindu festival of Holi was "abominable . . . yearly carnival of the polluted Hindus, during which they practise abominations such as may be supposed to be acceptable to the demon of lust".

The British differentiated between Aryans and the Dravidians. The Aryans, Caucasian, approximated European standards, not least those of beauty, and Britishers understood Brahmin pride in their light complexion, the result of their "splendid Aryan or Indo-Germanic stock". The Dravidians were despised as black, ape-like, woolly-haired, thick-lipped and "noseless"; Krishna, the god with a black skin, was regarded as the god of the "lower orders". They were regarded as the most inferior of the Indian peoples, whose kin were to be found in Africa, the Malay Peninsula and elsewhere. A writer in the *Contemporary Review* in 1901 said: "To this black race, passionate, magnetic, of wild imaginings, we must trace every lurid and demoniac element in the beliefs of India. This is their contribution to the common sun; a contribution fitting in the kin of the African Voodoo, the Australian cannibal, the Papuan head-hunter." Another English writer described the Dravidians as "an inferior type of human being, for the most part dark or black-skinned".

The essence of the Victorian attitude to Indian society was the superiority of the European. The president of the London Ethnological Society, John Crawford, writing in the 1860s, dismissed as absurd the notion that the Hindu and Europeans were of the same race. He justified this on the ground that the European surpassed the Hindu in brainpower, and was his superior in intellect, taste, invention, imagination, enterprise and moral sense. It reads strangely like Jefferson's doctrine of white superiority over black a century before.[10]

It followed logically from this, in the hands of Kipling, that there must be no miscegenation: "A man should, whatever happens, keep to his own caste, race and breed. Let the White go to the White and the Black to the Black." Viscount Bryce went the whole hog: apartheid. Expatiating on the control of India by so few European civilians, maintaining "peace and order on an immense population standing on a lower plane of civilization" (shades of Azurara!), on principles of strict justice, Bryce concluded: "The existence of a system securing these benefits is compatible with an absolute separation between the rulers and the ruled."

The Indian Mutiny of 1857, savagely suppressed, made the British very angry indeed. Here is one account two years later:

> It used to be said of the Hindoos that they were such a mild, amicable, and gentle race. . . . But what is the disclosure? That greater liars do not exist in the world than the Hindoos; that you cannot always trust them out of sight; that they are deceptive; and we have seen by recent events such outbursts of fanaticism, cruelty, bloodshed, and crime, that we wonder how any that knew them thirty years ago could have given them such and so splendid a character.

Especially among the military, during and after the mutiny, the vituperative epithet "nigger" was frequently heard. As one of India's journalists put it, "to the great unwashed abroad today, we are simply niggers – without past; perhaps without future. They do not choose to know us". It is not surprising that these views should have been echoed in the sugar colonies. A Trinidad chronicler described the Indians as liars, filthy in their habits, lazy and addicted to pilfering. The governor himself who said in 1848 that a race had been freed but a society had not been formed, Lord Harris, has given us this appraisal of the Indians and the Africans for good measure:

> The only independence which they would desire is idleness, according to their different tastes in the enjoyment of it; and the higher motives which actuate the European labourer . . . that to be industrious is a duty and a virtue; that to be independent in circumstances, whatever his station, raises a man in the moral scale amongst his race; and that his ability to perform his duties as a citizen, and, we may add, as a Christian, is increased by it. These, and such motives as these, are unknown to the fatalist worshippers of Mahomet and Brahma, and to the savages who go by the names of liberated Africans.
>
> After having given my best consideration to the subject, it appears to me that, in the first place, the immigrants must pass through an initiatory process; they are not, neither Africans nor Coolies, fit to be placed in a position which the labourers of civilized countries may at once occupy. They must be treated like children – and wayward ones, too; the former, from the utterly savage state in which they arrive; the latter from their habits and religion.[11]

Some features of Indian indentured immigration require special mention. The first was as it affected the Indians themselves. The 1870 commission of enquiry in British Guiana was particularly savage on this point: the system left the Indian no alternative but reindenture: "There is no provision for settling people on the soil and no trade or special calling can be said to be open to them. The reindenturing coolie has only once in his Industrial

202 | THE BLACKEST THING IN SLAVERY WAS NOT THE BLACK MAN

Residence of ten years the opportunity of acting and judging as a free man." Desertion was so widespread that often the whole plantation labour force was marked as absent. The commission emphasized: "By this means a technical offence was every day laid up in store for every immigrant who behaved badly." All the cards were stacked against the immigrant. His supposed protector was demoted in Guiana to the status of an office boy of the governor. Managers bringing cases against immigrants were, as justices of the peace, allowed to sit on the bench even during the trials of their own cases; the commission rejected proposals to correct this, arguing that "it is carrying a little too far the doctrine that all men are equal before the law to object to any customary arrangements whereby, in a crowded, ill ventilated court room, under a tropical sun, the few Europeans present are exempted from the necessity of standing close packed among a crowd of Asiatics".

The second feature deserving special mention is racism. Indian indentured immigration was openly designed to introduce an ethnic difference calculated to keep the labour force divided and the races separate. In Jamaica it was fully recognized by the Colonial Office that a large part of the black population was opposed to Indian immigration as financially burdensome and reducing the prospects of black employment: "The immigration system could not long survive the introduction of representative legislation into this island." The popular view among the agricultural societies was that the money voted for immigration should be spent, instead, on purchasing factory and field equipment. The council of 1888 declined to consider the renewal of Indian immigration unless the whole cost was thrown onto the planter. In British Guiana after 1879 there was serious unemployment, and a steady pressure on wages had become a permanent feature of the economy. From the inception of the system, Governor Barkly had assessed the safety of the whites as "dependent upon the want of union in the different races of labourers, and I should be glad to see more Madeiranese and, if possible, Chinese coming in; the coolies too would always hold by the whites . . . The Planters . . . look upon the Portuguese and coolies as their friends in any struggle which might take place". The 1870 commission stressed the mutual tendency of each race to despise the other – the Indian because he considered the black not so highly civilized, the black because the Indian was so immensely inferior to him in physical strength. There would never be much danger of seditious disturbances among the Indians, the commission concluded, so long as large numbers of blacks continued to be employed with them.[12] As one planter put it succinctly to the West Indian Royal Commission of 1897, "If the negroes were troublesome, every coolie on the estate would stand by me. If coolies attacked me, I could with confidence trust my negro friends for keeping me from injury."

It has been well said that "the British anti-slavery movement had become, by the mid-1850s very much a marginal affair, with more than its share of cranks, visionaries, and habitual schematics". Wilberforce thought it enough to dismiss the Africans as men, but "fallen men". Granville Sharp continued to believe that Hindu religion and Hindu law were quite literally the devil's work. James Mill, with a new note of cultural arrogance towards non-European peoples, was extremely unfriendly to the culture of India.

The essential point was that the Indians in the West Indies, however much they kept their religion and their priests, had abandoned the essence of Indianness – the caste system. The most significant characteristics of the Indian caste system were marital exclusiveness; ceremonial cleanliness (to avoid pollution by other castes and maintain food restrictions); economic position; and hereditary caste occupation. But as someone said in Trinidad, the sceptre of the Maharaja Brahmin dwindled to the insignificance of a hoe handle. No one in Trinidad bothered over the fact that the majority of immigrants to El Socorro, say, were the lower castes; for example, 9 per cent were Chamars alone in the 1879–1880 immigration year, and 21 per cent in 1889–1890, it being the greatest possible insult for one Hindu to call another a Chamar, a member of the leather-working caste. The food taboos seem to have been maintained for the most part, especially, in respect of pork; the taboo on beef seems to have been modified, by the toleration of canned beef from Argentina; and chicken and eggs, only slightly less polluting than beef in India, were widely adopted in Trinidad, as well as fish. Indians participated in All Saints, as everyone else. It was their practice to dig their graves to face the Himalayas. Which direction would that be in Trinidad? In effect, the Northern Range became to Indians what in Trinidad the Himalayas were to India.

8.

Black Power

Black is Beautiful.

Stokely Carmichael

Slavery an' freedom
Dey's most de same
No difference hardly
Cep' in de name

The black folk song expressed the mood of the blacks in America at the time the great powers set out to make the world safe for democracy. Some four hundred thousand American blacks served in the armed forces during the struggle, while black civilians at home enthusiastically purchased $250 million worth of bonds and stamps in the Liberty Loan drive. When the blacks set out to help hang the Kaiser, it was no longer true that, as Mr Dooley had once remarked, "the black has many fine qualities. He is joyous, light-hearted, an' aisily lynched". The blacks really had no choice. The Ku Klux Klan, revived after 1915 against blacks, Roman Catholics, Jews, Asians and all foreigners, was particularly emphatic about blacks: "We would not rob the colored population of their right, but we demand that they respect the rights of the white race in whose country they are permitted to reside." The death of Booker T. Washington in 1915, with his counsels of patience and moderation and how to gain white respect, removed one of the greatest obstacles to black militancy, which was essentially left to Du Bois and his National Association for the Advancement of Colored People, founded in 1910.

Due in part to the depredations of the boll weevil in the cotton belt, as well as to the low price of cotton, there was a heavy exodus of blacks from the South to the North in the decade 1910–1920, especially in the years 1916–1918. The black population of Gary, Indiana, increased more than 1,200 per cent in the decade; Chicago's increased by 150 per cent as compared with 21 per cent for the whites. The race riots then intervened. The savage penalties inflicted on the blacks of the Twenty-Fourth Infantry Regiment involved in a riot with white civilians in Houston in 1917 – thirteen executed, forty-seven sentenced to life imprisonment – was a warning to the blacks. The race riot in East St Louis, Illinois, in the same year was an indication that the riots would not be confined to the South. Arising out of the employment of blacks in a factory holding government war contracts, at least forty blacks were killed, hundreds wounded and about a million dollars' worth of property destroyed. This was the preview of the "Red Summer" of 1919, when there were twenty-six race riots in American cities. Whites learned much of the black ghetto in Longview, Texas. White servicemen played a prominent part in the riots in the capital, Washington, DC. The riot in Chicago was even more serious, involving the breakdown of law and order for thirteen days. The result was thirty-eight dead, hundreds injured more than a thousand families (mainly black) homeless. The riots spread far and wide, to Knoxville, Tennessee; Elaine, Arkansas; and Omaha, Nebraska.

This was the American climate which greeted Marcus Garvey, a Jamaican immigrant, who arrived in Harlem on 23 March 1916. He had hoped to meet Booker T. Washington, whom he admired greatly and was later to call "the great Sage of Tuskegee". From Jamaica he had written to Washington, who had, noncommittally, encouraged him to come to America; but Washington died before they could meet. Garvey had already worked on the banana plantations of the United Fruit Company, where he learned at first hand the plight of the black Jamaican worker and understood that the British authorities, indifferent to that plight, could, like all white men, never "regard the life of a black man equal to that of a white man". He had lived in Panama, where he saw the inferior status of black workers constructing the Panama Canal, which was nearing completion. He had seen black workers exploited at work in Ecuador, Nicaragua, Honduras, Colombia and Venezuela. He established contact in London with African and West Indian students, sailors and dock workers, and developed an avid interest in Africa. Washington's *Up from Slavery*, which he discovered in London, had an enormous impact on Garvey and aroused his interest in the blacks of the United States. In Garvey's own words:

> I read *Up from Slavery* by Booker T. Washington, and then my doom – if I may so call it – of being a race leader dawned upon me. . . . I asked: Where is the black man's government? Where is his King and his kingdom? Where is his President, his country, and his ambassador, his army, his navy, his men of big affairs? I could not find them, and then I declared, I will help to make them.[1]

Garvey returned to Jamaica full of plans and ideas of race redemption. He has told us: "My brain was afire", at the possibility of "uniting all the

206 | THE BLACKEST THING IN SLAVERY WAS NOT THE BLACK MAN

Negro peoples of the world into one great body to establish a country and Government absolutely their own"; he was "determined that the black man would not continue to be kicked about by all the other races and nations of the world". His vision was of "a new world of black men, not peons, serfs, dogs and slaves, but a nation of sturdy men making their impress upon civilization and causing a new light to dawn upon the human race". In Jamaica, on 1 August 1914 – the eighty-first anniversary of British emancipation of the slaves – he established an organization with the imposing title "The Universal Negro Improvement and Conservation Association and African Communities League", for the purpose of "drawing the peoples of the race together", recruiting "all people of Negro or African parentage" in a great crusade to rehabilitate the black race and put a stop to "the universal disunity existing among the people of the Negro or African race". The manifesto of the association recited its general objects as follows:

> To establish a Universal Confraternity among the race; to promote the spirit of race pride and love; to reclaim the fallen of the race, to administer to and assist the needy; to assist in civilizing the backward tribes of Africa; to strengthen the imperialism of independent African states; to establish Commissionaires or Agencies in the principal countries of the world for the protection of all Negroes, irrespective of nationality; to promote a conscientious Christian worship among the native tribes of Africa; to establish Universities, Colleges and Secondary Schools for the further education and culture of the boys and girls of the race; to conduct a worldwide commercial and industrial intercourse.[2]

The manifesto was subsequently edited to delete the reference to African imperialism, to substitute "spiritual" for "Christian" worship, and to add as a new object, "to establish a central nation for the race". The motto of the association was "One God! One Aim! One Destiny!" Garvey was designated president and travelling commissioner of the new organization, with headquarters in Kingston, Jamaica. A campaign was publicly launched for the establishment of a Jamaican Tuskegee, with opposition from some of the Jamaican mulattoes. Thus equipped, Garvey arrived in Harlem at the age of twenty-nine to solicit support for his programme of race improvement, to find the American blacks disenchanted, hopelessly frustrated, awaiting their black Moses to take them to the Promised Land.

The effect was instantaneous and electric. Harlem, the black metropolis, lapped up his resplendent uniforms, colourful parades, titles of nobility and grandiose dreams. Said Garvey, "Now we have started to speak, and I am only the forerunner of an awakened Africa that shall never go back to sleep." By 1918 Garvey had his own newspaper, *Negro World*, which claimed a circulation

Black Power | 207

somewhere between sixty thousand and two hundred thousand; one of its strongest points was its refusal to accept advertising for what it regarded as race-degrading items such as skin-whitening and hair-straightening compounds. If Garvey is to be believed, by 1919 the UNIA had more than two million members and thirty branches. He developed his Black Star shipping line. The UNIA headquarters was shifted from Kingston to Harlem, its new auditorium being christened Liberty Hall. The UNIA, through its Negro Factories Corporation, gave tangible evidence of its demands for black cooperative groceries, a restaurant, a steam laundry, a tailoring and dressmaking shop, a millinery store and a publishing house. The UNIA also operated as a fraternal organization, paying sick and death benefits.

The high-water mark of Garveyism was the international convention of 1920, attended by delegates from twenty-five countries. The parade staggered Harlem with its splendour and pageantry – the African Legion in dark blue uniforms with narrow red lines or stripes, the African Motor Corps, the Black Eagle Flying Corps, the Black Cross Nurses dressed in white, the juvenile auxiliary. An estimated audience of twenty-five thousand flocked to Madison Square Garden to hear Garvey, with African tribal chiefs present, with the anthem, "Ethiopia, Thou Land of Our Fathers". The convention drafted the "Declaration of the Rights of the Negro Peoples of the World", enumerating the rights in a series of fifty-four articles covering such topics as political and judicial equality, complete racial self-determination, and a free Africa under a black government; it repudiated the League of Nations. It approved the official colours of the movement, red, black and green – red for the blood of the race, black to symbolize pride in the colour of its skin and green for the promise of a new and better life in Africa. It appointed a provisional president of the African Republic. It created a nobility and bestowed titles – Knights of the Nile, Distinguished Service Order of Ethiopia.

The black man had emerged as a new force in America and the world. Glorying in his ancestry and colour, he was repudiating integration and assimilation. Tired of being three-fifths of a man, he announced his separate identity – equal but separate. "Back to Africa" would no longer be the white man's policy of removing blacks far from the taint of all mixture, it would be a self-repatriation: "We shall march out, yes, as black American citizens, as black British subjects, as black French citizens, as black Italians or as black Spaniards, but we shall march out in answer to the cry of our fathers, who cry out to us for the redemption of our own country, our motherland, Africa." No longer Sambo or Quashee, the white stereotype, the black was a new man; thundered Garvey, "Up, you mighty race, you can accomplish what you will . . . Black men, you were once great; you shall be great again . . . in the new program of building a racial empire of our own in our Motherland", with their own God, black, "the God of Ethiopia, and their own Church, the African Orthodox Church with its Black Holy Trinity, a Black Christ of Sorrow, and a Black Madonna".

Garvey never tired of making explicit his warning to the white man about Africa. A month after the convention, he spoke as follows in Carnegie Hall:

> The negroes of the world say, "We are striking homewards towards Africa to make her the big black republic." And in the making of Africa a big black republic, what is the barrier? The barrier is the white man, and we say to the white man who now dominates Africa that it is to his interest to clear out of Africa now, because we are coming not as in the time of Father Abraham, two hundred thousand strong, but we are coming four hundred million strong, and we mean to retake every square inch of the twelve million square miles of African territory belonging to us by right divine. . . . We are out to get what has belonged to us politically, socially, economically, and in every way. And what fifteen million of us cannot get we will call on four hundred million strong to help us get.

Pride of race based on Mother Africa – that was Garvey's message, that was Garvey's achievement. The distinguished black sociologist Professor Franklin Frazier stressed that Garvey made black people "feel like somebody among whites, people who have said they were nobody". The black Harlem politician Clayton Powell added that Garvey "brought to the Negro people for the first time a sense of pride in being black". Garvey could boast that the blacks of the world were "standing together as one man", and one of the delegates at the UNIA Harlem Convention in 1920 said that "it takes a thousand white men to lick one Negro". Garvey made no bones about it: "The Uncle Tom nigger has got to go, and his place must be taken by the new leader of the Negro race. That man will not be a white man with a black heart, nor a black man with a white heart, but a black man with a black heart." He had no use for the labour movement, where white workers repudiated black and at most tolerated separate black organizations.

But Garvey went much too far. It was one thing to have a strong distrust for any alliance with white labour organizations, quite another thing to tell blacks that the white employer was their best friend and they should accept a lower wage than the white worker. It was one thing to refuse to have anything to do with socialism or communism – "Fundamentally what social difference is there between a white Communist, Republican or Democrat?" – quite another thing to say that "Mussolini copied Fascism from me". It was going too far to congratulate a white president on his racism, saying that "all true Negroes are against social equality", going much too far to meet the Imperial Giant of the Ku Klux Klan, much too far to be lobbied by Germans for aid in securing the removal of black occupation troops in the Rhineland, a catastrophe for all blacks for him at a UNIA convention to call for the ostracism of Du Bois as "an enemy of the black people of the world".

His black American opponents, then and later, opposed West Indian domination of the black American movement: His conviction on grounds of fraud in relation to the sale of UNIA stock and the Black Star Line and his subsequent deportation to Jamaica were greeted enthusiastically by his opponents, but did little to detract from his mass popularity or to affect his political significance in the black man's claim to recognition, equality and respect. His opposition to miscegenation and "bastardy" offended many, but was an essential part of his philosophy of racial pride as an answer to white racism. His proud boast remained, that "the nations of the world are aware that the Negro of yesterday has disappeared from the scene of human activities and his place taken by a new Negro who stands erect, conscious of his manhood rights and fully determined to preserve them at all costs". The process had been completed. The orang-outang of Jefferson and Long, the monkey of Trollope, the faithful spaniel of Froude, had become the *Homo sapiens* of Marcus Garvey.

The Second World War was followed by the independence of a large number of black African states as well as Caribbean states with largely black governments in control. The decade of the 1960s saw the emergence of Castro in Cuba and the guerrilla philosophy of Che Guevara, the huge growth of organized crime in the United States related to gambling, narcotics, prostitution and the highest political connections, the wave of student protests and the wholesale resort to violence in connection with political protest. The key to the decade of alienation and violence was the war in Vietnam, which, in the American vernacular, had to be bombed into the stone age for acquiring a communist government.

The old integration of the National Association for the Advancement of Colored People under white liberal leadership and the non-violent mass action by blacks during the war, to achieve equal opportunities for employment in factories with government contracts, were equally passé in the world unrest of the 1960s. New men, new movements, new goals and new slogans arose to meet the need. The first was Martin Luther King on the civil rights issue, dramatized by his boycott in Montgomery, based on nonviolence and the active association of whites in the campaign. On 13 November 1956, the Supreme Court ruled that bus segregation was a violation of the US Constitution. King's leadership of the civil rights movement culminated in the march on Washington of 27 August 1963 (a tactic which was the innovation of Philip Randolph over twenty years before), when a quarter of a million blacks and whites heard, at the Lincoln Memorial, King's famous "I have a dream" speech, which ended as follows:

> When we allow freedom to ring – when we let it ring from every city and every hamlet, from every state and every city we will be able to speed up that day when all of God's children, black and white men, Jews and Gentiles, Protestants and Catholics, will be able to join hands and sing in the words of the old Negro spiritual, "Free at last, Free at last, great God a-mighty, we are free at last."

King made the non-violent direct action movement respectable; as has been said, he epitomized "conservative militancy", and the Student Nonviolent Coordinating Committee (later to become the Non-Student Violent Non-Coordinating Committee) satirically called him "De Lawd". King did not live to help overcome; he was assassinated in Memphis, Tennessee, on 4 April 1968.

The Rise of Stokely Carmichael

It was on the question of coalitions with whites that Stokely Carmichael, born in Trinidad, who had been made prime minister of the Black Panthers in 1968, broke with them. Carmichael charged the Panthers with being "dogmatic, dishonest, vicious and in collusion with whites. . . . The alliances formed by the party are alliances which I cannot politically agree with, because the history of Africans living in the US has shown that any premature alliance with white radicals has led to complete subversion of blacks by the whites through their direct or indirect control of the black organisation".

The split between Newton and Cleaver, between Newton and Carmichael, has been the dominant feature of the black political situation in America in the past decade. Coming from the National Association for the Advancement of Colored People via Martin Luther King's civil rights struggle, Carmichael was active in the campaign for the registration of voters in April 1965 in Lowndes County, where not a single black out of 12,500 (60 per cent of the population) was entitled to vote. It was in that region that Stokely Carmichael cried out for the world subsequently to hear, echoing a call made a week previously by Adam Clayton Powell at Howard University: "The only way we gonna stop white men from whipping us is to take over. We been saying freedom for six years and we ain't got nothing. What we gonna start saying now is black power."

By this Carmichael meant, as he explained in an article in the *New York Review of Books* in September 1966, "the coming together of black people

Black Power | 211

to elect representatives and to force those representatives to speak to their needs. It does not mean merely putting black faces into office. . . . The power must be that of a community, and emanate from there". Carmichael, including the black ghettoes among the colonies of the United States, opposed integration as speaking "not at all to the problem of poverty, only to the problem of blackness", and as "a subterfuge for the maintenance of white supremacy". Expressing the hope that eventually there would be a coalition between poor blacks and poor whites as "the major internal instrument of change in American society", Carmichael stressed black cooperatives in business and banking as the alternative to black capitalism. His goal was not civil rights but human rights.[3]

By the time he reached London in 1967 Carmichael had expanded his definition of the black ghettoes as colonies of the United States which must be liberated to identify poor black Americans not with poor white Americans, but with the people of the Third World living under colonial states. After his differences with the Black Panthers he abandoned the United States for Africa and went to join the deposed Kwame Nkrumah in Guinea to work for Pan-Africanism as the solution for the American black problem. In an open letter to Carmichael in July 1969, Elridge Cleaver publicly attacked and humiliated him, to the point of accusing him of being an FBI stooge. Cleaver wrote:

> By giving you the position of Prime Minister of the Black Panther Party, we were trying to rescue you from the black bourgeoisie that had latched onto your coattails and was riding you like a mule. Now they have stolen your football and run away for a touchdown. . . . In effect your cry for Black Power has become the grease to ease the black bourgeoisie into the power structure . . . on the international level . . . in the same bag with Papa Doc Duvalier, Joseph Mobutu, and Haile Selassie.

These splits and dissensions in the black movements were widened by the Black Power Conference of 1967 in Newark, which resolved that the conference "initiate a national dialogue on the desirability of partitioning the US into two separate and independent nations, one to be a homeland for white and the other to be a homeland for black Americans".

Mid-twentieth-century Caribbean

It was against this background that the ghetto riots took place. Fanned by the increasing savagery of apartheid in South Africa and Rhodesia, they drew sustenance, especially among the black students, from the popularity of the works and doctrines of Frantz Fanon. Another West Indian, this time from Martinique, a psychiatrist who ended up working for the Algerians in their war of independence, Fanon began his career in the field of political literature with a savage indictment of the effect of colonialism on the ex-slaves, *Black Skin, White Masks*, accusing the emancipated men of a century before of seeking to assimilate themselves to the metropolitan culture.

Fanon's *The Wretched of the Earth* became the classic of dissidents everywhere, especially the dissident and revolutionary blacks. Its particular appeal was the first chapter, "Concerning Violence": he described violence as a "cleansing force".[4] In later years a curious silence enveloped Fanon. The North Vietnamese in particular (but of course the Russians also) have massacred his theory of revolution and the role of the peasantry in that revolution.

Compared with their American counterparts, the blacks in the United Kingdom were fifty years behind. British racism is older and has far deeper roots than is generally thought; the first British exclusion attempt goes back to Queen Elizabeth I, in the middle of the sixteenth century, when she called for removal of the blacks because of food shortages and because they competed with whites for scarce jobs. Similarly, at the end of the eighteenth century, largely under abolitionist pressure, many of the indigent blacks who swarmed in London were taken up and sent out to the new British colony of Sierra Leone. Many old black residents of Britain will not forget the race riots of 1919, especially in Cardiff's "Nigger Town".

The thoughts of Martí notwithstanding, the Cuban blacks had not emerged, between the 1911 revolt and the rise of Castro, as a political force to be reckoned with – a minister here and there, a few senators, a few more representatives in the lower house, a couple of generals, an occasional major. Some blacks achieved prominence in the trade union movement, but seemed to have a special flair for getting themselves assassinated. President Batista was a mulatto with Chinese blood, and the best avenue for public service for Cuba's blacks and mulattoes seemed to be his army and police force – 4,039 blacks and mulattoes to 14,637 whites in the army, 947 black policemen and 5,492 white. A few of Castro's followers in the abortive 1953 revolt were black or mulatto. Castro's only black officer of importance was Almeida. In Thomas's words, "the black population as such never rallied to Castro before 1959". Castro's silence on the issue is particularly strange in the context of black domination of the arts in Cuba – the popular Cuban rhythms; the black musician Brindis de Salas; the mulatto poet Nicolás Guillén; the jungle paintings of Wifredo Lam, half black, half Chinese; the sculpture of the mulatto Ramos Blanco; as well as the *negrismo* and invention of black feelings in the novels of Alejo Carpentier, of French descent, Cuba's greatest novelist. But Castro's ban on racial discrimination in hotels and beaches, and the general improvements, in such areas as land reform, housing, and above all education and the elimination of illiteracy, would help to explain Maurice Zeitlin's findings, in a 1962 survey, that 80 per cent of the blacks were wholly in favour of the revolution as compared with 67 per cent of the whites.

Black Power in the Caribbean originated as a movement of literary protest and expression. Drawing sustenance principally from the independence of Haiti, the literary protest spread to Cuba and then to the French West Indies; the only opposition, so to speak, came from Puerto Rico and the Dominican Republic. The first and most important characteristic of this literary movement was negritude, pride in being black. The word is first used by Aimé Césaire of Martinique in his famous 1939 poem *Cahier d'un retour au pays natal*. It figures prominently also in the poetry of Léon Damas of French Guiana and of President Senghor of Senegal. Césaire's poem, a description of colonial Martinique with its poverty, decay and hopelessness, states the concept emphatically:

> My negritude is not a stone, its deafness thrown up against the
> clamour of the day,
> My negritude is not a pool of dead water on the dead eye of the earth
> My negritude is not a tower nor a cathedral
> It delves into the red flesh of the soil
> It plunges into the burning flesh of the day[5]

Nostalgia for Africa, as the ancestral motherland – what a Haitian poet called "the profound nostalgia of the transplanted ones of Africa" – was the principal feature of negritude. It began with the scientific call of Jean Price-Mars of Haiti, in his 1928 classic *Ainsi Parla l'Oncle*, not to repudiate any part of Haiti's ancestral heritage, which for 80 per cent of the population is a gift from Africa.[6] Starting off vaguely with an Africa as Black Arcadia, with its "racial drum", where the poet can drink blood out of human skulls, the protest against this Africanization of Haitian intellectuals was voiced by Dantès Bellegarde, the minister of education, who had opposed the Americanization of Haitian education: "They don't want to hear about French or even Latin culture. What is good enough for Walloon Belgium, for French Switzerland or French Canada, is not good enough for Haiti. It should therefore set itself the ideal of becoming in the middle of America a small Dahomeyan island, with a Bantu culture and a Congolese religion to entertain Yankee tourists."

Debilitating diseases, malnutrition, disgraceful housing, landlessness of the peasantry and starvation wages – were the norm. In one territory – Barbados – the weekly budget of the worker was less than two dollars, of which seven cents a day went on food; in Puerto Rico it was twenty-three cents a day on food for a family of six. In another territory – Trinidad – every adult over 20 was affected by deficiency diseases, and the working life of the population was reduced by at least one-half between 1900 and 1937. In another territory – Puerto Rico – the incidence of tuberculosis was between three and seven times the rate of such states in the United States as New Mexico, Tennessee, Nevada and Colorado. In another territory – British Guiana – the directors of the sugar company would vote no money to improve the housing of their workers; houses which, as seen in Trinidad, were officially condemned as "indescribable in their lack of elementary needs of decency." In one territory – Trinidad – the profits of the oil industry were four times the wages bill. In one territory – Jamaica – more than half of the total area was comprised in less than 1,400 properties each averaging a thousand acres; while in Barbados, three out of every four holdings were less than one acre. In Puerto Rico, of a quarter of a million workers in agriculture, only one in five owned the land he tilled, and foreign-owned sugar plantations of five hundred acres or more (that is, exceeding the statutory limit) were less than 1 per cent of all farms but occupied one-third of the area included in farms. A South African professor (who would know better?) summed it all up: "A social and economic study of the West Indian islands is necessarily a study of poverty."

Riots and revolts broke out everywhere. The first result was the legalization of trade unions. The second was the birth of political parties. The third was the acceleration of constitution reform in the direction of greater self-government – universal suffrage in the British areas, local and elected governors in Puerto Rico. In 1946 the French West Indians, on their insistence, became assimilated to France as overseas departments. A few years later the Dutch territories became self-governing parts of the tripartite Kingdom of the Netherlands. By the decade of the 1960s independence had arrived, with the independence of Jamaica and Trinidad and Tobago in 1962. There were black governments in the British Caribbean, black deputies and senators in the French Parliament, a few blacks in the Puerto Rican legislature, some blacks and Indians in Suriname.

The Black Power Movement

It is in this soil that Caribbean imitations of the American Black Power Movement have manifested themselves. Before the 1960s Jamaica had been the only Caribbean territory to reflect the Garvey movement and the inspiration of Africa. With the crowning of Haile Selassie in Ethiopia, followed by Italy's Fascist invasion, the Rastafarians emerged in Jamaica into national prominence, claiming that the Ethiopian emperor was the Living God. Their goal was repatriation to Ethiopia, in accordance with what they claimed were biblical prophecies as well as a prophecy of Marcus Garvey. Their general disregard for the ordinary amenities and dress; their refusal to shave and cut their hair – the "dreadlocks" hairstyle; their partiality for marijuana (ganja), to which they attached religious significance, while acclaiming its therapeutical effects; the squalor of the slums in which they congregated; the extent to which criminal elements were able to make use of their existence for their criminal interests; the violence of their language, which is taken from the Bible and especially the Old Testament – all these contrived to make of the Rastafarians a group regarded by police and by citizens as a social menace. The grant of five hundred acres of land by Haile Selassie for the settlement of "Blacks of the West" intensified the repatriation urge, which involved the total repudiation by the Rastafarians of any allegiance to Jamaica and its self-government. An official investigation undertaken by the University of the West Indies at the request of the government of Jamaica in 1960, in urging the government to take the initiative in arranging for emigration to Africa, concluded:

> The general public believes in a stereotype Ras Tafarian, who wears a beard, avoids work, steals, smokes ganja, and is liable to sudden violence. This type exists, but it is a minority. The real danger is that if all Ras Tafarians are treated as if they are like this, more and more will become extremists. What strikes the investigator, on the contrary, is how deeply religious the brethren are. Our meetings with them began and ended with the recitation of psalms and the singing of hymns, and were punctuated by frequent interludes of religious observance. A movement which is so deeply religious need not become a menace to society.

The Ras Tafari cult is unique; it is not seditious. Its adherents have, and should continue to have freedom to preach it. Their demand for freedom of speech and freedom of movement is wholly justifiable.

The Ras Tafari movement, unique to Jamaica, represents the first effective Caribbean repudiation of Europe – after Haiti – and return to the inspiration of Mother Africa. It was the literal expression of what the poets were calling negritude. When Haile Selassie visited Jamaica in 1966, the tumultuous welcome accorded him almost turned into a serious riot.[7]

The Black Power developments in the New World have been complicated by racial and linguistic antagonisms which have developed in various parts of the world, being particularly virulent in the last quarter of a century – in Ceylon against Indians, in Malaysia against Chinese and Indians, in Uganda against Indians and Pakistanis, politico-linguistic problems in India, Quebec and Flanders.

Now for the politico-linguistic problem. First, there is Quebec in Canada. In 1963, the government of Canada appointed a powerful royal commission on bilingualism and biculturalism in an attempt to seek accommodation between the French in Quebec and the English in the rest of Canada, with such smaller minority groups as Ukrainians, Germans, Italians, etc. The two dominant groups are the English and the French, English being the mother tongue of 58 per cent and French the mother tongue of 28 per cent of the population. This, however, has not helped the general situation or abated the demand of the Quebec separationists for secession and the division of Canada into two nations. Most recent developments have included the assumption of special powers by the Canadian Government to cope with what has been called "apprehended insurrection" in Quebec.

This is the world climate in which the Black Power movement in the Caribbean has emerged. On the one hand, drawing its inspiration from the black ghetto in the United States and the various conflicting and divergent protest movements and spokesmen, it is anti-white, especially in the tourist areas – witness the spate of recent murders in St Croix and the popularity of the slogan "tourism is whorism" and the protest against "nations of busboys". On the other hand, with large Indian populations in Guyana, Suriname and Trinidad, the Asian opposition to Indians in Malaysia and Ceylon, the African opposition to Indians in Uganda, have all had a political impact. This has been aggravated, for example, by the recent African-element's call for the introduction of Swahili and Yoruba into the school curriculum. This is in response to Indian demands for the inclusion of Urdu and Hindi.

A full-scale confrontation between the two elements took place in British Guiana in 1964 and has been simmering ever since. Serious and costly riots broke out against the Indian-dominated government of Jagan, who professed to be a Marxist; Jagan charged that the riots were inspired and financed by the United States, in line with its announced policy not to allow another Cuba on its doorstep. The African-dominated government of Burnham emerged after elections and this led to the independence of Guyana, under the Israeli system of proportional representation, and with provision for voting by Guyanese living overseas. In this explosive situation Stokely Carmichael, on an official visit to Guyana in 1970, explicitly stated

Black Power | 217

that Black Power was not something for the Indian population, which must develop its own solution. This naturally aggravated the existing racial antagonism.

The Black Power movement in Trinidad, by contrast and possibly also as a consequence, sought to define "black" as including both Africans and Indians – its slogan, "Indians and Africans unite now", has met with apparently little success so far. Disturbances broke out in 1970, originating in protests against the trials of West Indian students in Canada who had destroyed a computer room at Sir George Williams University, where they alleged racial discrimination. Black American influence was evident throughout – afro hairstyles, dashikis, attacks on the "Establishment" and the "white power structure", designation of the police as "fuzz" and "pigs", rejection of "conventional politics". The disturbances were complicated by an army mutiny when a state of emergency was declared. The protests were then directed against the emergency powers, the detention of the principal agitators, more stringent legislation, against the possession of firearms and to control marches and demonstrations. Casualties were low and property damage not high, despite the frequent resort to Molotov cocktails. Among the more serious aspects of the unrest were demands for the nationalization of oil, sugar and the banks.

The guerrilla has become an integral part of the international scene since the Second World War. But he was not unknown before, as was clear in the Spanish resistance to Bonaparte in the early nineteenth century and Irish resistance to the British Government at the time of the First World War. Since the Second World War the guerrilla has come into prominence, particularly in China with Mao Tse Tung; in Yugoslavia with Tito against Hitler and then against Stalin; in Vietnam, against the French and the Americans; in Cyprus and pre-war Palestine against the British; in Algeria against the French; in Cuba; in the contemporary liberation movement of freedom fighters against former Portuguese colonialism in Africa (Mozambique, Angola, Guinea); Rhodesia and South Africa. Apart from Castro in Cuba, all these guerrilla activities have one thing in common – they developed as an indigenous revolt against colonialism, and owe their success to this fact. One can see this even in the struggle of the Jewish terrorists against the British mandate in Palestine and the Cypriot guerrillas against British refusal to consider the independence of Cyprus. It was only in Cuba that a guerrilla movement succeeded which was not directly aimed at foreign colonialism. But that was merely on the surface, as Cuba before Castro was a notorious sugar colony of the United States, and Batista, who was deposed by Castro, was a mere puppet of the United States. If Castro did not have to fight a foreign power in Cuba before he took power, he had to do it after he took power, with the abortive invasion of the Bay of Pigs, and he still has to face the American naval base in Guantánamo, which Cuba had been forced to concede to the Americans after the First World War.

Notes

Introduction

1. Manuscript of *The Blackest Thing in Slavery Was Not the Black Man*, Eric Williams Memorial Collection (EWMC), file 1,328, chapter 3.

2. Eric Williams, *Forged from the Love of Liberty*, compiled by Paul Sutton (London: Longman Caribbean, 1981).

3. *Revista Inter-Americana*, vol. 3, no. 1 (1973).

4. EWMC, file 657. Williams to André Deutsch and Basil Davidson, 16 March 1973.

5. EWMC, file 1,877. Prime Minister's television interview on Trinidad and Tobago Television with Owen Mathurin, 2 July 1976.

6. EWMC, file 831.

7. J. Alexander, D. Lee, and M. McAllister, "Diaries", *TEXT*, vol 19, no. 1 (April 2015): 4.

8. Ibid., 5.

9. EWMC, file 627.

10. Erica Williams, "My Father", in *Eric Williams, the Man and the Leader*, ed. Ken Boodhoo (Boston, MA: University Press of America, 1986), 6.

11. Ibid., 10.

12. "Nationwide Address" (Port of Spain: Government Printing Office, 1970).

13. Colin Palmer, *Eric Williams and the Making of the Modern Caribbean* (Kingston: Ian Randle, 2006), 246.

14. EWMC, file 158, chapter 11.

15. *Hansard* (Trinidad and Tobago), vol. 18, 280–281.

16. For a more detailed study of the uprising of 1970 see B. Samaroo, "The February Revolution (1970) as a Catalyst for Change in Trinidad and Tobago", in *Black Power in the Caribbean*, ed. Kate Quinn (Gainesville, FL: University Press of Florida, 2014), 97–116.

17. Ken Boodhoo, *The Elusive Eric Williams* (Port of Spain: Prospect Press, 2001), 233.

18. See Hamid Ghany, "Commonwealth Caribbean Presidencies", in *Issues in the Government and Politics of the West Indies*, ed. J. La Guerre (Trinidad: School of Continuing Studies, UWI, 1997).

19. Louis Regis, *The Political Calypso: True Opposition in Trinidad and Tobago 1962–1987* (Kingston: University of the West Indies Press, 1999), 128.

20. Ibid. The other calypso is also taken from this source.

21. S. Ryan, *Eric Williams: The Myth and the Man* (Kingston: University of the West Indies Press, 2009), 726.

22. EWMC, file 627.

23. Ibid.

24. EWMC, folio 630, 1980 diary.

25. EWMC, vol. 158, chapter 11, 417.

26. Ibid., 418.

27. Ibid., 422.

28. EWMC, file 1,326, chapter 1, "Slavery and Racism".

29. EWMC, file 1,339, 857.

30. Ibid., 881.

31. Ibid., 903.

32. Ibid., 909.

Chapter 1. Europe 1492

1. Philip Hitti, *History of the Arabs* (London: Macmillan, 1972 [1937]), 41.

2. Hitti, chapter 27.

3. C. Verlinden, *The Beginnings of Modern Civilization* (New York: Cornell University Press, 1970), 39.

4. Verlinden, 40.

5. J. Hammond, *China, the Land and its People* (London: Macdonald Educational, 1974), 46–47.

6. C. Roth, *A History of the Jews in England* (Oxford: Clarendon Press, 1978), 81.

7. *Las Siete Partidas*, trans. S.P. Scott (Chicago: University of Chicago press, 1931), 980.

8. *Spenser's Faerie Queene*, ed. J.C. Smith (Oxford: Clarendon Press, 1964), vol. 1, book 2, canto 9.

9. G. Freyre, *The Mansions and the Shanties* (London: Weidenfield & Nicolson, 1963), chapter 2.

10. William Atkinson, *A History of Spain and Portugal* (London: Penguin, 1960), 6.

11. Thor Heyerdahl, *The Kon-Tiki Expedition* (London: George Allen and Unwin, 1950).

12. Cited in I. Van Sertima, *They Came before Columbus* (New York: Random House, 1976), 24.

13. Van Sertima, chapter 9.

Chapter 2. The European Exodus

1. This section is based on R. Davis, *The Rise of the Atlantic Economies* (London: Weidenfeld and Nicolson, 1973), chapter 2.

2. *Selected Writings of Bolívar*, ed. H. Bierck (New York: Colonial Press, 1951), vol. 1, 110.

Notes | 221

3. Bierck, vol. 2, 747.

4. *Readings in Latin American Civilization*, ed. B. Keen (Boston, MA: Houghton Mifflin, 1955), 254.

5. Lord Macaulay, *The History of England*, vol. 2 (1831, reprinted by Oxford University Press 1931).

6. Henry George, *The Land Question* (New York: D. Appleton, 1881, reprinted 1941), chapter 8.

7. M. Grant, *The Passing of the Great Race* (New York: Arno Press, 1970 [1916]), 89.

Chapter 3. The Amerindians

1. W. Whitman, *Leaves of Grass* (New York: Modern Library, 1921), 27.

2. M. Leon-Portilla, ed., *The Broken Spears* (Boston: Beacon Press, 1962), 74–76.

3. Alain Gheerbrant, ed., *The Royal Commentaries of the Inca Garcilaso de la Vega* (New York: Orion, 1961), 11–12.

4. Bernal Díaz del Castillo, *The Conquest of New Spain* (New York: Penguin, 1963).

5. Bartolomé de las Casas, *The Tears of the Indies* (New York: Oriole Chapbooks, 1972 [1656]), 176.

6. W.H. Prescott, *The Conquest of Peru* (London: Dent, 1963 [1908]), chapter 7.

7. Keen, 174.

8. Keen, 177.

9. For a full account see G. Stanley, *The Birth of Western Canada* (Toronto: University of Toronto Press, 1960 [1936]), passim.

Chapter 4. African Slavery in the New World

1. E. Long, *The History of Jamaica* (London: T. Lowndes, 1774), vol. 2, book 3, chapter 2.

2. John Newton, "Thoughts upon the African Slave Trade", in *Journal of a Slave Trader*, ed. B. Martin and M. Burrell (London: Epworth Press, 1962 [1788]).

3. P. Curtin, *The Atlantic Slave Trade: A Census* (Madison: University of Wisconsin Press, 1972), 268.

4. W. Rodney, *West Africa and the Slave Trade* (Nairobi: East African Publishing House, 1967), 4.

5. For Jamaica profitability see B. Edwards and W. Young, *The History, Civil and Commercial, of the British Colonies in the West Indies* (London: John Stockdale, 1801), vol. 1, book 2, chapter 5, 236, 237.

6. G.T.F. Raynal, *Histoire Philosophique et Politique des Etablissements et du Commerce des Européens dans les Deux Indes* (Paris: 1951 [1770]), 183, 184.

222 | Notes

Chapter 5. European Christianity and African Slavery

1. Caio Prado, *The Colonial Background to Modern Brazil* (Berkeley, CA: University of California Press, 1971), 321.

2. D.B. Davis, *The Problem of Slavery in the Age of Revolution* (Ithaca, NY: Cornell University Press, 1975), 254.

3. Roger Bastide, *African Civilization in the New World* (New York: Harper and Row, 1971), 138.

4. W.E.B. Du Bois, *The Souls of Black Folk* (Greenwich, CT: Fawcett, 1961 [1903]).

5. Jean Fouchard, *Les Marrons de la Liberté* (Paris: Editions de l'Ecole, 1972), chapter 2.

6. L. Hughes and A. Bontemps, *The Poetry of the Negro* (Garden City, NY: Doubleday, 1970 [1951]), 182.

7. J. Blassingame, *Slave Testimony: Two Centuries of Letters, Speeches, Interviews and Autobiographies* (Baton Rouge: Louisiana University Press, 1977).

Chapter 6. The Calvary of Free Blacks

1. University of Toronto Press, 1970, 192–214.

2. L.M. Fraser, *History of Trinidad* (London: Routledge, 1971 [1896]), vol. 2, 376.

3. V. Schoelcher, *Esclavage et Colonisation* (Paris: Presses Universitaire de France, 1948), 169–170.

4. W.G. Sewell, *The Ordeal of Free Labour in the West Indies* (London: Low, 1862), 38.

5. A. Trollope, *The West Indies and the Spanish Main* (London: Chapman and Hall, 1859).

6. D. Wood, *Trinidad in Transition: The Years after Slavery* (Oxford: Oxford University Press, 1968), 66, 67.

Chapter 7. Asiatic Labour

1. W. Roberts and J. Byrne, "Summary Statistics on Indenture and Associated Migration Affecting the West Indies", *Population Studies*, Vol. 2, no. 1 (1966): 130; H. Tinker, *A New System of Slavery* (London: Oxford University Press, 1974), 380.

2. Trollope, cited in Tinker, 16.

3. Gladstone, cited in Tinker, 63.

4. Mortality rates cited in Tinker, 162, 163.

5. G.W. Des Voeux, *Experiences of a Demerara Magistrate, 1863–1869* (Georgetown, BG: Daily chronicle, 1948), iii, 148.

6. A. Adamson, *Sugar without Slaves* (New Haven, CT: Yale University Press, 1972), 10, 11.

7. R.W. Beachey, *The British West Indian Sugar Industry in the Late 19th Century* (Oxford: Basil Blackwell, 1957), chapter 8.

8. Trollope, *The West Indies and the Spanish Main*, 190.

9. West Indian Royal Commission (Shannon: Irish University Press, 1971 [1898]), appendix C, vol. 12, part 5. 284–285.

10. C. Bolt, *Victorian Attitudes to Race* (London: Routledge and Kegan Paul, 1971), 16.

11. Cited in E. Williams, *History of the People of Trinidad and Tobago* (London: Andre Deutsch, 1964), 111.

12. British Guiana Commission report, cited in Des Voeux.

Chapter 8. Black Power

1. Marcus Garvey, *A Talk with Afro-West Indians: The Negro Race and Its Problems* (Kingston: African Communities League, 1914).

2. For a full account of the UNIA see Tony Martin, *Race First* (London: Greenwood Press, 1976).

3. For an elaboration of Carmichael's views see S. Carmichael and C. Hamilton, *Black Power: The Politics of Liberation in America* (New York: Vintage, 1967).

4. Frantz Fanon, *The Wretched of the Earth* (New York: Grove Weidenfeld, 1963), 73.

5. Aimé Césaire, *L'homme et l'oeuvre* (Paris: Présence Africaine, 1973), 24.

6. Jean Price-Mars, *Ainsi Parla L'Oncle* (New York: Parapsychology Association, 1928), 6,7.

7. J. Owens, *Dread* (Kingston: Sangster, 1976).

Bibliography

Aguirre Beltran, G., *La Población Negra de México, 1519–1810*. Mexico: Ediciones Fuente Cultural, 1946.

Bodard, L., *Green Hell: Massacre of the Brazilian Indians*. New York: Outerbridge and Dienstfrey, 1971.

Bolt, C., *Victorian Attitudes to Race*. London: Routledge and Kegan Paul, 1971.

Campbell, A.A., *St. Thomas Negroes – a Study of Personality and Culture*. Evanston, IL: American Psychological Association, 1943.

Collier, J., *The Indians of the Americas*. New York: W.W. Norton, 1947.

Curtin, Philip, *The Alantic Slave Trade, A Census*. Madison, WI: University of Wisconsin Press, 1969.

Davidson, Basil, *Old Africa Rediscovered*. London: Victor Gollancz, 1959.

———, *Black Mother. Africa: The Years of Trial*. London: Victor Gollancz, 1961.

———, *The African Past: Chronicles from Antiquity to Modern Times*. Boston, MA: Little, Brown, 1964.

De Castro, J., *The Black Book of Hunger*. New York: Funk and Wagnalls, 1967.

Diaz Soler, L.M., *Historia de la Esclavitud Negra en Puerto Rico (1493–1890)*. San Juan, PR: Universidad de Puerto Rico, 1974.

Ellison, M., *Support for Secession: Lancashire and the American Civil War*. Chicago, IL: University of Chicago Press, 1972.

Fernandes, F., *The Negro in Brazilian Society*. New York: Columbia University Press, 1969.

Freyre, G., *The Masters and the Slaves: A Study in the Development of Brazilian Civilization*. New York: Alfred A. Knopf, 1946.

———, *The Portuguese and the Tropics*. Lisbon: Executive Committee for the Commemoration of the Vth Centenary of the Death of Prince Henry the Navigator, 1961.

———, *The Mansions and the Shanties: The Making of Modern Brazil*. New York: Alfred A. Knopf, 1962.

Hanke, L., *The Spanish Struggle for Justice in the Conquest of America*. Philadelphia, PA: University of Pennsylvania Press, 1949.

Jordan, W.D., *White over Black: American Attitudes towards the Negro 1550–1812*. Chapel Hill, NC: University of North Carolina Press, 1968.

Knight, F.W., *Slave Society in Cuba during the Nineteenth Century*. Madison, WI: University of Wisconsin Press,1970.

Masur, G., *Simón Bolívar*. Albuquerque: University of New Mexico Press, 1948.

Prado, C., Jr., *The Colonial Background of Modern Brazil*. Berkeley, CA: University of California Press, 1971.

226 | Bibliography

Price, A.G., *White Settlers in the Tropics*. New York: American Geographical Society of New York, 1939.

Rodney, Walter, *How Britain Underdeveloped Africa*. Dar-es-Salaam: Tanzanian Publishing House, 1972.

Saignes, M.A., *Vida de los Esclavos Negros en Venezuela*. Caracas: Hespérides, 1967.

Segal, R., *The Race War: The World-Wide Conflict of Races*. London: Penguin, 1967.

Swellengrebel, N.H., *Health of White Settlers in Surinam*. Amsterdam: Colonial Institute, 1940.

Weller, J.A., *The East Indian Indenture in Trinidad*. Rio Piedras, PR: Institute of Caribbean Studies, University of Puerto Rico, 1968.

Williams, Eric, *Capitalism and Slavery*. Chapel Hill, NC: University of North Carolina Press, 1944.

————, "Historical Background of Race Relations in the Caribbean", in *Miscelánea de Estudios dedicados a Fernando Ortiz*, Vol. 3, La Habana, 1957.

————, *History of the People of Trinidad and Tobago*. London: André Deutsch, 1964.

————, *British Historians and the West Indies*. London: André Deutsch, 1966.

————, *From Columbus to Castro: The History of the Caribbean 1492–1969*. London: André Deutsch, 1970.

Index

absentee ownership, 196
adultery: Incas, 98–99
Africa/Africans: contract workers
from, 178; European views on,
11–13, 201; homewards towards/
repatriation to, 207–208, 215;
Indian indentureship in, 186;
nostalgia for, 213; number of
slaves exported from, 121–122;
ordeal after emancipation, 12;
racism against, 45–46; religion of,
26, 145–147
African Christianity, 146–147
African Muslims, 145
African slavery/slaves, 32–34,
45–46, 58; abolition of, 161–163;
and Christianity, 138–147, 149;
deference to whites, 151; diet of,
148–149; labour economy of,
122–127; language of, 153–154;
and law, 147–152; opposition to,
132–133; planters' views of, 162,
163; and rights of man, 128–135;
runaway slaves, 150–151, 159–160;
slave as three-fifths of a man, 12,
135–137; slave personality, 152–158;
slaves on, 158–160; suicide, 150;
surnames, 156; syncretism of New
World and, 154–156; in US South,
126–127, 148–149
African slave trade, 115–122;
intercolonial, 174–176
agricultural revolution, 16 17
agriculture: of Amerindians, 96–98;
in Puerto Rico, 169; in US, 127; in
West Indies, post-emancipation,
172–174
Alcazar, Henry, 199
Al-Ghazzali, 40
Almagro, Diego de, 103
Alonso, Juan, 109

Americas: colonial pact, 72–74;
discoveries of Asian art in, 47;
discovery of, 49–54; European
immigration, 55–63; European
immigration after colonial
independence, 81–90; European
society in, 69–72; European state
rivalries in, 63–69; independence
struggles and movements, 74–81;
industries and commodities,
117–118; syncretism of Africanisms
and, 154–156; white man's burden,
113–114
Amerindians, 46–47; British policy
towards, 103; conversion to
Christianity, 105–107; diseases,
112–113; European association of
bestiality with, 11–12; European
destruction of treasures of, 101, 114;
influences of, 91–92; Jefferson's
views and policy towards, 104;
linguistic diversity of, 93; Métis,
111–112; noble savage, 94, 105;
pro-Amerindian movements, 114;
resistance of, 107–112; slavery of,
102, 107; white man's burden,
113–114
ancient civilizations, 21–22, 199
Angola, 120–121, 141
Anguilla, 69, 143, 180
animal power, 38
Antigua, 163, 165–166, 171, 179–180,
196
anti-Semitism, 41
anti-slavery thought, 132–133
apartheid, 12
Apprenticeship Decree of 1840, 149
apprenticeship system, 163–169
Arabs: racism against, 44–45; rise of,
22–23
Arab scholarship: preeminence of, 23

228 | Index

Argentina: immigrants in, 88
Aristotle, 28
Atahualpa, Inca emperor, 65, 95, 96, 109
Augustine, St, 30, 47
Aurobindo, Sri, 3
Australia: Indian immigration to, 182–185; literacy tests for immigrants, 86; penal colony, 181–182; whites-only policy, 18
Aztec, 48, 95–99, 100, 102

Bacon, Francis, 17, 60
Bacon, Roger, 40
Barbados, 68–69, 132; burials in, 71–72; Consolidated Slave Act, 175; independence of, 75; Jews in, 61; post-emancipation, 170; Quakers in, 143; slave laws of, 57; sugar production, 174, 175–176, 196; white society in, 70–71
Barbuda, 179–180
Barkly, Sir Henry, 202
Basil, St, 30
Bastide, Roger, 153
Batista, Fulgencio, 212, 217–218
Becerrillo (dogs of conquistadores), 108
beet sugar, 193–195, 197
Bellegarde, Dantès, 213
Benezet, Anthony, 144
Bentinck, George, 162
Berkeley, George, Bishop, 58
Bermuda, 122
bestiality: European association of native races with, 11–12
Black Death, 35
The Blackest Thing in Slavery Was Not the Black Man (Williams), 2–3; 1973 version, 13–16; 1976–1979, later manuscript, 16–20; first draft, 10–13; significance of, 19–20
black ghettoes, 211
black movements: Jamaica, 214–215; splits and dissensions in, 210–211. See also Black Panthers; Black Power
Black Panthers, 6, 210, 211

Black Power, 5–6, 14–16; in America, 204–210; in Caribbean, 214–218
Bolívar, Simón, 77–78
Booker Bros McConnell and Co., 196
Brazil: abolition of slavery, 12; Africanization of, 154–155; American planters' immigration to, 177; destruction of archives, 114; discovery of, 49; European rivalry for, 63; German immigrants in, 88–90; *mazombo*, 89
Britain. See United Kingdom
British Guiana, 144–145; absentee ownership, 196; African-Indian confrontation in, 216–217; Indian indentureship in, 189, 191–193, 197–198; land distribution in, 164–165; sugar exports, 194; sugar production, 173–174
British Honduras, 166, 177
Bruce, Victor, 9–10
Bryce, James, Viscount, 200–201
Buddhism, 24–25, 47
Bulgarian emigrants, 84–85
Burke, Edmund, 61
Burma, 186, 187
Burnley, William, 177–178
Butler, Tubal Uriah, 7, 8
Buxton, Thomas Fowell, 135–136

Caballero, José de la Luz, 1
Cabral, Pedro Alvares, 49
Canada: Amerindian resistance in, 111–112; Caribbean immigration to, 130; early Europeans views of, 93–94; English deportation from, 85; French immigration to, 56; indentured labour in, 18; Irish immigration to, 83; Italian immigration to, 87; politico-linguistic problem in, 216, 217
Canary Islands, 34
Caribbean: African emigration from, 129–130; American immigration to, 177–178; anti-slavery movement in, 143; Black Power in, 214–218; disappearance of Amerindians from, 113; diseases

in, 214; independence movements, 80–81; Indian indentureship in, 19, 189–199; inefficiency of slave system of production, 123–125; in mid-twentieth century, 211–214; migration to Trinidad, 176–177; scholars/activists from, 1–2; sugar production, 193. *See also* West Indies; *specific nations, e.g.,* French Guiana; Suriname

Carlyle, Thomas, 168, 173

Carmichael, Stokely, 6, 14, 210–211, 216–217

Cartier, Jacques, 56, 61, 93–94

cassava, 96, 97

Castro, Fidel, 209, 212–213, 217–218

Catholicism/Catholics, 60–61; black and white, 154–155; land ownership by, 43–44; and Protestant rivalry, 105–106; sanction of colonization, 100–101

Central America: Afro-American contacts in, 48. *See also* Aztecs; Mexico

Césaire, Aimé, 15; *Cahier d'un retour au pays natal*, 213

Ceylon, 186, 187

Chamberlain, Joseph, 185

Champlain, Samuel de, 94

Charles II, King of Great Britain, 116, 179

Cherokee, 104

Chile: war of resistance, 109

China/Chinese, 184; guerrilla movement in, 217; indentureship of, 179, 184, 194; isolationism of, 51; maritime trade and naval technology, 50–51; religion in, 24–25; slavery in, 27–28; technological development, 37, 39

Choiseul, Étienne, 74

Christianity, 26; and African slavery, 138–147, 149; Amerindians' conversion to, 105–107; attitude towards Amerindians' religions, 98; and slavery, 29–31

Cicero, 29

Cieza de León, Pedro, 103

Clarkson, Thomas, 133, 137

Cleage, Albert, 145

Cleaver, Eldridge, 6, 210, 211

Clifford, Sir Bede, 188

Code Noir, 147–148, 149, 151, 159

Code of Tortosa (1272), 34

Código Negro Carolino, 148

Código Negro Español, 149–150

Codrington, Christopher, 143

Codrington family, 179–180

Colbert, Jean-Baptiste, 56

colonial trade, European, 72–74

colonization, European: Amerindian resistance to, 107–112; religious sanction of, 100–101

Columbus, Christopher, 35, 49, 50, 56, 93, 102, 109, 113

Confucius, 27–28

conversion (religious): Amerindian to Christianity, 105–107

convicts: as labour, 194–195; transportation to colonies, 60, 61–62, 181–182

coolieism, 17–19, 179; in African colonies, 185–189; in Asian colonies, 185–189; in Australia, 181–185; in Caribbean, 189–199; reindentureship, 201–202

Cooper, James Fenimore: *Last of the Mohicans*, 105

Corsica, 26

Cortés, Hernán, 62, 65, 100, 103, 108, 109, 112, 113

Creoles: creole Spaniard, 77; independence movements of, 78–79; *mazombo*, 89; Spanish contempt for, 75–76; West Indian, after emancipation, 169–172

Cromwell, Oliver, 60, 70, 76

Crowther, Samuel Ajayi, Bishop, 146

Crusades, 22, 101

Cuba: abolition of slavery, 12; African descent population in, 130, 212–213; African slaves and Christianity in, 140; guerrilla movement in, 217–218; slave code, 149–150; Spanish colonialism, 78

Curaço, 61, 64, 66, 120

230 | Index

Curtin, Philip, 121, 122, 129–130
Cyprus, 33

Da Costa, Emilia Viotti, 152
Dahomey, 11, 155
Damas, Lèon, 213
Danish Virgin Islands, 12, 61, 142;
    slave codes, 150–151
Da Nóbrega, Manuel, 106
Dario, Rubén, 89
Davidson, Basil, 2–3
De Boissière, Jean, 198
Declaration of Independence (US),
    128–129, 137
Deerr, Noel, 121
Defoe, Daniel, 4
Demerara, 174, 198
Demosthenes, 27
De Souza, Mervyn, 9–10
Deutsch, Andre, 2–3
diaries (of Williams), 3–5, 10
Díaz del Castillo, Bernal, 100
diseases and epidemics: in Caribbean,
    214; in Europe, 35–36; in New
    World, 112–113
doctor politics, 7
dogs of conquistadores, 108
Dominican Republic, 213; Santo
    Domingo, 148
Dominicans, 141–142
Donawa, Muriel, 9
Drake, Francis, 64–65, 119
Dravidians, 200
Drax, James, 70
drunkenness, repression of: Incas, 99
Du Bois, W. E. B., 124, 126, 153, 204,
    209
Durer, Albrecht, 100

Edwards, Jonathan, 142
El Socorro, 203
emigration: American, 177–178;
    Caribbean, 129–130, 176–177; early
    transatlantic, 46–47; European,
    55–63; European, after colonial
    independence, 81–90; European,
    post-emancipation, 178; European
    transient workers, 86

encomienda system, 102–103, 113
Encumbered Estates Act (1854),
    196–197
Ethiopia, 46, 145, 207, 208, 215
Europe: Africanization of, 154–155; diet
    in, 38–39; epidemics and famine
    in, 35–37; inequality of races,
    41–46; intellectual dynamism,
    39–41; overseas expansion, 51–54;
    technological development and
    progress, 37–39
European emigration, 55–63; after
    colonial independence, 81–90; of
    poor whites, 70–71; to US, 17
European superiority, 16–17, 37–41, 200
Explainer (Calypsonian): "Selwyn", 8

Fage, J.D., Professor, 121
Fanon, Frantz, 2, 6, 15, 211–212
feudalism: in Britain, 57; in Europe,
    30–31; Fiji, 18, 186; Indian
    immigrants in, 187–188; in New
    World, 124–125
Fletcher, Andrew, 58
floating magnetic compass, 40–41
Forbidden City, 51
Forged from the Love of Liberty
    (Williams), 1
Fouchard, Jean, 156–157
Fox, George, 143
France: and African slave trade,
    115, 116–117, 119, 122; Caribbean
    emigration to, 130; convict
    emigrants, 61–62; and Dutch
    rivalry in Tobago, 67–68;
    emancipation policy of, 168–169;
    emigration to Canada, 56; exclusif,
    72, 74; Huguenots' emigration, 61;
    Inca treasure, 65–66; Nantes, 118,
    119; religious sanction of African
    slavery, 138, 139; slave codes,
    147–148, 149, 151, 159; vagrancy,
    59–60
Fraser, Louis, 164
Frazier, Franklin, 153, 208
French Guiana, 74, 192
Freyre, Gilberto, 45, 126
Froude, James Anthony, 4

Index | 231

Gage, Thomas, 76
Gardelin code (code of 1733), 150–151
Garvey, Marcus, 15, 145, 205–209, 214–215
Genghis Khan, 23
Genovese, Eugene, 153
George I, King of Great Britain, 116
George II, King of Great Britain, 129
Germans: emigration, 61, 81–82; immigration to Brazil, 88–89
gold and silver, 65–66, 101–102
Gomes, Albert, 7–8
Gonzáles Martínez, Enrique, 89
Gordon, Marilyn, 9
Grant, Ulysses S., 111
Greek city states: role of women in, 26–27; slavery in, 29
Gregory X, Pope, 41, 42
Grotius, Hugo, 133
guerrillas, 15, 217
Guevara, Che, 207
Guinea: initiation of African slave trade, 21, 138; repatriation of slaves to, 115, 116; slaves, 32–33, 142

Haile Selassie, Emperor of Ethiopia, 215
Haiti, 50, 125–126, 153–154, 155, 213
Hall, Gwendolyn, 149, 151–152
Hammond, James Henry, 137
Harappa, 21, 199
Harlem Convention (1920), 207, 208–209
Harris, George Francis Robert, Lord, 201
Hawkins, John, 115–116
Hebrew bondsmen, 29
Heegard, Anna, 132
Hegel, Georg Wilhelm Friedrich, 133
Hemings, Sally, 12, 131–132, 160
Heren XIX, 68, 120
Heyerdahl, Thor, 47
Heyn, Piet, 64
Hidalgos, 36, 79
Hinduism, 24, 200–201, 203
Hobbes, Thomas, 133
horses, 38, 108
houses of correction, 57–58

Howick, Charles Grey, Lord, 162–163
Hudson's Bay Company, 107
Hume, David, 133
Hutcheson, Francis, 58, 135

Ibn Khaldun, 40
Ibn Rushd, 40
Incas, 65, 94–95; agriculture of, 96–98; architecture of, 99–100; military society of, 95–96; religion of, 98; society and life of, 98–99; Spanish colonization of, 107
indentured labour/servitude, 122–123; engagés, 56–61. See also coolieism
India/Indians: ancient civilization, 21–22; British views of, 199–203; caste system, 203; Portuguese colonialism in, 52–53. See also coolieism
Innocent III, Pope, 41
Ireland/Irish: deportations from Canada, 85; immigration to US, 82–84; racism against, 42–44
Isabella, Queen of Spain, 102
Islam, 25–26; and Africa, 145; second Islam, 52; spread of, 22
Islamic scholarship, 23, 39–40
Italy: 'birds of passage', 87; immigration to New World, 84, 85–86, 89; Siena, 35

jade, 102
Jagan, Cheddi, 216
Jamaica: black movement in, 214–215; immigration to Panama, 129–130; independence struggle, 80–81; Jews in, 61; opposition to Indian indentureship, 202; post-emancipation, 166–167, 168, 171, 172–173, 178–179; slave laws of, 57; white society in, 70, 71
James, Cyril Lionel Robert, 14
Japan/Japanese, 12, 17, 20, 47, 53; emigration of, 87, 181, 183; isolationism, 51
Jefferson, Thomas, 11, 12; relationship with Sally Hemings, 130–132, 160; views and policy towards Amerindians, 104

232 | Index

Jesuits, 39, 53, 63, 106–107, 139, 141, 142
Jews: discrimination against, 41–42; immigration to New World, 61, 86–87; and non-Jewish slaves, 30
John Chrysostom, St, 30, 51
Johnson, Samuel, 63–64
Juan II, King of Portugal, 49
Julien, Ken, 9–10
Juvenal, 29

Kanakas, 18, 20, 183–184
King, Martin Luther, 209–210
Kingsley, Charles, 4
Kingsley, Mary, 146
Kublai Khan, 23
Ku Klux clan, 204, 209

Labat, Pierre, 61, 125, 138, 139
labour: African slave labour economy, 122–126; *encomienda* system, 102, 103, 113; indentured, 56–61, 122–123. *See also* coolieism
Landa, Diego de, Bishop of Yucatan, 101
land distribution and ownership: in Ireland, 43–44; in West Indies, 164–167, 177, 198, 214
language: of African slaves, 152–154; of Amerindians, 93; Quechua, 94
Las Casas, Bartolome, 102–103, 109, 142, 178–179
Las Siete Partidas, 34, 42
Latin America: assimilation of immigrants, 88–90. *See also* Incas; *specific nations, e.g.*, Brazil
Lazarus, Emma, 55
Lettsom, John Coakley, 143
Lindemark code (code of 1755), 150–151
literacy: among immigrants, 85–86; and Christianity, 26; denial for slaves, 141
literary protest movements, 213
Locke, John, 58, 134
Lok, John, 116
Long, Edward, 11
Longfellow, Henry: *Song of Hiawatha*, 92, 105

Louis XIII, King of France, 138, 139
Louis XIV, King of France, 116
Louisiana, 77, 148–149, 194–195

Macaulay, Thomas Babington, Lord, 82
Macdonald, John A., 111
Madison, James, 134–135
maguey, 97, 99
Mahabir, Errol, 9, 10
maize, 96, 97–98
malaria, 35
Manifest Destiny, 10, 109
maritime trade: China, 50–51. *See also* colonial trade, European
Martí, José, 2
Martinique, 69, 139, 156, 190; French convicts in, 61–62
Maryland: racial inequality in, 122
Massachusetts, 116, 136
Mauritius: Indian immigrants in, 185–190
Mayas, 100, 102; *Popol Vuh*, 95–96
mazombo, 89
McShine, Halsey, 5
measles, 112
mechanization, 38
medieval geography, 50
Mediterranean, 51–52; slavery in, 33–34
Mexico: African influences and presence in, 48; gold and silver in, 66; independence of, 79; resistance to Spanish colonization, 108; smallpox epidemic, 112; Tepexpan man, 49
Milton, John, 73
missionaries, 140–141, 144–145
Modyford, Thomas, 70
Mohenjodaro, 21, 199
Mongols, 23–24
Montadouin, Jean-Gabriel, 119
Montezuma, Aztec emperor, 95, 96, 100, 108, 109
Moors, 45–46
Morant Bay, 12
Moravians, 142
Moreau de Saint-Méry, M. L. E., 69, 125

Morgan, Henry, 65, 119
Morison, Samuel, 153
Morton, John, 4
Morton, Sarah, 4
mulattoes, 12, 131, 147, 212
mumps, 112
Myrdal, Gunnar, 153

Nahuatl, 93
Naipaul, Vidya, 69
Narváez, Pánfilo de, 109
National Association for the
Advancement of Colored People,
204, 209
National Union of Freedom Fighters,
6, 15–16
Navigation Acts (Britain), 72–75
negritude, 213, 215
Nehru, Jawaharlal, 3, 5, 187
Netherlands: African slave trade,
115, 116, 120; challenge to Iberian
claims to New World, 64; colonial
pact, 73; emigration, 82; and
French rivalry in Tobago, 67–68;
salt agreement with Spain, 66–67
New England, 70–71, 75, 80, 84, 116,
136
New Hampshire, 135
Newton, John, 6, 119–120, 144, 210
New World. See Americas
New Zealand, 86, 181, 191
Nicholas V, Pope, 101
Nile Valley, 21
non-European people and culture:
American attitude towards, 17;
inferiority of, 11
North American colonies:
independence of, 74–75; resistance
movement in, 111–112. See also
Canada; United States; specific
colonies, e.g., Virginia

O'Halloran, John, 5, 9, 10
Olmsted, Frederick, 158
Oviedo, 103, 113

Panchacuti, Inca emperor, 95
Paul, St, 30

Paul III, Pope, 105
Penn, William, 142–143
Persia, 22, 23
Peru, 47, 79, 108; encomendero, 124–
125; epidemics, 112; Gamonalismo,
114. See also Incas
Phillips, Ulrich B., 152–153
Philpotts, H., Bishop of Exeter, 146
Pizarro, Francisco, 101, 107, 108,
109
Pizarro, Hernando, 101
plantocracy and plantation economy,
59; apprentice system, 163–169;
emergence of, 55; and intercolonial
slave trade, 174–176; planters' life,
124–127; and slave labour, 118,
122–126, 161–163; West Indian, 70
Plutarch, 29
Pocahontas, 45, 92
Portugal: African slavery in, 32–34;
African slave trade share of, 122;
Christianity and African slaves,
141–142; claims to Amazonia,
63; colonialism in India, 52–53;
Madeira, 33, 34, 189–190; papal
sanction of colonization, 101;
religious sanction of African
slavery, 139; views of native races,
11; white labour refusal to work in
the colonies, 62–63
potato, 96–97
poverty: and emigration, 83–85; in
Europe, 36–37; in West Indies, 214
Powell, Adam Clayton, 210
Price, Sir Rose, 161–162
Price, Thomas, 162
Price-Mars, Jean, 213
prostitution, 27
Protestantism/Protestants, 60–61;
and Catholic rivalry, 105–106; land
ownership, 43–44; and legality
of slave system, 142; sanction of
colonization, 100–101
Providencia Island, 122–123
Puerto Rico, 169, 194, 213, 214
Pufendorf, Samuel von, 135
Puritans, 61, 75, 122–123
Pym, John, 122

234 | Index

Quakers: participation in slave trade, 142–143
Quechua, 94
Quesada, Gonzalo Jiménez de, 107, 108

racial inequality, 122
racism, 10–12; against Arabs, 44–45; British, 212; against Indian indentured immigrants, 202–203; against Irish, 42–44; against Jews, 41–42; in West Indies, 202–203
Rampersad, Frank, 10
Rampersad, Isidore, 10
Ramsay, James, 136
Ras Tafari, 145, 215
Raynal, Abbe', 132–133, 137
religions, 24–27; Mauritius, 188–189. *See also specific religion*
religious dissent: and white emigration, 60–62
religious instruction: for African slaves, 140–141
religious syncretism, 154–156
Renaissance, 53
Revista Interamericana, 2, 10, 14
Rhode Island, 143
Richardson, Selwyn, 8
Riel, Louis, 111–112
rights of man, 128–135
Rochford, Philip, 9–10
Rodney, Walter, 2, 121
Romans: and slavery, 28–29
Rostovtzeff, Michael, 27
Rousseau, Jean, 94, 134
Royal African Company, 116, 134, 143
royalty: and Amerindian slavery, 102, 107; and slave trade, 116
Ruffin, Thomas, 147
runaway slaves, 150–151, 159–160

Sáenz, Moisés, 114
salt, 66–67
Sambo, 153, 158
San Juan de Ulúa, 77, 79
Sannon, Pauleus, 152
Saxe, Maurice, comte de, 67–68
Schoelcher, Victor, 168–169

Scotland: deportations from Canada, 85; immigration to Americas, 81; immigration to West Indies, 168, 178
Seneca, 28–29
Senghor, Léopold, 213
Sewell, William G., 169–172
Shakespeare, William, 46
Shorty (Calypsonian), 8
Sicily, 34
Sioux, 111
slave laws, 57, 147–152, 159
slavery, 1, 27–34; abolition of, 12; Amerindian, 102, 107; Iberian, 34; non-Hebrew slaves, 29; as punishment for idleness, 58. *See also* African slavery/slaves; African slave trade
slave songs, 152, 155–159
smallpox, 112
Smith, Adam, 107, 132, 133
social criticism, 94
Society for the Propagation of the Gospel (SPG), 143–144
Society of Friends, 143
Sokoto, 11
South Africa: apartheid, 11, 211–212; indentured labour in, 18, 181, 185
South America: pro-Amerindian movements, 114. *See also specific nations*
South Carolina, 70, 80, 120, 127
Spain: African slavery in, 32, 33; Amerindian resistance to, 107–111; Anglo-Spanish rivalry, 64–65, 74–75; Christianity and African slaves, 142; claims to New World, 63–67; colonization, 100–104; immigration to New World, 56; independence of colonies of, 75–79; interest in gold and silver, 101–102; *Las Siete Partidas*, 34, 42; overseas expansion of, 51–52, 54; pacte colonial, 72–74; papal sanction of colonization, 101; race relations in, 45; religious conversion of Amerindians, 106–107; religious sanction of African

slavery, 138; Seville, 56, 72; slave code, 148, 149–150; war against Incas and Aztecs, 95–96
Spenser, Edmund, 43
SPG. *See* Society for the Propagation of the Gospel
spices, 66
Statute of Artificers (1563) (Britain), 57
Statute of Labourers (1495) (Britain), 57
St Bartholomew, 68, 74
St Croix, 65, 68, 173, 216
St Domingue, 68, 74, 133, 141, 152, 155
Stephen, James, 183
St Kitts, 68, 69, 118, 166
St Lucia, 74
St Vincent, 170
sugar industry, 117–118; apprentice system, 163–169; and slave labour, 33–34, 149–150; technological development, 193–196; West Indies post-emancipation, 173–178
suicide: African slaves, 150
Suriname, 68–69, 142; German immigrants in, 61; language, 153; post-emancipation, 163; *watramama* dance, 154
Sweden, 68, 74
syphilis, 35–36

Tamerlane, 23–24
Taney, Roger B., 128
technological development: Europe, 37–41, 193; and slavery, 28–29
Temple, Sir William, 58
tenant slaves, 31
Thornton, William, 143
Tortola, 143, 175, 177
Tortuga, 65, 122
Trinidad and Tobago: 1976 general elections, 7; Black Power, 217; Dutch and French rivalry in, 67–68; 'guerrillas', 15; Indian indentureship in, 189–192, 197–198; land distribution and ownership in, 164, 198; living conditions in, 214; post-emancipation, 170, 176–178; prime

minister's governance, 7; race relations in, 6; sugar exports, 194; sugar production, 173–175
Trollope, Anthony, 4, 168, 172–173, 186
Tucker, St George, 128–129
Túpac Amaru II, 110–111
Turkey, 52
Tyler, Wat, 31

Umbanda spiritual movement, 145
UNIA. *See* Universal Negro Improvement Association
United Kingdom: African slave trade, 115–116, 122; Caribbean immigration to, 130; colonization, 103–104; concerns with unemployed, vagrants and the poor, 56–58, 60; discrimination of Irish, 42–44; emancipation policy, 161–169; independence of Caribbean colonies, 80–81; independence of North American colonies of, 74–75, 79–80; legislation relevant to colonies, 57–58, 72–75, 165; Peasants' Revolt of 1381, 31–32; political exiles, 60; Protestant authorization of colonization, 100–101; slave compensation claims, 146; and Spain rivalry, 64–65, 74–78; views on Indians, 199–203
United States: African immigration from Caribbean, 129–130; African slaves, 148–149; agriculture in, 127; coloured immigration to Caribbean, 177–178; European immigrants, 17, 60–61, 85–86; independence of, 74–75, 79–80; industries in, 127–128; Irish immigration to, 81–84; Italian immigration to, 85, 89; new states, 126; race riots in, 204–205; races in, 104; views and policy towards Amerindians, 104–105; Westwards move, 126–128
Universal Negro Improvement Association (UNIA), 15, 206–209

236 | Index

Urracá, Cacique, 109
Usselinx, William, 68
Utrecht, 116

vagrants: state-aided immigration of, 56–60
Venezuela: German immigrants in, 89; independence of, 79
Vera Cruz, 77, 79
Vespasian, Roman emperor, 28
Vespucci, Amerigo, 93
villeinage: English laws on, 57
Virginia: Bill of Rights, 128–129; colonial independence of, 75; definition of mulatto, 131; English servitude in, 58–59; introduction of African slavery, 116
Vodun, 155
Voltaire, 52, 67, 92, 94, 119
von Scholten, Peter, 132

Wadström, Carl Bernhard, 123–124
Walcott, Derek: "The Spoiler's Return", 9
Washington, Booker T., 152, 204, 205
Washington, Joseph R., 145
Webster, Noah, 131
West Indies: anti-slavery movement, 143; Asian indentureship in, 178–179; colonists' life in, 69–71; European death rate, 123; European rivalry in, 67–68; independence, 214; land distribution and ownership in, 164–167, 177;

ownership of, 118–119; post-emancipation, 167–180; poverty, 214; sale of encumbered estates, 196–197; Spanish immigration to, 56. *See also* Caribbean
wheat, 98, 127
Whitefield, George, 142
white labour: and African slave labour compared, 161–162; indentured, 56–61, 72, 122–123; industries, 127–128; refusal to do manual work in the colonies, 62–63; unsuitability in tropics, 11
white supremacy, 53
Wilberforce, William, 135–136, 203
Williams, Eric: 1976 TV interview, 3, 16; advisors of, 9–10; criticism of, 8–9; disengagement with public life, 5–8; literary exemplars, 1–2; manuscript preparation, 2–4, 10; works of, 14
Williams, Erica, 5
women: emigration to New World, 62–63; inclusion in Trinidad's governance, 9; role in ancient societies, 26–27
Wooding Commission, 6, 7
Wyke, Marguerite, 9

Ximenes, Cardinal, 53

Zambesi, 141–142
Zeelanders, 67, 68–69
Zimbabwe, 11

Printed in the USA
CPSIA information can be obtained
at www.ICGtesting.com
LVHW041553140923
758098LV00001B/115